The Human Mind

A Psychological View of Theological Concepts

Eric J. Kolb, Ph.D.

authorHOUSE®

AuthorHouse™ UK
1663 Liberty Drive
Bloomington, IN 47403 USA
www.authorhouse.co.uk
Phone: UK TFN: 0800 0148641 (Toll Free inside the UK)
UK Local: (02) 0369 56322 (+44 20 3695 6322 from outside the UK)

Published by AuthorHouse 04/21/2022

ISBN: 978-1-6655-9807-1 (sc)
ISBN: 978-1-6655-9806-4 (e)

Print information available on the last page.

To Him and all who are earnestly seeking
the Way, the Truth, and the Life.

CONTENTS

INTRODUCTION

This book is the first of a series of four books that I felt compelled to write while I was still writing my first book, *The Psychology of God*. In that book, I dedicated one chapter to Jesus's statement: You shall love thy Lord, you God with all of your heart, body, mind, and soul (Luke 10:27). In that chapter, I examined these four components of the human being. The heart represents the emotional component, which is designed to influence our behaviour in response to emotionally provoking stimuli. The soul represents the moral goodness of an individual. As a person's identity describes who a person is, the soul describes who a person wants to become. The body, including the brain, is the fleshy material from which we are composed. And then there is the mind, which refers to the cognitive processes and the topic of this book. In my previous book, I illustrated how each of these four components work together and influence the development of the other three components. However, one chapter was not nearly enough to adequately cover each of these four components. Thus, I decided then to write a book on each of the four components of the human being. In this edition, we will explore the human mind.

The four components of the body work together very intricately, each drawing from and influencing each other. They are so interwoven that it is impossible to discuss any one component without addressing aspects of the other three. Very often in scientific literature, theological literature, and in life in general, these four terms—heart, body, mind, and soul—are often used interchangeably, as well as reduced into fewer terms. Materialists, as I will later discuss, argue that the body is really the only component, because heart, mind, and soul are all contained in the body. From a neurophysiological perspective, the limbic system, which controls our emotions, is contained in the brain but indeed functions distinctly separate from the mind, which is yet to be located in the brain, or in any other part of the body for that matter.

During the publication process of this book, I promptly began researching for my next book on the human soul. In doing so, I have come up with a visual model that illustrates how these four components work together. If you have already read my last book, *The Psychology of God*, you will notice that I have tweaked my theory a bit since then. Instead of four separate components that are integrated together to make up the human being, I am now proposing that the fourth component, the human soul, is not a distinct and separate component as the other three are. Rather, the soul is the intersection of the other three components.

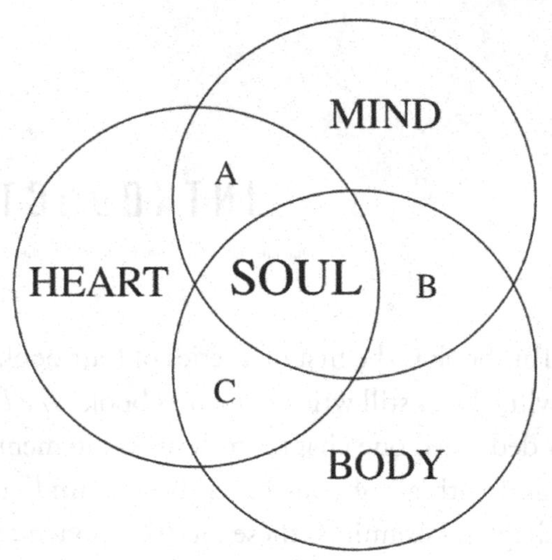

The areas labelled A, B, and C are the intersections of each pair of circles. In each of these paired intersections, something very interesting is going on. Intersection A represents the duality of the heart and mind. Generally, our behaviour is governed by the mind, but upon the perception of emotionally provoking stimuli, our emotions take over and dictate our behaviour. Intersection B represents the highly debated mind/body duality. It is generally understood that our behaviour is governed through our mind, but at some point, neurons have to be activated for behaviour to take place. But the problem is the mind does not consist of

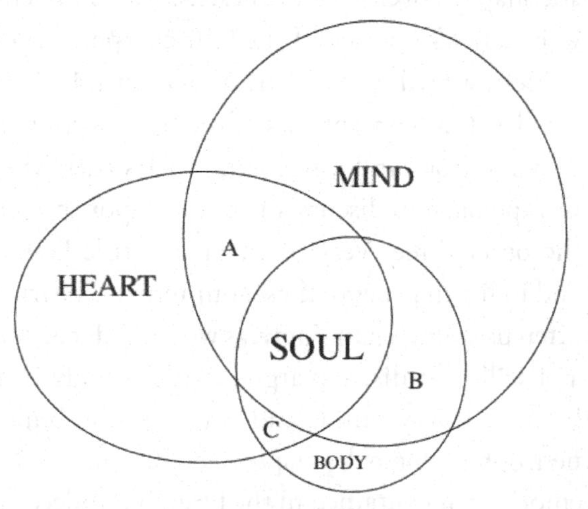

neurons, so how does the mind activate the neurons in the brain? Finally, intersection C represents passion. Passion is what happens when one's emotions fully take over a particular behaviour, such as dance, music, art, sport, and other such meaningful hobbies or activities. The areas of this diagram that will be discussed in this book will be the area labelled mind, and areas A and B.

It should be noted that the size and symmetry of the circles are indeed very flexible from person to person. For example, the diagram of my person may look something like this. I am certainly much more rational than emotional, so my heart circle would be more oval and drawn into the mind, while my mind circle is larger and more symmetrical. I would also suggest that area A is only slightly more dominated by my mind while area B is predominately more dominated by my mind. Due to my physical disability, the muscles in my body, and particularly my face, are very week, so it takes strong conscious effort to project emotion through my body, thus area C is relatively small. Generally, I don't allow my body to influence my heart and mind, but I use my mind to significantly influence my body. Finally, it should also be noted that these circles are not at all stagnant. The above diagram illustrates my preferred state. But some days, the pain is simply unbearable, making any sort of concentration impossible, and that also makes me very emotional in a negative way, so much so that I don't even want to draw that diagram.

This book will be a deliberation of the mind, its development, and the various cognitive processes and systems. For this discussion, we will first have to establish an understanding of the concept of belief. In chapter 1, we will be viewing belief both in the broadest sense as well as individual beliefs. Everything an individual believes, all of their collective individual beliefs, are formed in what we will call a belief system.

First, it will be demonstrated that one's belief system serves as the lens through which an individual perceives their subjective reality, and upon which they build an identity. Second, it will be demonstrated that the human belief system is unique in that only humans have the ability to choose what they want to believe. Studies will be discussed that demonstrate that the human beliefs system is an innate process that begins in early childhood development and continues throughout a lifetime. It would seem as if humans are born not only with the capacity to form beliefs but also with the inclination to do so intuitively and non-consciously.

The concept of core beliefs will be a major focus in my next book on the human soul, but because the soul and the mind are so intricately interwoven, it is necessary to at least briefly define the concepts here. Thus, core beliefs are defined as those beliefs that become so embedded into an individual's mind that they become a part of their identity. As such, I will argue later that 'I believe, therefore I am' would be a more accurate test of consciousness than 'I think, therefore I am' because if one would equate computing with thinking, then one could argue that even computers are technically conscious and have belief systems. It will be illustrated that identity, as each of us subjectively perceives as the self, develops through experience. And all of this experience, all of the sensations that come into our minds and everything we perceive, is perceived in relation to our core beliefs.

While our belief system is an innate process, driven initially with an intuitive cognitive thinking style, humans still essentially choose what they want to believe. One belief to which all humans will have formed a subjective opinion is the belief about God's existence. Whether one believes in God, a god, or anything of spiritual nature, or one believes that there is no supernatural force that brought life and the universe into existence, this one specific belief will have a significant effect on the development of the individual's mind, and thus, ultimately their personality and behaviour.

Because each of us forms a belief concerning God, I found it necessary to outline the basic arguments upon which believers and non-believers base their beliefs. In doing so, it will become obvious that it is not the arguments that create belief, but rather individuals choose to believe what they want to and then find the evidence to support this belief. This is true for believers and non-believers alike.

After having laid out the foundation of belief upon which the human mind develops, we will then discuss the various processes that have been associated with the mind. Beginning with the blank slate, the term often used to describe the newborn mind, we will outline the processes of the development of the human mind. These include the concepts of objective and subjective self-awareness, theory of mind (ToM), identity, consciousness, and behaviour. Then in conclusion, after having outlined the developmental processes of the human mind, we will examine the developmental process of one specific human mind, that of Jesus of Nazareth.

Two last notes pertaining to the structure of and format of this book. Scattered through the book, you will find in text citations in what is called APA format. These citations are in the format (Author, Date of Publication). Although these citations may significantly disturb the flow of the reading, they are extremely important. They serve the purpose of proving that the cited statements are not merely my opinions but rather are based on a scientific, peer-reviewed study. At the end of the book, I have listed all of the references of the in-text citations, so you can find and read the original article for yourself. In a few cases, you will find the citation in the form (as cited in Author, Date). This means that I am referring to something that someone else said about what someone else said. This is generally frowned upon in APA format, but on a few occasions, I simply could not get my hands on the original source, and so the APA format dictates that I must illustrate that in such cases, I am not referring to the original source but to a secondary source.

Also, throughout the book, you will find text boxes. This is information that did not make the final cut of the final draft but is interesting enough to get an honourable mention, an interesting side note, a suitable quote, or any such gem of information that is interesting and fitting to the topic but, if included in the main text, may distract from the main point. Finally, it should be noted that unless otherwise indicated, all Bible verses are taken from the New International Version (NIV). But I do very much encourage the reader to compare and contrast versions. In fact, originally, I had a section where I demonstrated that the terms *heart*, *soul*, and *mind* were used interchangeable from version to version, and I compared these verses to the original Greek and Hebrew. However, because this is a book on scientific psychology and not on the linguistics of the Holy Scripture, I deemed it sufficient to simply point out that the King James Version (KJV) tends to use the term *heart* where the NIV uses the term *mind*. Some examples are Proverbs 23:33, 'Thine heart shall utter' (KJV) versus 'your mind will imagine' (NIV), and Isiah 44:18, 'shut their eyes, that they cannot see, and their heart, that they cannot understand' (KJV) versus 'Their eyes are plastered over so they cannot see, and their minds closed so they cannot understand' (NIV). Furthermore, the KJV often uses the term *soul*, where the NIV often uses a more specific term for the context. For example, Psalm 86:4, 'I lift up my soul' (KJV) versus 'I put my trust in you' (NIV); Proverbs 13:4, 'the soul of the sluggard desireth' (KJV) versus 'A sluggard's appetite' (NIV). The inconsistent use of the terms in the Bible does not surprise me very much because even scientific psychological literature also uses the terms interchangeably, and many even admit to doing so (Farris, 2015; Landro, 2019). However, I for one do believe that the heart, body, soul, and mind of the human being, interwoven as they are, are nevertheless distinct elements. Unfortunately, it will take an entire book to describe and define the distinctness of each component. With that said, let us begin with the human mind.

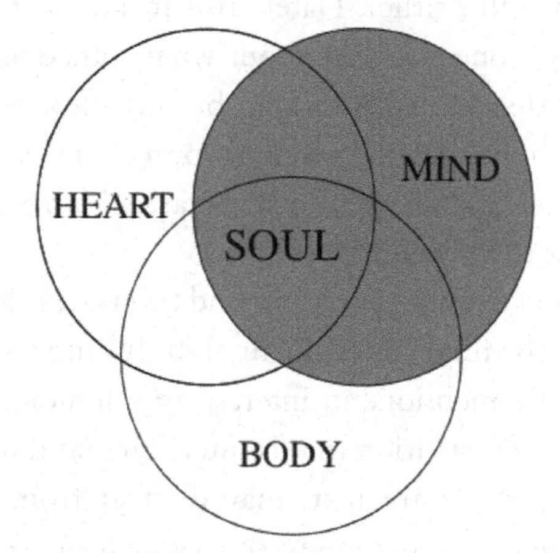

CHAPTER 1

Belief, the Lens of Reality

Everything we perceive, everything that enters our minds through our senses, and everything we experience is first filtered through our belief system. One's entire belief system serves as the lens through which we perceive reality. This includes one's belief in God, gods, superstitions, and any matters pertaining to the supernatural or spirituality, as well as science. It will be shown that science is just as much based on our individual and subjective belief system as other cognitions. Whatever any individual believes, be it a deeply embedded core belief or a seemingly insignificant and petty belief, our beliefs collectively form the basis upon which our minds develop.

However, while seeing is believing, humans also have the innate tendency to see what they believe. Belief is a very broad topic and ranges from opinions to ideals. Everyone has their own set of personal and subjective beliefs through which they experience their environment. The COVID-19 pandemic is a prime example. An individual's belief pertaining to the coronavirus, vaccine, and all related topics will determine how they will react in response to stimuli associated with the virus, which right now is a very common stimulus. If one believes it is all a malicious hoax used to gain world domination, one will react accordingly. If one believes it is a plague, which may wipe out humanity, then one will react in a manner according to that. Clearly, one can understand that a person's belief about a dramatic situation will inevitably affect one's behaviour; however, the same is true for less dramatic situations. Right now, I am trying to think of a situation that is so insignificant that anyone's belief about it would not affect his or her behaviour. I can think of no situation. Anything can be, and most likely is, extremely important to someone.

It could be easily argued that the most significant belief that an individual can form is their belief in God, because this one belief significantly influences the development of one's mind and behaviour throughout their lives. Every human being forms a subjective belief about the existence of God. Whatever it may be, this belief greatly influences one's identity development, social-emotional development, cognitive development, and communication.

The question of the existence of God comes down to this: Is this world, consisting of physical matter, energy, and life, a result of chance or God? Both science and theology agree that it can be only one or the other. Either there is a God who is in control, or chance rules. Sure, God may have some systems like the migration patterns of birds or the weather that seemingly operate on random systems, but God must have the ability to access any element of nature in any way and at any time, or He is not God.

Thus, when we perceive the situations in our environment, we have the choice to believe one of two things. This situation, no matter how good or bad, no matter how relevant or irrelevant, either serves a purpose or does not serve a purpose. There can be no middle ground. To take this to a theological level, either chance is, or God is. As Einstein put it, 'God does not play with dice.' Evolution is chance; God is purpose. Sproul and Mathison (1994, p. 19–20) quoted Arthur Koestler: 'God is an anachronism,' which is a fancy way of saying something is outdated and old fashion.

Sproul and Mathison (1994, p. 19–20) agreed with Koestler's argument that 'if chance rules, God cannot', adding, 'It is not necessary for chance to rule in order to supplant God.' In fact, chance requires little authority to depose God; all it needs to do the job is to exist. 'The mere existence of chance is enough to rip God from his cosmic throne. Chance does not need to rule; it does not need to be sovereign. If it exists as a mere impotent, humble servant, it leaves God not only out of date but also out of a job. … If chance existed, it would destroy God's sovereignty. If God is not sovereign, he is not God. If he is not God, he simply is not. If chance is, God is not. If God is, chance is not. The two cannot coexist by reason of the impossibility of the contrary.'

Similarly, Leconte DuNouy wrote, 'Chance alone is radically incapable of explaining an irreversible evolutive phenomenon.' However, as Barbour previously pointed out, Darwinian evolution implies chance with loaded dice. Still, many claim that no dice are loaded enough in lieu of such a complicated creation (as cited in Barbour, 1990, p.182).

Dawkins (2006b, p. 139) clarified that something to come about by chance means to 'come about in the absence of deliberate design.' Each of us is free to choose whether we believe all of this has a purpose and God is in control, or all of this is simply chance, and no one and nothing is in control. Some may claim that they themselves are in control. I disagree. Such control is merely an illusion. Take driving for an example. People may feel like they are in control because they have their hands on the steering wheel and their feet on the brake and gas pedals. However, how many components are involved in exerting that proclaimed control between the perception of an obstacle and the avoidance of that obstacle? So many things can go wrong, and they can do so very fast. As if that is not enough, while one may claim at least limited control over their own vehicle, they have absolutely no control of the many other cars on the road. Such as it is also in life. The only thing that humans have the capacity to control is that of their own behaviour. But even doing that is difficult because of our animalistic nature of drives, instincts, and reflexes.

When individuals are in an emotional state of mind, they may literally not be in control of their behaviour because the autonomic nervous system can override the central nervous system at any time in response to an emotionally provoking stimulus. Nevertheless, humans are the only animals capable of self-reflection and are able to become consciously aware of our emotional and mental states, giving us the ability to ultimately choose how we want to perceive a situation and regain control of our behaviour.

Nevertheless, one's belief in God is not limited to yes, God exists, or no, God does not exist. One's belief in God, either for or against, goes much deeper and wider. It has been found to have a significant influence on how people think, develop, and behave. Suppose an individual does not believe in God. In that case, this individual will perceive and experience the world differently than an individual who believes in God or in a god of some kind, simply because one's belief in God dictates what the world, life, and humanity mean.

The belief in the hereafter is the most common example of this; however, the hereafter is greatly misunderstood by believers and non-believers alike. Salvation, which may be defined as the assurance that one will go to heaven, should not be the goal of Christian life but the starting point. And, not going to hell may perhaps be a reason to believe, but it should certainly not be the main reason. Nevertheless, one's belief in the hereafter, whatever this belief may be, will inevitably have a significant effect on a person's perception of reality.

About anything that happens, and something is always happening, every single living human will have a belief associated with God's, the Devil's, or Chance's role in that situation. The personal significance of one's belief will determine the level of awareness one might have of this belief at any given time. Nevertheless, one's belief in God determines one's perspective of reality. As such, belief is essentially the engine of the mind because our perception of our environment is filtered through it.

Of course, one's belief in God is not the only belief that influences one's perception of reality. Everything a person believes, all that they hold true, including mere opinions, which sport's team is the best, which political party is the best, which anything is anything, collectively forms an individual's belief system upon which their reality is perceived. People have opinions about everything; some are strong and important, others are less important, but everything anyone believes about anything and in any way will influence how they perceive the world.

Perception

Russel (2008) described two systems of perception: bottom-up and top-down. Bottom-up perception is perception as one generally understands it. This kind of perception is data driven and takes place through sensory integration, in which our senses perceive information of the environment. Simply put, in bottom-up perception seeing is believing. However, top-down perception is more intuitive. This kind of perception occurs when our background knowledge of past experiences influences our perception. For example, a bump in the night is often perceived much differently than the same sound heard during the day. Our perception of something, be it a physical object like a painting or an abstract construct like the idea implied through a painting, is not a material thing, nor is it a mental thing. It is something in between. This may be illustrated in that two people cannot have the same exact perception of the same object, whether it is physical or abstract. All a person can see is the light reflecting off the object, but two different sets of eyes cannot see the same object because their eyes do not catch the same light, sound, or any other perceivable sensation.

Thus, to begin this journey, we will first discuss the topic of belief. Most books on the human mind would not begin with the topic of belief, but unlike most psychological books on the human mind, this one includes the Christian theological perspective as well as the scientific psychological perspective. Sometimes these perspectives are very similar, and sometimes they are very different. The purpose of this book is not to evangelize but rather to educate. Thus, the point to be made here is not whether or not God exists but the fact that our belief in God serves as a lens through which each of us, individually and subjectively, experiences reality. If a person believes they evolved from primates, then their subjective reality is perceived through this belief. If another person believes in reincarnation, Ra, Thor, Buddha, or whatever, their subjective reality is perceived through this belief.

Nevertheless, belief does not influence objective reality. No amount of belief in something can cause that something to materialize into existence. In other words, God's existence (or the existence of any such unobserved entity) does not depend on extraneous belief. No one can believe something into existence. God exists or does not exist regardless of what I, you, or anyone in the world believes.

Fowler (1981) outlined six stages of faith in terms of human development. The kind and level of belief that an individual demonstrates changes over time. As such, each stage builds upon the previous one and prepares one for the proceeding stage of belief. The first stage is the intuitive stage, which begins in early childhood. In this stage, beliefs are based primarily on intuition. In this stage, a child faced with an unknown will derive an understanding of this unknown intuitively, based on better known associations. For example, when a child sees the moon and contemplates the nature of the moon, it will perceive the craters on the moon and then associate that with other objects of similar appearance. Thus, a child may conclude that the moon is made out of cheese, because the moon appears to have holes in it just like cheese. This is followed by the mythical stage, during which myths are interpreted literally. In this stage, a child's beliefs are influenced by the parents and other adults. Thus, when an adult tells a child that they will get strong like Popeye from eating spinach, the child will believe this. The third stage, beginning in early adolescence, is the synthetic conventional, which is still dependent on external authority, but now a child may incorporate not only the beliefs of adults but also the proposed believes, as well as the scepticisms of peers. In this stage, beliefs tend to conform to the general consensus. For this reason, children are extremely susceptible to advertisement and peer pressure. Some individuals remain at this stage throughout their lifetime. During the fourth, individuative-reflective stage, people begin to question, doubt, and assume responsibility for their own beliefs. At this point, one's beliefs are embedded in one's personality and are no longer significantly vulnerable to suggestion. Fifth, the conjunctive stage of mature faith is marked by security. At this stage, an individual is able to show respect for other's beliefs while also maintaining a strong commitment to their own. Finally, the universalising stage is reached only by individuals who are committed to radical inclusiveness, a greater depth of religious experience, a vision of a transformed world, and a love that reaches out to others.

As such, people's belief systems are established and developed throughout their life experiences. I would even suggest that one's belief in God, or anything else for that matter, may fluctuate considerably while it develops. I can imagine that many Christians reading this book may cringe at the last statement, and many non-believers will chalk that last statement up as a confession of disbelief. Thank you both for making my point. It is your belief that induces such thoughts, not God's existence or nonexistence. God (or anything else for that matter) either exists or does not exist, independently from what anyone believes. With the scientific method, it can be determined that something exists. But science is useless in trying to show that something does not exist. No one can prove that God, the Easter Bunny, mermaids, Pegasus, honest politicians, and the like do not exist using the scientific method.

In the age of modern science, a person who believes in the Easter Bunny and such mythical things is rarely taken seriously. Nevertheless, belief in God, in some way or form, is still quite predominant. Several scientific psychological studies have been conducted to address why people still believe in God. The most frequent answer to this question is that belief in God is passed down from parents to their children. However, a close examination of the data suggests that humans have been created to believe, just as the Holy Scriptures claim.

Children's Belief in God: Created to Believe

In search of an answer to why people believe in God, one could begin with an investigation into how beliefs of the supernatural form in children and then extrapolate from that point and question why adults continue to believe in matters of the supernatural. Many of the studies, which I will review in this section, were conducted with the sometimes subtle, sometimes direct, intent of demonstrating that it is childish to believe in God, and thus adults who believe in God are childish. But like so often in life, when we try to run from something, we very often end up running right into the very thing we are trying to avoid. Thus, although the following studies were designed to discredit the belief in God, had the authors also been familiar with the Holy Scriptures, they might have realised that these studies actually support exactly what the Bible says.

As outlined previously in Fowler's (1981) stages of faith, the basic premise of the following studies is that children intuitively believe what people tell them. But when they grow up, they begin to think rationally and thus question and then eventually dismiss their irrational, childish beliefs. The following studies offer fairly conclusive support to the theory that adults who believe in God tend to think intuitively rather than rationally. While the data seems to support this claim, it is often misinterpreted to mean that adults who believe in God do so because they don't think rationally. But before we get into the interpretation of this data, allow me to first outline some of these studies.

Studies from Epley et al. (2009) and Ross et al. (2012) investigated the extent to which children and adults distinguish between God's mind and human minds when attributing moral beliefs. Participants were asked to distinguished amongst agents' minds in three ways: viewing God as especially similar to themselves and conceiving of other people as the 'odd ones out, viewing God as especially similar to other people, and conceptualizing themselves as the odd one out' (Fromkin and Snyder, 1980); or viewing themselves as especially similar to other people and conceiving of God as the 'odd one out' (Lane et al., 2010). These results demonstrated that religious believers are particularly likely to use their own beliefs as a guide when reasoning about God's beliefs compared to when reasoning about other people's beliefs. That is, people who believe in God tend to believe they know God better than people. To an atheist, this is an inconceivable notion, which again illustrates that it is one's belief system that lays the foundation upon which reality is perceived, regardless of what an individual believes. These studies may be interesting, but they seem to want to suggest that believing in God is an odd and childish thing to do, and they offer no additional information that is not already explicitly pointed out in the Bible—and that is that believers should not be surprised if the world hates us (1 John 3:13).

Heiphetz et al. (2018) investigated the extent to which children and adults distinguish their beliefs and other humans' beliefs from God's beliefs. In their first study, they found adults believed that God was less likely than humans to view behaviours as morally acceptable, while children believed God was more understanding and lenient. A second study replicated these findings and additionally revealed that adults (but not children) reported that God was less likely than any other agent to think that controversial behaviours were morally acceptable; furthermore, across ages, participants reported that another person's beliefs were more likely to change than either God's beliefs or their own beliefs. These findings then led to a discussion about the implications of an individual's belief on their moral cognition.

Moral cognition is an argument that many believers often use as evidence of God. While it is actually a good argument for the existence of God, it is often presented incorrectly. A believer may argue that if it were not for God, humans would have no morals, but we do have morals, and thus God exists. This is very simply faulty logic (Alexander, 1987). Although our morals come from God, they do not depend on our belief in God. As such, an individual who believes that Jesus Christ is Lord may still live a very sinful life. At the same time, someone who does not believe that Jesus Christ is Lord may still live a very peaceful life. This is because God made all humans in His image and has given all humans the ability to judge between right and wrong, along with the free will to choose for themselves to do right or wrong.

Richert et al. (2017) asked 272 Protestant Christian, Roman Catholic, Muslim, and religiously non-affiliated parents and their preschool-aged children what the difference was between the capabilities of human minds and God's mind. Children of Muslim parents are differentiated the most, suggesting that human minds are fallible but not God's. The results showed that children who had greater differentiation between God's and humans' minds had parents who attributed fewer human-like qualities to God's mind. Additionally, children of religious parents differentiated between humans and God the least, and their differentiation was unrelated to a religious context. The authors interpreted that data to mean that a child's belief in God was merely a result of their parents' beliefs. Thus, God does not exist because if He did, a child's belief would come from Him and not the parents. It was clear throughout the paper that the authors were serving an unrevealed agenda, with the underlining proposal that those who believe in God are simply stupid. However, what the authors neglected to report was that their finding corresponded exactly to what the Holy Scriptures have to say about parents raising their children to believe God created them, loves them, and has a specific plan for their lives: 'Start children off on the way they should go, and even when they are old they will not turn from it' (Proverbs 22:6–7). In addition to this—and this will be discussed later in greater detail—it has been found that one's DNA has been found to have a greater influence on one's behaviour than one's environment. However, when it comes to religious behaviours, one is very quick to say that this comes from the parents, while all other behaviours are a result of DNA. Obviously, it is ridiculous to claim that only religious behaviour comes from the parents and all other behaviours from the DNA, but more on that in chapter 2.

Nyhof and Johnson (2007) conducted an experiment that aimed

to gain knowledge about children's image, belief, and understanding of God. They examined how readily children acquire God concepts that resemble or contrast from that of a human father in the context of different religious traditions and found that even four-year-olds from different religious backgrounds could distinguish concepts relating to God or the supernatural and concepts relating to the natural world. Thus, the argument some radical atheists bring forth that raising a child to love God and love all people should be equated with brainwashing and thus also child abuse is completely unfounded.

While science tries to interpret such data to mean that belief in God is childish and that these studies show that God does not exist, when one compares these research findings to the Holy Scriptures, three key points surface.

1. As children, we are born with the innate capacity and even the tendency to want to believe in God.
2. Indeed, the way a child's belief develops is significantly influenced by their parents' belief, but behaviour studies demonstrate that behaviour, and thus also religious behaviour, is more influenced through our DNA. Thus, it would seem we were created to believe. In fact, one could argue that this is exactly what Jesus was talking about when He said, 'Unless you change and become like little children, you will never enter the kingdom of heaven' (Matthew18:3).
3. Despite all this, people are inspired by other people's beliefs, especially if they seem irrational.

Hollywood, Bollywood, and film production worldwide is a multi-trillion-dollar business which ultimately consists of portraying an artificial reality of irrational beliefs, and people all over the world love it. We love to see people rise above all odds and do things that we wish we had the courage to do. In any story ever made, there is a moment in which a character is called from the place they were into an unknown adventure of some kind. People love to sit there and watch as actors portray an artificial reality. The audience knows it is not real; the people they are watching are simply actors on a movie set. But we are nevertheless drawn in, inspired, and motivated to watch an artificial reality of people doing what they believe in. Why? Because we rational, intelligent, and critically thinking adults also want to follow our intuitive beliefs against all rational thought. But most of us simply do not have the courage to do it for ourselves.

Studies have shown that supernatural beliefs are an innate setting of the human mind (Heiphetz et al., 2018; Nyhof and Johnson, 2007; Richer et al., 2017). That is, humans seem to have an innate predisposition to form beliefs. Moreover, this capacity to form beliefs accounts for human intelligence based on intuition and rationalisation. The acquisition and formation of childhood beliefs have been found to be related to the development of cognition, which begins in early childhood development (Hutson, 2013; Lloyd, 1996; Pennycook et al., 2012; Shenhav et al., 2012). From the theologian to the preschool child, everyone contemplates God's existence and nature until they reach a point where their curiosity is satisfied, or enough animosity arises to render the conundrum a moot point. So while the discussion of God's existence is often futile because of the human ability and inclination to believe, the discussion of belief itself may prove more productive. Because belief, as it will be shown, is a choice. When it comes to belief systems, religious or any other manner, one's belief is a choice. A great deal of thought or very little thought may be applied in making this choice, but belief in anything is essentially a choice made, stored, and regulated in the mind.

Belief Is a Choice

One thing that theists and atheists may agree upon is that agnosticism is a cop-out. When an individual is posed with the question, 'Does God exist?' neither the theist nor the atheist can offer conclusive and irrefutable evidence. Thus, when the agnostic replies, 'I don't know,' the theist and the atheist respond in unison, 'No one can know with certainty, but what do you believe?' In the next few pages, I will be discussing some of the popular arguments for and against the existence of God. My motivation for doing so is to inform rather than to convince. You will choose to believe what you will, but the more educated the choice, the stronger the faith will be.

When contemplating the existence of God, one can entertain various methods of thought. Science and theology are two fields of study that are based on significantly different thought systems. Theology is based on our intuitive cognition, whereas science is based on our rational cognition. The theological method of thought teaches us what to think but not how to think, whereas the scientific method of thought teaches us how to think but not what to think. When contemplating God's existence, the universe, and life itself—which, as we will show, is significantly related to the development of the human mind—one can only get so far with science. The scientific method is a great method of gaining knowledge, but it can only be implemented in matters that can be observed and measured. Thus philosophy, which has its basis in logic, has been used to explore the concepts of God, nature, and the human mind.

Before I became a psychologist, I was a performing artist. Amongst other things, I performed some magic tricks. Some people enjoy such illusions and simply leave it at that. Others do not enjoy the illusion but are enticed by the mystery and want to know how I made it seem like something disappeared, appeared, or changed. They see the illusion as something to be explained rather than merely enjoyed. But before they begin thinking about how I did it, they disregard the possibility that I might have Harry Potter–like magical abilities because they believe such powers do not exist. Thus, with this predetermined knowledge, they immediately consider how I might have created the illusion without true magical abilities.

After every show, at least one audience member would approach me, compliment me for an entertaining show, and then present me with a theory of how I did a particular trick. This is a situation with which every illusionist is familiar; learning to deal with this is as important as learning to do the tricks in the first place. An inexperienced performer will prove to the ambitious audience member that their theory is wrong, which leads to the person to devise a new theory that, when again proven wrong, will motivate the individual to comprise a new theory again, and again, until the performer either caves and explains how the trick works or the discussion becomes heated and aggressive, destroying the performer-audience relationship. Over time, I have learned that the best way to handle this situation is to simply confirm the suspicious audience member that their first theory is correct, even though it is not. In doing so, the sceptic feels satisfied and vindicated, promises to keep my secret, and gives me a huge tip.

> *Magic is just science that we don't understand yet. Any sufficiently advanced technology is indistinguishable from magic.*
>
> —*Arthur Clarke*

> *Science without religion is lame, religion without science is blind. The more I study science the more I believe in God*
>
> —*Albert Einstein*

Belief in God versus Science

In scientific discussions about God's existence, the same sort of dialogue occurs between the magician and the spectator. Scientists begin their thinking process with the assumption that there is no God. As such, any scientific study results will be based on the assumption that there is no God. Thus thc conclusion is predetermined. Of course, one could approach the question of God's existence with the method of a contrapositive. That is, one first assumes that there is no God, and then if this assumption leads to contradictions, then one would have to conclude that the assumption is false. The problem with that is that people ultimately choose to believe what they want and interpret data in a way that supports their beliefs.

By employing the contrapositive method of proof, one can demonstrate that God, the Creator of life, and the universe must exist. After applying this method of proof, we begin by assuming that no form of intelligent design is responsible for the existence of matter, energy, and life. As such, chance must be responsible for the existence of matter, energy, and life. So what is the probability that matter, energy, and life came into existence by random chance? Believe it or not, this can be and has been calculated, and it has been come to be known as the anthropic cosmological principle.

Anthropic Cosmological Principle

Barrow and Tipler (2009) offered as close to scientific proof of intelligent design as one may possibly suggest. Although I cannot claim to have understood it in its entire complexity, my understanding of math and chemistry was sufficient to follow the more than seven hundred pages of arguments. Essentially, the authors outlined the many various attributes of the universe, which allow for life on the Earth as we know it, and demonstrate how unbelievably fine-tuned these many attributes are. In this work, Barrow and Tipler define the weak anthropic principle (WAP) and the strong anthropic principle (SAP). The WAP merely states that life had to come to pass; otherwise, we would not be here to contemplate the question. The WAP is a circular argument which claims life exists in the universe because we are here, and we are here because life exists in the universe.

The SAP goes much further, suggesting that the universe is set up in such a way that life is a necessary result. It claims that the laws of physics themselves are the causes of life. As such, the SAP stops just shy of suggesting intelligent design and begs the question, Could the universe be any different than it is and still support the development of life? When one examines the laws of physics, it would seem that the universe is so fine-tuned for life that two main theories arise. Either there was indeed an intelligent designer, or we live in a multiverse, consisting of an infinite number of universes, so regardless of how unlikely the evolution of life may be, in a set of infinite universes, the odds are indeed good that in at least one of them, life should evolve. Either way, one must refrain from using the term *evolution* when suggesting that the universe is set up in such a way that humans should be the resulting 'end product', as Lovejoy (1981) put it. As I suggested earlier, these and similar statements are actually totally contrary to what Darwinian evolution claims. Darwinian evolution claims that there was no goal or end product, but rather that it was blind and random. This contradiction arises quite often in statements which attempt to support Darwinian evolution.

It would seem I am beating a dead horse, and I feel I have little hope in getting evolutionists to conform to using their own terminology according to their own definitions of these terms. Nevertheless, Barrow and Tipler do an excellent job in reporting all of the factors that have contributed to the development of life and how exactly each of these factors had to be for life as we know it to have come to be. However, they disagree that human life is merely the inevitable result of a finely tuned universe that has come about by chance: 'For the above reasons, and many others which we omit for reasons of space, there has developed a general consensus among evolutionists that the evolution of intelligent life, comparable in information-processing ability to that of Homo sapiens, is so improbable that it is unlikely to have occurred on any other planet in the entire visible universe.... in short, there is no indication in the geological record that the evolution of intelligence is at all inevitable; in fact, quite the reverse' (Barrow and Tipler, 2009, p. 133).

Barrow and Tippler (2009) list and examine the many factors that make up our 'Goldilocks universe'. The term *Goldilocks* refers to the fact that if just any one of the many life-supporting factors were only very slightly different than they are, then life as we know it could not exist. Some of these factors are, but are not limited to, the strength and properties of the four universal forces: electromagnetic, strong nuclear (holds atoms together), weak nuclear (radiation), and gravity; stars; black holes; and the position, size, and nature of the Earth, moon, and sun, which is also dependent on the other planets in our solar system. To very briefly summarise Barrow and Tippler's 706 pages of very small print: If electro-magnet forces were any stronger, they would destroy us. If they were any weaker, the Earth's magnetic field would not protect us. If the strong nuclear forces were any stronger, all material would collapse into itself; if it were any weaker, it would all fly apart. If gravity was any stronger, then the whole universe would be one giant black hole; no stars or planets could have formed if it were any weaker. If the Earth were any closer to the sun, we would burn. If it were any farther from the sun, we would freeze. If the moon was any different in size or distance to the Earth, all sorts of things would go very bad for us. The list goes on and on. These are only the things necessary to have Earth in a position to support life as we know it. Once that is done, DNA would have to assemble itself randomly. And the chances of that happening are between 4.3×10^{109} and 1.8×10^{217}. The odds against assembling the human genome spontaneously are even more enormous: $(4 \times 10^{180})^{110{,}000}$.

So how do intelligent scientists rationally explain that all of this came to pass by chance against such unfathomable odds? The simple solution to this question is the multiverse. They believe it is irrational that a God should exist, so they believe there must be an infinite number of universes that exist instead. That way, as astronomically unlikely that all of this should happen by chance, if there were an infinite number of universes, with a countless number of planets in each of them, then it would again be very likely that in at least one of them, the Goldilocks jackpot should hit. Thus, instead of believing that there is a God because there is no empirical evidence to support such a belief, they believe that there is an infinite number of universes, for which there is also no empirical supporting evidence.

This belief gave rise to the many-worlds interpretation (MWI), which Everett first proposed in 1957. However, it should be abundantly clear that the WMI is merely a scapegoat for those who simply refuse to accept the conclusion based on the evidence from the contrapositive method of proof, which is found in the anthropic principle, weak or strong. Instead of interpreting the data to mean that the universe must have had an intelligent designer, because the odds of all of this coming about by pure chance are more than astronomically small, many choose to believe in the WMI. Those who support the WMI do not question the minuscule odds of the universe coming about by chance; they simply allow themselves an infinite number of chances in order to even out the odds.

A common question posed by both believers and non-believers towards the other party is this: What evidence would convince you that there is no God or that there is a God? To this, the non-believer may reply, 'God Himself would have to tell me face to face that He exists.' But the believer may reply, 'God Himself would have to tell me face to face that He does not exist.'

Religion, science, and philosophy have offered numerous and various explanations of life and the universe. Curiously, each person who has formed a belief seems satisfied with their belief, although they know other people have other beliefs. As such, if we believe in God, then we most likely believe that God created humans with the innate tendency to form beliefs, which gives us comfort and the ability to adapt to things we do not understand or cannot readily observe. But if we do not believe in God, then we most likely believe that humans seem to have the innate tendency to form beliefs, which give us comfort and the ability to adapt to things we do not understand or cannot readily observe. Either way, humans have the innate ability to form beliefs about things that they cannot truly know.

When an individual sees the vast universe and the variety of life on this wondrous planet, and they ponder the origin of all of this, the answer they come up with will be directly dependent on their belief in God. Let me restate that very carefully and purposefully. An individual's answer to the question of the origin of life and the universe will depend directly on the individual's belief in God. If they believe in God, they will attribute the origin of life and the universe to God. If they do not believe in God, they will attribute the origin to something else. As such, if a person does not believe in God, they will find some other explanation for the origin of life and the universe.

Why do some people believe in God and the supernatural whereas others do not? Numerous authors have thoroughly investigated this question in various experiments with conclusive results. Much later in this book, I will discuss cognitive behaviour, but for now, to give a concise answer to this question, studies have demonstrated that we humans are born with an intuitive thinking style through which we form beliefs. Later, we begin to develop a rational thinking style, which enables us to rationalise, question, and ultimately choose what we want to believe.

Scientific psychological evidence has demonstrated that one's subjective understanding of God may significantly influence the development of one's mind. It has been shown that children, regardless of their theological upbringing, seem to develop some significant understanding of the concept of a god (Nyhof and Johnson, 2007). (I purposefully use a lower-case *god* in this case because I strictly differentiate between a god, which can be anything that is a person's heart's desire, and God, the Creator of life and the universe.) Other studies have yielded evidence that humans are born with the innate intuition to believe in some sort of god or supernatural phenomena, but the development of rational thinking skills may later recant such intuitional beliefs. These findings are often used to negate God's existence, but a thorough review of the Holy Scriptures illustrates that humans are created in exactly this manner. Furthermore, the Bible also recognises the difference between intuitive and rational thought and warns against the latter.

Knowledge versus Belief

'Trust in the Lord with all your heart and lean not on your own understanding; in all your ways submit to him, and he will make your paths straight' (Proverbs 3:5–6). This is a Bible verse which many atheists use to argue that religious people are stupid. While many Christians may do tend to be somewhat narrowminded, take a moment to think about what you know and distinguish it from what you believe. Do you know the sun will rise tomorrow? Do you know your car will slow down when you apply the brakes? Do you know that if you are a kind person, people will be kind to you? Do you know your parents, children, or anybody for that matter? The fact of the matter is we know much less than we think we do. In reality, we do not know. We merely believe to a significant level of certainty.

Here again, we see how the scientific interpretation of data is formed to demonstrate the scientific assumption that God does not exist, whereas the data actually validates the Holy Scriptures. Many would like to interpret this data to mean that if one thinks rationally, one will choose to believe there is no God. However, the data actually says humans are born first with the intuitive understanding that there is something, a greater force, something that cannot be explained rationally. Intuitively, we seem to know that we are the children of God created in His image; however, grasping that rationally is for some more difficult. Nevertheless, theologically and scientifically, a rational explanation can be offered that is simple and that claims more evidence than blind faith. Faith in anything is blind simply because we cannot see into the future. But blind as it is, faith does not have to be ignorant.

Suppose humans alone, and no other animals, are created in the image of God. In that case, this difference must be reflected through some quality. This quality is illustrated in the fact that humans are the only animals that are not completely dominated by their animalistic desires, drives, instincts, and reflexes. This capacity to override our animalistic nature is what gives us the ability and the very meaning of sin. Regardless of how vicious or ferocious it may be, any animal does not have the aptness to commit a sin because it has no understanding of right and wrong. Humans can choose to forgive rather than condemn, give instead of take, accept rather than reject, and love those who hate them.

Created to Know God

'For God knows that when you eat from it your eyes will be opened, and you will be like God, knowing good and evil' (Genesis 3:5). This event is often depicted as if God quickly had to scurry and come up with a plan B. Jesus's death on the cross was not plan B but only phase three of plan A. Phase one was create. Phase two was growth; without resistance, there can be no growth. Phase three was redemption. Humans were created with the innate desire to have a relationship with God. 'Man knows God naturally as he desires Him naturally. Now man desires Him naturally in as much as he naturally desires happiness, which is a certain likeness to the divine goodness. Thus, it is not necessary that God, considered in Himself, should be naturally known to man, but a certain likeness of God. Hence, man must be led to a knowledge of God through His likenesses that are found in the effects which He works' (Aquina, 1975, p. 9).

A Critical Examination of Darwinian Evolution

In contrast, Darwinian evolution argues that humans are not cousins of angels but rather of apes. If one perceives reality through this belief, this does not mean that they cannot know love or morality, as some have falsely argued. But it does mean that their perspective of this world is decisively different in that they are not living with the kind of hope that only comes from God. Regardless of whether one believes he is a child of God or a product of evolution, this belief serves as a foundation upon which reality is experienced. The studies we discussed in the previous chapter illustrated that humans are born with the intuitive understanding that there is something to believe in, but as our cognitive capacities develop, our rational cognition begins to question our intuitive beliefs. At some point in this process, humans gain the ability to choose how they want to perceive a situation (Frankl, 2006). Frankl, a survivor of the Nazi concentration camps and psychologist, observed that when fellow prisoners lost hope, their demise seemed to follow quickly. Frankl found that as long as one can perceive a purpose, one can maintain a spark of hope even in a suffering situation.

Whether or not one believes in God, one will have to endure hardship, suffering, and malicious evil acts in this world. Thus in reaction to this, one can believe that only the strong survive, and this is good because it weeds out the weak that burden us all. Or one believes that the world is simply evil, and all one can do is keep one's head down and try not to draw attention. Or it is a dog eat dog world, so become the boss dog and do unto others before they do unto you. Or always be prepared to run, and when problems arise, run. It is a simple, animalistic 'fight, flight, or fright' response. However, one can also choose to see the world as described in the Holy Scriptures and choose to endure hardship with the belief that suffering produces perseverance, and perseverance builds character and character hope (Romans 5:3–5).

We choose what we want to believe. Some make this choice with little thought, some with more. Blind faith is not the same as ignorant faith. I am aware of several followers of Christ who mistake blind faith with ignorant faith. Some believers reject science altogether and justify that by saying that science rejects God; therefore, I reject science. Science does indeed reject God, but as a scientist, I understand why. Science is a method of thinking based on the assumptions that our observations reflect reality as we experience and that the physical laws governing this reality are embedded in this same reality. In short, it means that what we see is what we get. Scientists must assume that data reflect the observations and that no other forces are at work other than what we experience. Otherwise, there would be no point in measuring observations and then building hypotheses based on these observations. For example, when conducting experiments with the coefficient of sliding friction to determine which material is best suited for the construction of a tire, scientists do not consider how much the driver might be praying at the time he slams on the breaks.

Similarly, when science tests the effectiveness of a drug, it is the drug that is being tested and not the level of faith that the user may possess. Thus, science must assume that God, gods, spirituality, crystals, magic, spells, enchantments, and the like are not factors which should undergo consideration in the outcomes of scientific experiments. If this were not so, then science could not make any conclusion without someone holding up their hand and asking how much of the variance can be attributed to the hand of God.

Nevertheless, belief is still a very important aspect of science. Scientists make theories based upon what they think or believe to be true. Then they create an experiment to test this belief, otherwise known as a hypothesis. Of course, problems often arise when scientists try to puzzle data into their beliefs instead of forming a belief based objectively on data. Ruse (1986) demonstrated how one's personal beliefs could lead to gross misinterpretations of the data. In his work *Taking Darwin Seriously*, Ruse projects his spitefulness and animosity towards God in his scientific work. He writes as if he is talking about someone he does not like but is in the company of friends of that disliked individual. He speaks of the integrity of science but ignores the fact that this integrity is balanced on the scientist's ability to avoid the kind of bias rhetoric that is clearly portrayed in his work. This is most clearly illustrated in that he begins his work by stating evolution is a fact, which is the very point he is trying to demonstrate.

He repeats this many times without offering any supporting evidence, other than references to his own previous works. Essentially, he is saying, 'It is so because I said it is so.' And on a couple of occasions, he stated things that were simply known to be wrong, such as claims about speech, language, and communication. Take all of that away, and what is left over is an interesting book on natural selection, which is indeed a fact but not a preliminary step to evolution.

Natural Selection Is Fact; Evolution Is Grand Assumption

The Bible clearly supports the concept of natural selection, in that God created Adam, who was either black, white, red, or yellow, but one skin colour. Now we have various skin colours, which happened through what is now referred to as natural selection. However, just because small changes can occur does not mean that many small changes can lead to one big change over time. Still, that is the grand assumption behind the theory of Darwinian evolution.

In many works supporting evolution, the authors' faulty logic is underlined with outright distortion from the facts. Rana and Ross (2015) reported on incidences in which fossil data was purposefully manipulated to support the theory of evolution, explaining that scientific investigation is often motivated by the pursuit of recognition and fame rather than the pursuit of knowledge. When one desperately wants to find connections between human and ape, one can formulate a theory and then interpret the data to support that theory. In fact, while the fossilized remains of other species of primates have been found, none of them have been deemed 'half man, half ape'. Instead, they have all been deemed simply not human and not any more or less primate than the primates that are living today. All that has been found are primates that have gone extinct.

But when one wants to categorise the various fossils of all the various prehistoric primates, one can arrange the categorical data horizontally or vertically. Horizontal categorization displays the data parallel to each other like on a bar graph. The very idea of a bar graph is to visually demonstrate that nothing from any category pours into another category. That is, no family of primates is a descendant of another family. However, when charts are made that attempt to illustrate humans' 'evolution', these categorical data are placed in a timeline according to their assumed age. This exact alignment creates the illusion that one species evolved into the next if one arranges the categories linearly by time. In a discussion of the proposed ape to human transition phase, Washburn and Moore (1974, p. 68) admitted, 'Only a few scant fossils tell of this stage in evolution.' Thus, the assumptions required to make such an idea plausible are much too great to allow for an acceptable amount of reliability and validity for this interpretation of the data.

Similarly, in Matsuzawa's (2009) work *The Chimpanzee Mind: In Search of the Evolutionary Roots of the Human Mind*, I seriously wondered if the author did not understand the difference between communication and language or whether they were purposefully deceptive. The purpose of this work was to present a theoretical framework for comparative cognitive science, which employs various methods to investigate the minds of non-human animals to understand the evolutionary origins of the human mind. In doing so, science has found ways to communicate with animals, which seems extraordinary only if one equates communication with language.

Communication versus Language

Communication is based on relational meaning, whereas language is based on symbolic meaning. The difference is that almost all animals communicate through relational meaning. The chirping of a bird, the croaking of a frog, and the hissing of a cat are examples of relational communication. These sounds mean something in that they are related to something. Such sounds are no different in communication through the rattling of a snake's tail, displaying a peacock's feathers, or a gorilla beating on his chest. Indeed, through classical conditioning, humans have been able to expand the relational vocabulary of many non-human animals, but only humans are able to communicate through symbolic communication. The difference is best explained through an example: the word lunch. The sounds used to create that word are in and of themselves in no relation to that word. In fact, some of the sounds have a meaning of their own. If I asked you, 'Lunch?' and you responded with the n sound in that word, I might think you do not want lunch. Or if you responded with the u sound in the word, I may think you are unsure if you want lunch or not. As such, the individual sounds have no relational meaning to the word lunch, but only in this specific construction. Furthermore, the symbolism continues on the next level because if I say the word lunch, it still has no relational meaning in that you still do not know if I am offering lunch, requesting lunch, or referring to a time, location, or activity. In order to convey meaning through symbolic communication, many symbols are needed, and more time is required, but the conciseness of the communication is immense compared to relational communication, which is fast and simple but unable to communicate a significant amount of information.

In *Man, Animal, or Both? Problems in the Interpretation of Early Symbolic Behavior*, Petru (2012) illustrated another problem in the interpretation of data, which is made to support the idea of Darwinian evolution. This work is a perfect example of how anthropologists make statements of factual implication based on data that in no way justifies this level of certainty. In psychology, even if the data express a 90 per cent likelihood of causal relation, a level which is hardly ever reached, the analyses would be stated with a high degree of certainty, A is very likely to cause B, but even at this high level of a causal relationship, it would be considered in poor taste or even bad science to claim A absolutely causes B without any other factors or issues needing to be addressed.

Unfortunately, in Darwinian evolution, the data has been sorted to fit their theory, which proposes to demonstrate that the world could have come to be without a creator. The theory first assumes that there is no God and then demonstrates how the data may be sorted in a way, which offers an explanation of how humanity and the universe could have come to be without the supernatural interventions of an intelligent designer. However, there are two problems in that logic as I see it. First, they are doing the science backwards. The steps of the scientific method are as follows: observation, question, hypothesis (belief), record data, interpret data, present data.

However, this process cannot be followed in the field of anthropology, which is the study of human societies and cultures and their development. However, the only scientific data available in the exploration of early human development is fossils. As such, the anthropologist does not collect data through experiments; he simply digs and digs and finds various fossils. By naming the fossils and determining their age, the fossils become data. Thus, an anthropologist cannot formulate any research questions based on observations. Thus, they formulate their research questions based only on their assumptions and fantasy. That is, they assume that there is no God who created life and the universe. But life and the universe are here now.

So, without having had made any previous observations of how this came to be, they formulate the research question: How could life have come into existence without a supernatural creator? Then they dig up some old bones and proceed with the next step of the scientific method, belief (aka hypothesis).

Everyone wants to make a name for themselves, and scientists are no exception. The anthropologists are motivated to interpret the data in a way, which best supports their beliefs because that is all they have to go on. Anthropology freely claims 'A causes B' as fact without question, although the theory is based only on very little data. It is like finding the same word in two different books and then suggesting that the two books must have some sort of relation. Or it's like having five pieces to a five-thousand-piece puzzle and claiming to know exactly which picture the completed puzzle reveals.

Dawkins (2006) suggested that natural selection is the blind watchmaker. It is blind because it does not see ahead, does not plan consequences, and has no purpose in view; the design is only an illusion. But at the same time, he claimed that Darwinian evolution has the characteristic to converge, and he compared this to the characteristic of convergent designs by human engineers. However, convergence without intelligence is useless. As such, attempts to prove that the human mind emerged during the Palaeolithic period were based on meagre findings which were questionably linked to rituals and funerals, illustrating that a child wanting to believe in Santa will accept cookie crumbs as evidence of the fact.

The point that I am trying to make is that it is the nature of humanity to question where he came from, and only humans have the capacity to ponder and make assessments of their existence. Those who choose to believe that God does not exist make the fossil puzzle fit their belief. Those who choose to believe that God created life point out that the fossil puzzle is not a puzzle at all. As such, the debate goes back and forth as claims about fossils are made, disproven, redated, rearranged, renamed, and essentially laid out as anyone with a degree chooses. However, evolutionary psychology is a different matter altogether. In the framework of evolutionary psychology, we have no data aside from a few partial skull sizes, which are used to explain the increasing intelligence of humans over time. The theory is based on the idea that there is a causal relationship between skull size and intelligence. The idea is highly questionable when one considers the intelligence of some animals, such as octopuses, which do not even have a skull. Nevertheless, in evolutionary psychology, this is a well-established belief, although it is very poorly supported with empirical evidence of any kind.

Buss (1999) is considered the leading authority on evolutionary psychology. Nevertheless, throughout his book *Evolutionary Psychology: The New Science of the Mind*, Buss often uses the word *design*, which is totally the opposite of the concept of evolution. In addition, the word *evolution* is often used to describe development processes, which is also categorically incorrect. The difference is quite simple. *Development* and *design* imply a goal or pinnacle, whereas *evolution* is and must remain completely random, continuous, and with no known or preconceived outcome. According to Buss (p. 3), evolutionary psychology focuses on four key questions:

1. Why is the mind designed the way it is—that is what causal processes created, fashioned, or shaped the human mind into its current form?
2. How is the human mind designed—What are its mechanisms or components parts, and how are they organized?
3. What are the functions of the components and their organized structure—that is, what is the mind designed to do?
4. How does input from the current environment, especially the social environment, interact with the design of the human mind to produce observable behavior?

As I read these points, I cannot help but think, 'What?' My brief response to each of these four points are as follows.

1. If the human mind is a product of evolution, how can it be designed?
2. Seriously, design is the opposite of evolution.
3. Are you trying to make my point for me?

4. I understand now why Ruse's book was entitled 'Taking Darwin Seriously'.

It is a little-known fact that in his iconic work, *The Origin of Species: By Means of Natural Selection*, Darwin (1994) never used the word *evolution*. Washburn and Moore (1974) pointed out it was actually Thomas H. Huxley who pushed the concept of natural selection into a concept of evolution.

During his expedition, Darwin found that the beaks of various finches differed from island to island depending on the kinds of food sources that were available to the finches on each island. This is evidence of natural selection but certainly not evidence of evolution. A change from A to B does not support a change from all possible points to any other conceivable point. In no other field of science would such an idea have any credibility. But as I said, anthropologists begin their scientific process with the third step, belief (hypothesis). Thus, they tend to choose to believe what they want to and find the evidence they need to support their beliefs.

The theory of Darwinian evolution by means of natural selection also has a problem with the timeline in which life appeared in the fossil records. Buss, Dawkins, and many other pro-evolution authors have asserted that natural selection is a very slow process, with lots of very small changes over a very long period. However, if it is as slow as it has been proposed to be, it is not fast enough to account for the appearance of life in fossil records. That is, there is not much time between fossils of the first evidence of any kind of life and the fossils of the first human. And the more they dig, the older the human fossils they find. This is often referred to as the problem of punctuated equilibrium (Gould and Eldredge, 1977). As such, pro-evolutionists have had to tweak their theory and say that sometimes evolution suddenly made large changes and not always small ones (Dawkins, 2006a).

Dumsday (2019) questioned the theory of Darwinian evolution by asking, If the universe is supposedly fine-tuned for the eventual development of biological life, why did it take billions of years for life to develop? If the universe came into existence four billion years ago, why did life pop up relatively recently and quickly? In contrast, John Haught doubled down and used the same point against creationism: 'Our question then is why, if God exists, evolution has been so slow. If God is a creator, why is the divine production of life so much more inefficient than the projects of human engineers? Certainly, if the universe was created by an intelligent deity, the emergence of living and thinking beings would not have taken so long or been so circuitous' (Dumsday, 2019, p. 317).

Another source of weak evidence comes from DNA studies, which point out that human beings and chimpanzees share more than 98 per cent of each other's DNA. However, Rana and Ross (2015) illustrated that this is true only if one only considers the parts of the DNA that are even comparable. That is, of the 60 per cent of the DNA that is even comparable, 98 per cent of that is identical in structures that have the same form. Additionally, the relation between human and primate DNA is very overexaggerated, in that mice and men share about 80 per cent DNA sequences. Thus, as different as mice are from humans and still have such a high correlation in DNA, it would seem those correlations in DNA are not at all very indicative of an ancestorial relationship between species.

Thus, it could even be argued that the similarities in DNA found between species are evidence of a designer rather than evolution. Otherwise, species that are very different in form would have a much greater difference in DNA. But as it is, the difference in DNA between mice and humans is not all that much greater than the difference in DNA between humans and chimpanzees, considering that mice and humans are much more different in physical form than humans and chimpanzees. The similarity in the DNA is simply due to the Creator using the same material to make all animals, just as it is stated in the Bible. Still, only the humans were made in his image, meaning only humans know and understand the difference between right and wrong (Rana and Ross, 2015) and choose how to perceive a situation based on a personal subjective core belief. Moreover, the similarities in the DNA of humans and primates should not allow one to assume any similarities in the nature of the two beings, because as in all fields of science, similarities in structure do not imply similarity in nature. Take salt (NaCl), for example, a substance we ingest daily. However, if we ingest sodium (Na) alone, we would literally explode, and if we ingested chlorine (Cl) alone, we would also die. But mix the two together first, and then it is not only harmless but also good and useful.

The form and function argument is another example of how

pro-evolutionists interpret data in a way that supports their preconceived beliefs. It is undeniable that many animals share various forms and structures. This too is often given as evidence of Darwinian evolution. Anthropologists have found that many animals share similar physical structures and conclude that their physical form changes slightly as animals evolve from one species to another (Washburn and Moore, 1974). For example, the structure of the human hand is said to be very similar to the fins of a whale or the wings of a bat. However, this is not very strong evidence of evolution by natural selection because an intelligent designer would use various forms in His creation as well, just like humans do in their creations. Since its invention, the wheel has been improved, but it is still round.

Finally, we come to the difference of degree or kind debate. Darwin (1871, p. 104) acknowledged 'that the difference between the minds of the lowest man and that of the highest animal is immense'. But then he added, 'Nevertheless, the difference in mind between man and the higher animals, great as it is, is certainly one of degree and not of kind' (Darwin, 1871, p. 105). Gaylin (1990) further illustrated this difference by suggesting the difference between the mind of human and ape is greater than the difference between ape and amoeba. As vast as this difference is, evolutionists maintain that this difference is one of degree and not of kind.

Humans and no other animals build fires and wheels and create from fantasy. We imitate reality for entertainment. We diagnose each other's illnesses, communicate using symbols, navigate with maps, and think about thinking, and in doing so, we improve our means of thinking. We risk our lives for ideas, and unfortunately we kill for them as well. We collaborate with each other on an unprecedented level and explain the world in terms of hypothetical causes. We create rules based on an innate morality and punish others for breaking these rules. We have the capacity to imagine impossible scenarios that exceed our perceptions and even our reality, and in doing so, we have even been able to make these previously unimaginable perceptions reality. Above all, we have the capacity to choose and differentiate between right and wrong and teach each other how to do all of the above. It should be clear to everyone—and I believe deep down it is—that the human mind is not just qualitatively different from that of other animals. It is completely different. But alas, this difference allows humans to choose what they want to believe. And so on this point, many scientists choose to downplay the differences as one of degree and not of a kind, and they focus on the similarities between animal minds and human minds (Penn et al., 2008).

Conclusion

Psychologically speaking, the mind is essentially a mystery. It is something for which there seems to be significant empirical data. However, atomistic arguments can be made which attempt to make empirical data seem invalid by reducing the mind to neurochemistry and nothing more. Francis Crick, the discoverer of DNA, affirmed that the ultimate aim of scientific biology is to explain biology in terms of physics and chemistry (Peacocke, 1993, p. 40). So what is the mind? A clear difference between the human mind and the animal mind could be significantly associated with the concept of the image of God if you choose to believe such a thing exists. If not, one is forced to develop an alternative hypothesis or simply reject the discussion before your coffee gets cold.

Heiphetz et al. (2018) explained that some Judeo-Christian theologies portray God as mysterious. Nevertheless, some individuals claim to know what God's mind is like (Bader, et al., 2005; Luhrmann, 2012). One way of making sense of the unexplainable is to personify it (Waytz et al., 2010). Such a practice is often equated with mythology, in which stories and legends are created to offer explanations to unexplained phenomena. Thus, one might simply argue that humans have a mind because God, our Creator, has a mind. Whether one believes that humans are naturally good but with the capacity to be evil, or whether they are naturally evil but with the capacity to be good, one must accept the fact that humans not only have the capacity to judge between good and bad but also do it frequently and with great passion.

In this section, we have discussed some of the psychological data that provides evidence that the human mind is significantly different from other animals' minds. I would like to conclude with one final argument: sin. Whether or not you believe in God, in the course of your life, having gained the cognitive capacity to read this book, you will have come to a subjective understanding of what sin is. Although all humans may have a subjectively different understanding of what sin is, we all have developed a subjective understanding of what it is. Therein lies the difference in the kind of mind humans have and how it differs in the kind of mind that animals have. I believe this difference is the result of being made in God's image. Ultimately, I believe this because I choose to believe this, and others choose to believe something else.

The Bible says seek, and ye shall find. Science proclaims the same thing. However, thinking purely scientifically requires that one assume that God does not exist before you begin to think. At the same time, one could claim religion asserts that one assumes that God does exist and then stops thinking about it. In my opinion, both of these methods of thinking are narrow-minded. Nevertheless, regardless of what one chooses to believe, all humans understand the difference between right and wrong and have the capacity to override their animalistic nature. Humans alone have the capacity not to lash out and cause harm, even when they are angry. Humans alone have the capacity to show love to those who do not show love in return. And only humans have the capacity to not only believe in God but also love Him. It is this difference that is a result of humans being made in God's image.

I could continue in this manner and demonstrate many more examples in which the theory of evolution is based on biased science. But at this point, let me take a step back and assure you I am not trying to convince you to believe in one thing or another. I am merely objectively describing the data and illustrating the point of this chapter. People choose to believe what they want to and then find evidence to support that. And yes, I am very well aware that I can be accused of the same. If I were asked to offer proof that God does exist, then I would lay out other data which would support my belief. However, the difference is I have read the works of those I do not believe, and I have learned from them. I said in my previous book, and I will say it again, that I have learned much about God from Hitchens, Dawkins, and Kraus. Christian authors write what I already believe to know, whereas secular authors are more likely to write something, which is new to me and causes me to think more. Therefore, allow me to encourage you to research all of this for yourself. I have included an extensive reference list. Look up the studies I am referring to in this book for yourself and draw your own conclusions. Though our faith is destined to be blind, it need not be ignorant.

CHAPTER 2

The Blank Slate

The blank slate is a concept found in any Psychology 101 textbook and the first pages of any work on the human mind. The term *blank slate* is fairly straightforward. A baby's mind is a blank slate that has yet to be written on through experience. Throughout one's lifetime, one's so-called blank slate *will* be formatted through life experience into one's core beliefs. Core beliefs are our definitions of the world, other people, and ourselves. However, the newly born mind has no memories, experience, or knowledge of itself or its surroundings. Nevertheless, the term *blank slate* is inaccurate because the slate is certainly not blank. Science has shown that the minds of newborn babies are equipped with drives, instincts, and reflexes. These preinstalled processes get the learning process started even before the baby is born.

The concept of the blank slate may be compared to the factory setting of a new cell phone. There are no pictures or telephone numbers, nor has the owner put any information at all on the phone. But the phone is not technically totally a blank slate. Even when it is still in the box, a new phone has some working programs and apps preinstalled so when the owner does take it out of the box, they can begin using it right away. However, unlike the new phone, in which each model has the same exact factory settings, the blank slates of newborn babies are unique. Not even identical twins are believed to have the same exact slate (Miele, 2004). The concept seems simple enough, but I have hardly come across it in all my studies since Psych 101. However, for the purpose of this book, I thought maybe I should look to see if there have been any new thoughts on the concept. In my research, I quickly came across a book from Steven Pinker titled *The Blank Slate: The Modern Denial of Human Nature.*

I immediately began reading until I came across a question Pinker posed to his readers. He asked why behaviourists focus on learning through experience and greatly ignore the overwhelming significance of our DNA's influence on our learning, behaviour, personality, and essentially everything else that makes us, us. Having just answered that question in my last book, I abruptly stopped reading and wrote Pinker, a professor at Harvard University.

> I am reading *The Blank Slate* now in preparation for my next book. Loving it.
>
> I totally agree that both are significant, and there is still a missing variance.
>
> But as a therapist working with families with children with behavioural problems, I encourage the parents to not search for a WHY and not to get wrapped up in genetics because there is nothing we can do about that now. The cards are dealt, and Nurture plays out the hand. It may not be the strongest determinant of behaviour, but it is the only one we have any hope of influencing today.
>
> Alles Gute und Liebe,
> eric

Almost immediately, I got a response. It read:

> Dear Correspondent,
>
> Email has been coming in far more quickly than I can reply to it. I am prioritizing the time-sensitive messages and cannot promise to reply to the growing backlog of non-urgent correspondence in a timely fashion. I will save

> your letter though, and reply as time permits. Thanks for your patience and understanding.
>
> Best,
> Steve Pinker

What was I expecting? After all, he is a professor at Harvard and a best-selling author. But then only a few hours later, I received another email from him:

> That's reasonable, Eric, though I also think that an acknowledgment of inborn temperament can identify some of the intrapersonal challenges we need to face and can lift the blame of moral failing from individuals and their parents.
>
> Best,
> Steve

I thought that exchange would make for an interesting introduction to this chapter. But it was not until a bit later in my research that I discovered how heated the debate between nature and nurture had gotten since I took Psych 101.

In his book, Pinker seemed to push back hard against the behaviourist standpoint that behaviour, in relation to the experience of the environment, is all that matters because it is all that we have any hope of controlling. Jane and John, who is having a baby Jessica, do not influence Jessica's DNA, and Jessica does not have any say in the matter either. We get our DNA, that is, the hand we are dealt and with which we have to play, at conception. So the behaviourist may say the DNA does not matter; the child has to learn. But in contrast, studies have clearly shown our DNA does matter. In fact, it has been scientifically proven that our DNA has a greater influence on behaviour than our environment does.

In driving this point home, Pinker stepped on some toes, as he pointed out the arrogance that some behaviourists may project in claiming to be able to make out of any random child any sort of person one chooses by carefully controlling a child's learning environment. My father and I would serve as perfect examples. As a professional athlete, he was able to provide me with the environment of working out with the Steelers 1970s Superbowl championship teams. As such, I became a very good athlete until my DNA stepped in and claimed to have something to say about it. I did not know it at the time, but I had muscular dystrophy (FSH MD), and no amount of environmental influence could train my muscles to be strong once the FSH MD reared its ugly head. And when it did, it put a strain on my family environment, which literally blew the family apart. So I can clearly see where Pinker is coming from.

Pinker (2003) pointed out that correlations between parents and children may be a result of the parents' genes rather than their parenting skills, in that parents, who are loving yet authoritative, talkative yet well-mannered, may tend to raise articulate, self-confident, and well-behaved children not because of their parenting skills but rather because of their own DNA-based nature. Thus, Pinker claimed that it is a false belief that parents must be loving, authoritative, and talkative and that if children do not turn out well, it must be the parents' fault. In my work with parents of children with behavioural problems, I cannot think of a single client who has not broken down at some point in frustration because their child seems to want to prove the parenting method wrong. As such, parents can do everything right or do everything wrong, but they cannot train out of the child what they bred into them, which can be a great source of stress in the family. 'The theory that parents can mould their children like clay has inflicted child-rearing regimes on parents that are unnatural and sometimes cruel' (Pinker, 2003, p. 40).

However, when Pinker suggested that crime, addiction, and other inappropriate behaviours demonstrated by individuals are more significantly a result of their DNA rather than their upbringing, the psychological community drew battle lines as to who was at fault for such behaviours. If our DNA so significantly determines our behaviour, why should we even try to raise our children the right way? And what is the right way—if there even is a right way to raise a child? Such questions would destroy any dinner party. Still, these are questions that each of us needs to come to terms with one way or another.

For this reason, this book on the human mind did not begin with the concept of the blank slate but rather with the concept of belief. In a moment, we will talk about what the blank slate is and how blank it really is, but one thing everyone will agree with is the slate is certainly void of belief when a baby is born. But it is certainly not void of the ability to form beliefs. Moreover, it will be demonstrated that humans have a prenatal inclination to form beliefs in the absence of understanding. As such, Pinker (2006, p. 1) pointed out that human nature has been traditionally tied to religion instead of psychology and biology:

> For example, the theory of the mind in the Judeo-Christian tradition is a modular theory, positing the mind consists of several separate faculties, such as a capacity for love, a moral sense, and a capability for choice or free will. Although our free will is not the effect of any prior cause, it has an innate tendency towards sin. There is also a theory of perception and cognition in the Bible, namely, that our faculties keep us in touch with reality because God is no deceiver, and He designed them to give us an accurate picture of the world. There is even a theory of mental health: that psychological well-being comes from accepting God's purpose, loving God, and loving our fellow humans for the sake of God.

I was excited when I read this. I thought, Wow, a fellow believer and psychologist. But then he continued: 'No scientifically literate person can believe that the events narrated in the book of Genesis actually took place' (Pinker, 2006, p. 1). Oh, well, no matter; Genesis is not the topic of this discussion. As such, Pinker is spot on in that our traditional beliefs may be viewed as the formatting process of our minds' hard drive, to put it in computer terms. A common argument against religion is that one's religion is more significantly a result of one's upbringing than the validity of any spiritual truth. It is a statement that is very hard to deny against the statistical evidence that a child brought up in a Christian home tends to become a Christian, a child brought up in an Islamic home tends to become a Muslim, and a child brought up in an atheist home tends to become an atheist. Of course, one hears stories of people changing their religious viewpoints against their families and environmental traditions, but statistically their religion is more significantly based on their environment rather than their own personal convictions. But do you see the contradiction? Science says our behaviour is a result of our DNA, but it also says our religious behaviour is strictly a result of our environment. It simply is not possible that only our religious behaviour is a result of the environment, whereas all other behaviours are a result of the DNA. The only explanation for this is the human tendency to want to believe in God intuitively is preprogrammed in our DNA.

The following study offers a good description of the influence the environment and DNA have on human nature. Based on genetic studies of IQ scores, Miele (2004) illustrated that the genetic influence on behaviour could not be as powerful as it would seem to be, and environmental influence could not be as weak as it would seem to be. If it were all in the genes, then purely genetic identical twins, whether reared together or apart, would have a 100 per cent correlation, and unrelated persons, whether reared together or apart, would have a 0 per cent correlation. In actuality, the correlations in IQ scores between identical twins is about 86 per cent if they are raised in the same environment and 78 per cent if they are raised in different environments, and the correlation in IQ scores between unrelated children raised in the same environment is about 32 per cent. This represents yet another contradiction in the theory that it's all in genetics. And Pinker himself pointed out, 'Logicians tell us that a single contradiction can corrupt a set of statements and allow falsehoods to proliferate through it (Pinker, 2003, p.39). Thus, instead of examining how genetic and environmental influences work separately, one should assess how they work together (Miele, 2004). However, doing this would require integrating psychology and theology, and as Dacey (2003) pointed out, the goal of evolutionary psychology seems to be to show that humans are biological machines rather than spiritual beings created by God.

It simply does not make any sense, and it would be very unscientific to suggest that our environment determines our religious behaviours completely while our DNA determines all our other behaviours. Thus, it is not only conceivable but also scientifically probable that God has set within the human DNA a spiritual component. As such, it would seem that once again, science and Christian theology agree on the drive behind religious behaviour. John 15:16 states that it is not us who choose God, but

God who chooses us. Verses such as 1 Thessalonians 5:24; Romans 8:28; 1 Corinthians 1:9, 28–29; 2 Thessalonians 2:14; 1 Peter 2:21; Philippians 3:14; 2 Timothy 1:9; Isaiah 65:1; Ephesians 4:4; and many others speak of a calling from God to us, not the other way around. In addition to this, numerous Bible verses instruct parents to raise their children to follow God (Proverbs 22:6–7; Psalm 34:11; Deuteronomy 11:19). And of course, many verses instruct us to create a loving environment, the golden rule being the epidemy of this: 'Do unto others, as you would have them do unto you' (Luke 6:3).

Scientific studies have come to the same conclusion. Humans are born with the ability and inclination to believe in God, and this attribute is embedded in our DNA. However, it is our environment in which we grow and develop. Regardless of our DNA and environment, it is up to each adult individual to either choose to follow God or choose not to do so. Thus, in religious terms, one may say that it was God who planted the seed, but it is our environment which waters the seed. Nevertheless, it is up to each individual to decide for themselves what they want to do with the harvest.

Furthermore, the Bible clearly states that our sinful nature is embedded in our flesh (Romans 8:3), which coincides with Pinker's (2003) conclusions that inappropriate behaviours result from DNA and not the environment. Thus, logically, our calling and spirituality should also be embedded in our DNA and not the environment. It would seem that our genes transact with the environment and our environment with our genes, just as Miele (2004) proposed.

Miele (2004) described three kinds of gene-environment correlation (as cited in Rose, 1995). Passive correlation readily occurs because in most cases, parents provide both their children's genes and their environment. In such cases, it is impossible to assess whether a specific behaviour is a result of the DNA or the environment. Evocative correlation occurs because individuals want to be individuals and not copies, whether from their environment or from DNA. Active correlation takes it one step further, describing the resistance individuals express towards learning and change. People simply do not like to be manipulated, and when they suspect they are being manipulated, they resist. It does not matter if that manipulation is for the good or the bad; when detected, people tend to shut down. This is generally referred to as stubbornness, a universal human trait embedded in our primal fear.

When it comes to protecting our thoughts, ideas, and opinions, humans react stubbornly towards communication and teaching because communication and teaching are essentially manipulations. It is the act of one person embedding an idea in the mind of another. Unfortunately, it does not matter if the manipulation is for the receiver's benefit or harm; one is always cautious about abandoning one's own comfortable ideas and beliefs for one coming from another's mind, regardless of what the communication is or from whom it is coming. To counteract this, humans are also born with various instincts and reflexes that foster the early learning process. For example, Schlinger (2004) claimed that humans have a 'predisposition to learn fears quickly from such unpredictable and uncontrollable events. But we must learn the fear of snakes nonetheless'.

As it is now, humans are at the top of the food chain. We can move about relatively freely, without the fear of getting eaten by something. Still, we have the inborn tendency to be safe rather than sorry. That means we would rather make the mistake that something bad is just around the corner when it is not (false-positive) than to make the mistake that there is nothing bad around the corner when there is (false-negative). A false-negative can be deadly, but a false-positive only wastes time and energy.

With that said, let us examine the scientific understanding of the newborn human mind. We will begin with how science has determined the overwhelming significance of our DNA's influence on our behaviour. A great amount of research has been dedicated to studying the correlation between our DNA and our behaviours. Since Francis Crick discovered the DNA molecule, longitudinal studies have been done on fraternal, identical, and adopted siblings raised together and apart. Very generally, they compare siblings' behaviours on many various factors and constellations. It has been found that identical twins who have been given up for adoption and raised in different homes displayed significantly more similar behaviours than fraternal twins raised in the same home. However, identical twins raised in the same home were not significantly more similar than identical twins raised apart.

Furthermore, non-related children adopted into the same home did not demonstrate significantly fewer similarities in behaviour than fraternal siblings raised in the same home. The similarities in behaviours between identical twins raised together or apart persisted and even increased in adulthood, whereas similarities between fraternal and adopted siblings dissipated over time. These studies have been conducted again and again and have consistently demonstrated that our DNA has an overwhelming significance on our behaviour. The data is so overwhelming, in fact, that one could pose the question: What is the point in parenting at all?

Dauphin (2003, p. 2) railed against Pinker's critic of virtually every aspect of parenting and suggested 'that all books or manuals which seek to give advice to parents about how to bring up their children are actually perpetuating a grand hoax'. However, Pinker is correct in that the entire field of research regarding child-rearing techniques is hopelessly confounded with genetics because one cannot determine whether the influences on the child's behaviour is a result of the parents' parenting or their genes. This would be a stronger argument if it were not for foster care, in which the caregiver gives only parenting and no genes into the works. Still, Pinker seems to sincerely believe that parents have little to no influence on what 'kind' of person the child becomes. So should we simply give birth, care for the child's physical needs, offer the child education, and let it pursue its own interests without offering any direction?

Although some parents agree with this and allow their children to misbehave without any consequence whatsoever, scientific studies on behaviour maintain that when consequences follow inappropriate behaviour, such behaviour generally becomes less frequent; however, such studies on the anti-disciplinary style of parenting have also shown that harsh physical punishment as a consequence of very inappropriate behaviour is significantly less effective than other forms of punishment (Kolb, 2021). Thus, once again, the great Counsellor and scientific psychology agree that children need direction through loving discipline.

> And have you completely forgotten this word of encouragement that addresses you as a father addresses his son? It says, 'My son, do not make light of the Lord's discipline, and do not lose heart when he rebukes you, because the Lord disciplines the one he loves, and he chastens everyone he accepts as his son.' Endure hardship

> as discipline; God is treating you as his children. For what children are not disciplined by their father? If you are not disciplined—and everyone undergoes discipline—then you are not legitimate, not true sons and daughters at all. Moreover, we have all had human fathers who disciplined us, and we respected them for it. How much more should we submit to the Father of spirits and live! They disciplined us for a little while as they thought best, but God disciplines us for our good in order that we may share in His holiness. No discipline seems pleasant at the time but painful. Later on, however, it produces a harvest of righteousness and peace for those who have been trained by it (Hebrews 12:5–11).

Sensory Integration and Learning

Despite the overwhelming powerful influence DNA has on us, I could argue that the influence of our environment is indeed greater when it comes to learning behaviours. Simply because as it is now, our DNA cannot be changed or corrected. Science is working on that now, and progress has been made. However, the Netflix documentary series *Unnatural Selection* illustrated that costs, application, reliability, and availability do not make gene alteration a viable alternative for learning through sensory integration. Furthermore, as astronomically large as the various combinations our genes may be construed to create a human being, the number is mathematically limited. But the influence of our environment is unlimited. Everything that happens and everything that does not happen in each moment of our life affects us in unknown ways.

For example, I bought instant coffee on Tuesday; I don't know why, because I usually drink the good stuff. On Wednesday morning, my five-year-old woke up at the break of dawn and called out, 'Dad, do you want a coffee?' I murmured, 'Yeah.' Moments later, she called me into the kitchen, where I found she had put at least one heaping tablespoon of instant coffee into a small cup and filled it half full with warm water out of the spout. But more important, she had set up the chessboard. On this morning, she seemed to have made a huge leap in her understanding of how the pieces work together to form a checkmate, as she explained to me a series of 'if … then' sequences that astounded me. Sure, she would have come to this understanding eventually anyway, but isn't timing everything? This morning together was in some way particularly special. But had I bought my usual espresso beans, the event would not have happened, at least not on that morning at that time. Thus, whether one believes that the events we experience are a wilful construction of God or a series of random and unrelated coincidences, it is undeniable that the events we experience are significant for learning and development.

So how do we learn through experience? Humans are born with a blank slate with a preinstalled learnings system called sensory integration. Through sensory integration of our six senses, we take in information about our environment through what we see, hear, smell, touch, taste, and the sense of balance.

The Sixth Sense

Anne Jean Ayres argued that the vestibular system is the unifying system for all sensory input, providing a 'framework for the other aspects of our experience'. She claimed 'that in order for a child's brain to function properly, it must be able to organize and integrate the bombardment of sensory input it receives (as cited in McCriedie, 2007, pp. 147–48). Ayre's work in the 1970s led to the concept of sensory integration (SI). SI is the term used to describe the process of taking in information through our sight, hearing, smell, taste, touch, and most importantly our sense of balance, which is the first of these systems to fully develop, the only one to always be active in during consciousness, and the only one without which we could not survive. The sense of balance is highly underrated and often totally forgotten. One can live without the ability to see, hear, smell, taste, or feel. But if we had no sense of balance, we would die a miserable death like a blob on the ground, unable to move or focus on anything. So next time someone mentions the five senses, please give a shout-out to the true sixth sense, balance.

Pavlov became famous for illustrating how sensory integration is used in learning in terms of conditioned and unconditioned responses and unconditioned and unconditioned stimuli. This learning system builds upon the innate survival instincts preprogrammed to learn survival behaviour. Thus, various animals demonstrate various learning behaviour that was motivated through food (positive reinforcement) or not being shocked (negative reinforcement). The ability to learn in this manner is coded in our DNA, which causes the human brain to develop the way it does.

Now we will examine how brain development leads to mind development. Although the mind and the brain are clearly distinct entities, they are very intricately interwoven through sensory integration. Our sensory organs are of material nature, made up of atoms. These organs are sensitive to material and energy in the physical environment. This sensory integration occurs in the physical brain, but then it is stored and processed in the mind. Since the brain begins to develop while the baby is still in the womb, one must concur that the mind begins to develop before birth as well. The development of the mind begins with the development of the vestibular system, commonly referred to as the sense of balance.

While the baby is still in the womb, the baby achieves a fundamental state of consciousness, which means it becomes rudimentarily aware of itself in that it distinguishes itself from sensory input from its environment. It hears its mom's voice and heartbeat and understands that these sounds are coming from outside itself (Sieratzki and Woll, 1996). And with that, the self begins to form. Somehow, the baby decides it is time to be born and turns itself upside down, again illustrating a fundamental awareness of its environment and self. This is the reason that the sense of balance needs to be fully functional before birth. If not, the baby could not know where up and down is and could not correctly position itself (McCredie, 2007).

But as soon as the baby is born, that is when the real sensory integration begins. Lights, sounds, the cold, the touch of people, and smells of disinfectant overwhelm the baby and cast it into consciousness. From that point on, the baby's mind begins downloading information like crazy. Our adult minds cannot fathom the shock that a newborn baby must experience as its environment of the womb is stripped away and replaced with our environment. As terrifying as that might be, it seems the sweet taste of breast milk counteracts that well. From that position, a familiar sound of mom's heartbeat brings comfort, and at least one of the voices sounds vaguely familiar. At that moment, the slate is no longer blank as the mind begins to integrate experience through the six senses. This information is then used to drive the various cognitive developmental processes such as identity, personality, and attitude that become observable through our behaviour.

Neural Plasticity

Neural plasticity is the process of building neuro-pathways through the various parts of the brain. Whenever we learn a new skill or gain a new understanding, this is attributed to neuron having created new connections between two or more brain areas. Thus, Schlinger (2004, p. 37) very accurately stated, 'Neural plasticity is just another name for learning and development.'

Geddes (2015) noted that the brain undergoes more change during the first two years of life than it does in the rest of the lifetime. So what happens next? Let us consider day two. The mother and child are well-rested, and both are relieved that the previous day is over. What might be going on in the baby's mind? The preinstalled apps such as hunger, sleep, emotions, desires, instincts, and reflexes will have started to send a barrage of notifications. These are not things that the baby consciously wants but rather things the baby is preprogrammed to want, and the baby is also preprogrammed with the behaviours needed to have those wants fulfilled. Please note that I am using the word *want* and not the word *need.* A baby has no idea what it needs (some adults do not even know that). All it knows at this point is want and how to get it, and a baby knows this instinctively, not through learning.

In her book *What's Going on in There? How the Brain and Mind Develop in the First Five Years of Life*, Lisa Eliot cites a study from 1972 in which researchers, working with babies two and four days old, tested various 'soothing methods. The babies were (1) lifted from their beds and cradled in a researcher's arm (tactile, vestibular, and body heat); (2) given contact without being lifted (tactile and heat); (3) placed in an infant seat and moved up and down, or side to side (vestibular only), or (4) stimulated with voice (auditory only). In the end, those methods that involved vestibular stimulation were more effective than those that relied only on touch or contact ... rocking a baby in an infant seat, without any caregiver physical contact—was more effective than contact alone' (McCredie, 2007, p. 144).

Humans do not only differ from all other animals in that their minds become the most capable, but they also differ from all other animals in that their minds begin the least capable: 'All other species rely more upon reflexes or fixed-action patterns that, although not insensitive to learning experiences, are relatively stable: aggression, mating, migration, imprinting, and care of young' (Schlinger, 2004, p. 35). Some animals are born and then immediately go about their independent lives. Mammals get their name because they are nursed and by their mother, but it is up to the newborn to become mobile enough to find its mother's mammary glands. Other animals are equipped with a wide range of instincts that foster survival and rush them through what would be, in human terms, child development and learning processes. However, most of what humans know how to do are not present at birth and must be learned through experience.

Kostrubiec et al. (2012) quantified the predisposition and capabilities that each learner brought to the learning environment and developed a dynamical account of sensorimotor learning to examine how new skills are acquired and old ones modified. However, these authors discovered that the quantification of such learning behaviours, especially in a laboratory setting, may not be as valid a measurement as one would like to have:

Performance in learning and memory studies is typically assessed by accuracy, that is, by the mismatch between what is required and what is produced.... However, this is not how learning works. As the saying goes, 'We learn from our mistakes.' Let us say a nine-month-old baby, who is able to crawl and sit, is hungry because it did not finish its bottle. The baby sees the bottle, crawls to it, sits up, and puts the nipple in its mouth. But nothing comes out because the bottle is already half empty and the baby is not tilting the bottle enough. A learning opportunity is at hand. If, in its attempt to drink, the baby loses its balance and falls backward, the baby will have unknowingly stumbled upon the solution without having learned anything at this point yet. But, the next time the baby is in this situation, it may remember the experience and then perform the correct behaviour to get the milk. Then it will have learned.

However, if the baby does not fall backwards and stumble unknowingly upon the solution, one of three things is likely to happen. Most likely, the baby will eventually get frustrated and start to cry. When this happens, parents, please recognise the learning opportunity and do not simply solve the baby's problem. If you do this, you will have taught your child to cry whenever faced with a challenge. Instead of simply solving the baby's problem, prompt the child towards the solution. When it comes to prompting a child to learn, the golden rule is this: Help as little as possible, but as much is necessary for success. So, if the parent were to tilt the bottle back, so that the milk hits the baby's lips for just a moment and repeats this a few times, the baby is likely to draw the connection between the required behaviour (tilting the bottle) and the reward (milk). Once the connection is made, the behaviour is learned. Of course, the baby could make this connection with enough trial and error without a prompt. If this happens, the baby not only learns this 'tilting bottle' behaviour but also learns that trial and error is an effective way of learning and exploring. The third possible outcome is that the baby's desire for the bottle's contents is not enough to warrant further attempts or crying, and the baby simply looks for something else to put in its mouth.

This learning situation would be impossible to recreate in the laboratory because nowhere in the above situation did anyone want the baby to do anything in particular. The desire and the resulting behaviour originated from the baby, not from anyone else. But, in lab situations, the researchers want to see if a baby performs a certain behaviour. Externally, we can only see if the baby performs the behaviour or not, but that does not necessarily reflect the baby's knowledge and understanding of the behaviour. When behaviours are generated on their own, rather than required in a test situation, then no accuracy measures can exist. Otherwise, it is like throwing a dart in any direction or manner and then drawing the target around the place where it landed. The accuracy of measurements made in this manner depend on the experimenter, not the performance of a target behaviour (Kostrubiec et al., 2012).

Educators much too often fail to understand that it is not how children are educated that matters but rather how children learn. At an institution I used to work for, we had a very appropriate saying: If a child does not learn the way it is taught, teach it the way it learns. Only with great effort—and still she is sceptical—have I told my daughter that I am far less concerned with her grades than her effort. I cannot stress this enough to parents, but it is not about getting the answers right; it is about getting the thinking right. The strength of human cognition is not in getting more right and less wrong. It is about creating theories, testing them, examining them, and then improving them. And above all, it is about learning from mistakes.

Naude (2015) noted that a child's intuitive theory about a phenomenon is not merely replaced or abandoned but rather serves as a foundation for new concepts. For example, the childhood theory that the moon is made of cheese is based on the observation of the cheese-like holes in the moon. This is completely wrong, but this false theory can serve as a basis for the understanding that meteoroids regularly collide with the moon. This, in turn, may bring rise to the understanding of an atmosphere and other cosmological concepts.

Schlinger (2004) agreed that *learning* is defined as specific changes in behaviour due to one of two kinds of experiences: classical and operant learning. In classical learning, an otherwise neutral stimulus elicits a specific behaviour. Our mind is full of such associations. Red means stop, green means go, and dogs bark and may even bite. Thus, the sight of a dog may prompt one specific behavioural response, while the sight of a red light prompts another. Humans learn to associate various stimuli with various behaviours quickly and often subconsciously. This kind of learning continues throughout one's life but is especially prominent in the earlier stages of development. Operant learning is slower, more complex, and defined by the universal equation of behaviour: Behaviour = (Reinforcement / Consequence) + Motivation. That is, an individual will do what it has to, to get what it wants if it wants it bad enough. In operant learning, behaviours are either strengthened (reinforced) or weakened (punished) by their consequences. Schlinger (2004, p. 38) noted that 'Operant learning has been shown to account for a much wider range of behaviours, including most if not all actions involving skeletal muscle activity. Operant learning has been observed in species ranging from simple to complex and has even been observed in individual nerve cells' (as cited in Stein and Belluzzi, 1988). Schlinger noted that the reinforcement of babbling explains how humans learn a language in terms of automatic reinforcement.

The acquisition of language is a prime example of all of this. First of all, babies have a reflex to babble at about nine months that lasts until about thirty-six months. Parents, especially mothers, have a reflex that makes their hearts melt when they hear this, so they pick up the child and dance around, sing, and coo with the child. This behaviour reinforces the baby's verbal behaviour, which then increases and prompts more reinforcing behaviours from the parents until the baby makes a vocalisation that sounds remotely like any word. This sound is often *ma* or *ba* because they are two of the easiest sounds to make. If the mother hears something like *ma*, then one can imagine what happens next. The mom totally flips out, rejoicing and saying, 'That's right, I'm your mama, mama,' over and over. In reality, the baby has no idea what it is saying, what a mama is, or what speech is, but the child likes the mother's reaction and also hears the mom saying 'mama', and so the child imitates the sound. It does not even have to be a very successful imitation, but merely the slightest effort will prompt all kinds of reinforcing behaviours from the mother. And so the child vocalises more and more, and each time it says something the more closely resembles a real word, the reinforcement that follows begins to prompt the child to assemble a vocabulary. Fathers are the same way, and even perhaps a bit more ridiculous, because if the baby says *ba*, the dad could hear *da* and then reinforce the *ba* into *dada*, just like the mom did. In this manner, a baby's instinctual vocalisations get shaped into language.

Like the example just used, Kostrubiec et al. (2012) outlined and simplified the universal laws of learning and associated attention and memory processes and demonstrated that these are formed based on spontaneous behaviours rather than formal teaching. So often during this pandemic, I have heard and read about parents expressing the stresses of homeschooling. This surprised and alarmed me greatly because parents teach their children so much more than any teacher could because a child is always learning. And because children are always learning, parents would do well to know that they are always teaching. Even if you are not aware that you are 'teaching' your child, your child is still always learning from you and their environment. I was shocked when the principal addressed the parents at my daughter's first-grade orientation and warned them not to interfere with their child's education. She meant policies and regulations, but still. Many parents tend to think teaching the child is the teacher's responsibility; after all, they are being paid for it. But in the words of Samuel Clemens, we should make an effort not to allow a child's schooling to interfere with the child's education. We educate children in groups of classes, one succeeding the next, but as Kostrubiec et al. (2012) point out, learning behaviours are specific to each child and occur spontaneously according to the child, not according to the teacher.

So what can be done about this? Unfortunately, not much. We cannot have one-on-one teaching for every child. We have to put them in groups not only for an administrative purpose but also for the sake of learning social skills. Sorry to leave you hanging like this, but we are discussing learning and not education, and unfortunately, these are not the same things. So if I have made you aware of a problem you did not know you had, allow me to make just one general suggestion. Reward good study behaviours, not good grades. Show interest in the creativeness of your child's work rather than its quality. Because learning is a process that is specific and unique to each child, I can say no more about the learning of one child without being completely wrong about the learning of another child.

Conclusion

Let me reiterate that the blank slate is not blank, and it is not a slate. It is not blank because various drives, instincts, and reflexes are preprogrammed into the DNA upon conception. These drives, instincts, and reflexes kick in at just the right time and jump-start various learning processes, such as controlled motor movement, speech, feeding behaviours, and attention to environmental and interpersonal stimuli. Within a typical child developmental process, each child will normally demonstrate the same instincts, drives, and reflexes, and these will set in and fade out at a typical time and in a standard order. Developmental disorders result when, for various reasons, one or more of the preprogrammed instincts, drives, and reflexes do not kick in when they should. Nevertheless, not even identical twins, who share the same DNA, will have the same development.

Thus, not only is the slate not blank, but also each slate is absolutely unique to each individual. As such, the term *slate*, which implies a uniformed structure, is also misleading.

By the time a baby is born, its cognitive systems will have already begun to process sensory input from its environment. The sense of balance is the first sensory system to become fully functional, enabling the baby to know where up and down is, which is the foundation for movement and attention. Studies have demonstrated that even a newborn baby can instinctually recognise its mother's voice, and shortly after birth, the baby can also recognise its mother's face. Such instincts foster attachment between mother and child, which later becomes crucial in social and emotional development. Reflexes, such as the reflex to hold on to anything that touches the baby's hand or suck on anything that touches the baby's mouth, help ensure the baby's ability to ingest nourishments. Drives such as hunger spark behaviours like crying, which lay the foundation for communication and other developmental processes.

Although humans have much more cognitive potential than any other animal, no animal is as incapable as humans are at birth. Perhaps this is the reason that the inherently false term *blank slate* has persisted for so long. All other newly born mammals can manoeuvre themselves to their mother's mammary glands, while the newly born human is incapable of controlled movement at birth. Nevertheless, as the various innate drives, instincts, and reflexes kick in to foster development, sensory integration enables learning through the environment. By the age of four, a typically developed human will have far surpassed the cognitive abilities of all other animal species but still not have begun to approach its adult cognitive potential. Before that can happen, much more needs to take place.

CHAPTER 3

Objective and Subjective Self-Awareness

> The human dilemma is that which arises out of a man's capacity to experience himself as both subject and object at the same time. Both are necessary—for the science of psychology, for therapy, and for gratifying living.
>
> —May (1967, p. 8)

The term *awareness* is often used in a very broad sense. However, as it is used in psychology, it has a more specific meaning and may be defined as the acute perception of an event. Thus, the term *awareness* is not synonymous with the term *consciousness*. The term *aware* is used in conjunction with the preposition *of*. That is, one is not simply aware but rather aware of something in particular. However, one can simply be conscious without being conscious of anything in particular. In fact, while you are reading these words, you are conscious. But, until just now, you were probably not conscious of your posture at this very moment. But now, having brought the idea of your posture to your attention, you have now become aware of your posture and may have even corrected it a bit or even stretched your back and shoulders. So let us define consciousness as a state of mind, ranging from unconscious to fully alert. *Awareness* is the consciousness of something in particular, and *attention* is a heightened level of awareness, which may be synonymous with *focus*.

Incidentally, explaining these concepts in the German language is even more difficult because the German word for *awareness* and *consciousness* is the same, *bewusstsein*, and the distinction between the two terms is made only with the addition of a prepositional phrase.

Pictorially, one could illustrate the difference between conscious awareness and focused concentration like this. At the risk of sounding esoteric, it would seem that an individual who is aware of his surrounding environment may be described as having vectors of attention going out from his centre in all directions. The feeling of being watched is a mysterious thing. And even though we do not have eyes in the back of our heads, one may nevertheless be able to gain some awareness of what is going on behind oneself, out of sight. However, if someone is concentrating on something—a specific stimulus—then it would seem as if all (or most) vectors of attention are focused in one direction, and thus, one becomes more oblivious to that which is going on behind them out of sight.

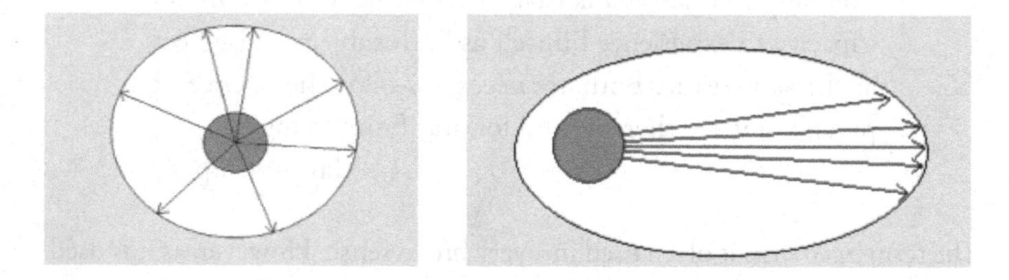

Now that the term *conscious awareness* has been defined, we can proceed to the term *self-awareness*, which again differs distinctly from the term *self-consciousness*. Self-consciousness relates to one's confidence in oneself rather than the term *consciousness*, as discussed thus far. As we are discussing it, the term *self-awareness* is merely a specific kind of awareness: the awareness of one's thoughts, feelings, and perception. Finally, self-awareness occurs in one of two forms: objective and subjective. Subjective self-awareness is when an individual perceives themself as the subject of its environment, whereas objective self-awareness is when an individual perceives themself as an object in its environment. Our subjective self-awareness is present at birth, whereas our objective self-awareness develops much later in parallel with our theory of mind (ToM), which will be discussed in the next chapter.

Objective versus Subjective

If you have come across these terms before, you may have noticed that I have reversed them. Duval and Wicklund (1972), who are generally accredited with defining these terms, did so from the perspective of a therapist outside the body of the perceiver. Hence, from this vantage point, objective self-awareness was defined as behaviour in which one subjects themself to the objectives of others, and subjective self-awareness is the opposite of that. Hence, the common terms of one's objective and subjective opinions do not coincide with my definitions. Still, I find my definitions much easier to follow. In any case, the terms themselves do not matter. It is important only that one understands the difference between the two modes of thought.

When we are born, we are born with only subjective self-awareness. A newborn perceives itself as the subject of its environment. Thus, they cry out relentlessly for what they want without considering the wants and needs of others. Everything and everyone a baby perceives in their environment is there to serve the baby's purpose. As you may well be imagining at this moment, one's subjective self-awareness does not dissipate in adulthood. Indeed, subjective self-awareness is and remains the default modus throughout one's life. If I am in my subjective self-awareness mode, then it is all about me, what I think, what I say, and what I do. Right now, writing this book, that is the mode in which I need to be. I need to concentrate on what I am thinking and writing. WhatsApp texts, my neighbours above me, and the cars passing by—none of that matters. Right now, it is all about me, what I am doing, and what I want to communicate.

However, when I am driving on the highway, this is not the frame of mind I need to be in; that would be very dangerous. I am one of many drivers on the highway, and I must understand that I have limited control of my own car and no control of any other cars. I am only one object among many, and I need to maintain that frame of reference. If I get too wrapped up in me, with what I want, and with where I am going, doing, and thinking, I might very well get in an accident. Thus, while driving, one would do well to maintain an objective self-awareness. Sometimes a person needs to focus on what they are doing, and sometimes we need to focus on what we are all doing collectively. Curiously, one can only assume objective self-awareness or subjective self-awareness, but not both simultaneously. The best we can do is flip back and forth quickly, but doing this considerably decreases the focus of both perspectives.

It should be clear that objective and subjective self-awareness are very important, and neither is more important than the other. But one must exhibit a significant level of awareness in both modes of perception and be able to adjust to the more appropriate mode of perception as the environmental situations demand. As previously mentioned, one can perceive objectively or subjectively, but not both at the same time. While you are reading this, you are probably in the subjective mode of awareness because you are focused on gaining an understanding for yourself. But if you are like me, sometimes you will discover that while you are reading, you have been thinking about something entirely different while your eyes continue to glide over the lines of text. Suddenly, you realise that you have not perceived a single word despite having read the whole page. The reason for this is our objective and subjective self-awareness, and the fact that we can only function in one mode or the other. Some may be able to fluctuate between the two modes of perception relatively quickly, but this will significantly decrease the level of awareness one can maintain in either mode of perception. For this reason, some may be able to read and watch TV at the same time. But in doing so, one's reading comprehension, as well as one's ability to follow the TV program, will both be significantly decreased.

Whether one's perception is in the objective or subjective mode of awareness, the greater the level of awareness, the better. The reason for this is simple: more information is received and processed. The more information one has, the better decisions one can make. At the risk of oversimplifying life, a person's life is basically a series of decisions. Sure, one may be faced with circumstances that are not a direct result of one's own decisions; nevertheless, one always has the decision to choose, how they want to perceive any given situation, and how they will react to it. Emotional processes can kick in at any time and override rational thought processes momentarily. Still, as difficult as it sometimes is, humans have the ability to become consciously aware of their emotional state and regain or maintain rational thought processes (Bucci, 2003).

One could raise their level of awareness in many aspects of life. But again, I am not talking about raising one's level of awareness in terms of the ice bucket challenge, the Me Too movement, or Black Lives Matter, as the term more commonly implies. Instead, I am referring to raising one's awareness about their situational environment, communication, spirituality, emotional and cognitive thought processes, and the like. While an increase in awareness on any of these facets would be an interesting discussion, we will focus on communication for brevity. I am sure that most would agree that a heightened level of awareness of one's projected and perceived communication would positively affect their awareness of spirituality, situational environment, and cognition. Moreover, I would argue that raising one's awareness of communication is easier to explain and easier to do. Therefore, we will focus on communication for now.

Bucci's (1995) multiple code theory outlined three levels of communication. Bucci defined *speech* as symbolic verbal communication, the first level of communication. As previously explained, speech is a very complex and relatively slow process. In order to form and articulate a thought, at least five different brain areas are activated in sequence. The prefrontal cortex formulates a thought; the Broca's area transforms the thought into language; the Wernicke's area transforms the language into speech by activating a specific area of the motor cortex, which controls the muscles necessary to pronounce words; and the hearing area checks the results in real time as words are spoken. If you have ever been on the phone and heard a delayed echo of your voice while you are talking, then you have experienced how important hearing is for speech. Any problems in any of these junctions can have serious effects on one's ability to speak. The process is comparable to a journey in which one has to change planes five times. A problem with any connecting flight will delay the entire journey. This process, unless we are talking in our sleep, takes place within our conscious awareness. Even if we are not fully aware of what we are saying or how it is being perceived, as is often the case with many politicians lately, one is distinctly aware that one is communicating.

The next level of communication may or may not take place within one's awareness. This level of communication is the non-verbal symbolic communication, which could be simply described as sign language. This level of communication is projected through our facial expressions, gestures, postures, and bodily actions. Some examples of this would be the well-known thumbs-up, the middle finger, sticking out the tongue, shrugging the shoulders, rolling of the eyes, the impatient tapping of the foot, and shaking the head yes or no. All of these gestures have specific symbolic meanings. Sometimes, they occur consciously, in replace of or in addition to speech. And sometimes they occur outside of our conscious awareness. Until muscular dystrophy began attacking my trapezius muscle, I had not been consciously aware of how often I shrug my shoulders when I say, 'I don't know.'

The last level of communication generally takes place completely outside of one's conscious awareness. This is commonly but very incorrectly referred to as body language. Bucci (2001) pointed out that the term body language is inherently incorrect because language implies symbolic meaning, however this level of communication is non-verbal and non-symbolic. Such communications consist of our facial expressions, gestures, postures, and actions that do not have any meaning in and of themselves but may nevertheless significantly contribute to the overall communication that is projected and perceived. This level of communication is more accurately described as emotional communication. Examples of this may be illustrated in the difference between a fake and genuine smile. While I was collecting data for my dissertation on emotional communication, I set up a display to attract potential subjects for my experiment. I displayed pictures of about fifteen different smiles, but only one was a picture of a genuine smile. I was surprised that nearly everyone could pick out the genuine smile from all the fakes, but no one could explain what it was about that smile that made it look genuine. This illustrates how far outside conscious awareness emotional communication takes place.

Danger Detection

In one study, participants were shown a 3×3 picture matrix of faces. One of these nine faces projected an angry facial expression. Although the picture was displayed for only a split second, participants were able to point to the grid where the angry face was with significant accuracy. A high level of accuracy was demonstrated only when the subjects were asked to identify an angry face. Faces displaying joy, surprise, and sadness were not as easy to pick out of a crowd so quickly. The reason most commonly given for this phenomenon is that humans are programmed to detect danger more quickly, and an angry face may be indicative of a dangerous situation.

While we are communicating consciously, the whole body communicates non-consciously, as if underlining, supporting, or even rejecting verbal communication. This is commonly referred to as leakage through micro-expressions. Ekman (1992, 2003) is accredited with the discovery of micro-expressions. These are split-second expressions of emotion that occur outside of an individual's conscious awareness, which often flashes upon a person's face when their verbal communication does not coincide with their emotional state. While emotional communication generally takes place outside of one's conscious awareness, Navarro and Karlins (2008) maintained that individuals can obtain conscious awareness of their emotional communication. This is essentially what actors learn to do through their training. Thus, the best way to increase one's conscious awareness of their emotional communication is to take acting classes, particularly improv.

Keith Johnstone (1981) described emotional communication from the performing arts perspective in much the same way Bucci (2002, 2003) did in her psychological studies on emotional communication. Johnstone described emotional communication as the friction between two minds due to the transference of thought never being 100 per cent accurate. Johnstone observed that when actors are reciting their lines, no matter how well they deliver them, if the spoken language does not affect them emotionally with each and every exchange, then the presentation will look like a presentation. However, acting is the art of creating reality. This is done by imitating the friction in one's emotional communication with the concept of status. Johnston (1981) and Spolin (2002) recognised that the improvisation exercises that actors use to develop their skills had entertainment potential in and of themselves on the comedy stage.

This later became what has been lovingly known as improv. Improv, as well as clowning, was a big craze amongst those who sought their inner … whatever. Performing improv is truly magical, and I loved it. But because my legs could no longer hold me for the duration of a show, my interest in improv shifted from the practical to the theoretical.

I considered that if acting, and improv particularly, is the art of creating reality, then the method and means by which actors induce artificial emotional episodes may offer significant insight into how emotional processing functions in reality. There are essentially three kinds of acting, each requiring a specific skill set and used for specific purposes. In traditional theatre acting, the challenge lies in the amplification and duration of one's emotional communication. That is, subtle emotional communications must be perceivable to the viewer in the back row without appearing overplayed to those viewers in the front row. In addition to this, theatre actors must be able to remain in character for long periods of time. To do this, actors implement techniques that ignite, maintain, and control emotional episodes by varying degrees of somatic and mental impulses.

In film acting, the challenge is much different. Movie actors do not often need to remain in character for exceedingly long periods, but rather they must be able to recall, re-experience, and reproject the same exact emotional communication again and again, take for take, over the course of days, weeks, or even months. Otherwise, after the takes are edited and spliced back into one flowing scene, inconsistencies in the emotional communication may obtrude in the final product. I know from personal experience how different this kind of acting is from theatre because I found out the hard way how bad I was at film acting. In the film *Stockflame*, my character displayed so many emotional discontinuities that the scenes with my character had to be drastically cut, because the character I played before lunch was emotionally different than after lunch. The director seemed to like every scene I played, but as an improv actor, I had great difficulty playing the same scene consistently, making it difficult to put various camera angles into one scene. Method acting, very simplified, is a technique in which an actor will associate a specific cognition with a specific emotional feeling. Once this association is established, an actor can recall and re-establish the same emotional episode any time they want.

The skillset of the improv actor is much different. In improvisation, the actors do not have time to dive into a character and explore all the many facets of the character they are portraying. Neither do they have time to establish any cognitive-somatic connection as in method acting. Improv actors have to pop into a character without any preparation. In addition to this, improv games traditionally include additional mental activities, like speaking in rhyme, speaking words without specific letters, or any mental activity to occupy the mind and mental capacity to collectively tell an improvised story. These extra mental activities are sold to the audience, as if these mental activities make the improvisation more difficult. Guess what; they do not; they make it easier. The key to improv is remaining in the moment through impulses out of the body. To be spontaneous is to react rather than to act. Action implies contemplation, thinking about what to do. Responding, in contrast, is instinctual and reflexive. By occupying the mind with various mental activities, the improv actor's mind is preoccupied with the proposed mental challenges from the audience, forcing the improv actor to act spontaneously through the somatic impulses they feel in the mimic, gestures, postures, and action that spontaneously come out of the body in terms of emotional communication.

Definition of Status

In my dissertation, *Directed Expression: Quantifying Emotional Expression with Concepts Derived from the Performing Arts*, I adopted the concept of status, as it is used and understood in the field of the performing arts, as a means of describing, inducing, and controlling emotional communication. Since my aim was to measure emotional communication, which par definition is non-verbal, I excluded the vocal components of status such as volume, timbre, melody, and the many various other aspects of voice that do attribute to an individual's status but are very difficult to explain in written form. Nevertheless, let it be said that status is also very clearly projected in the voice.

The term *status* is used in many fields of study, such as finance, medicine, and politics. A common concept behind all these uses is that one entity is being compared to another or to a standard, and this comparison is being continually or at least regularly monitored. This also holds true for the concept of status, as understood in the field of performing arts. The status relationship between two actors is ever-changing and is constantly and consciously being monitored by the actor. This corresponds exactly to the appraisal models of emotional processing (Patten, 2011; Scherer and Ceschi, 1997). In performing arts, the concept of status includes a few additional axioms (Kolb, 2010). First, the status relationship between two entities is never exactly equal but is continually under friction and fluctuating (Johnstone, 1981; Plonka, 2007). Next, unless people suffer from some sort of disorder or illness, they will prefer to maintain a higher rather than a lower status (Cialdini, 2007). Finally, when the difference in status between two individuals approaches zero, the two individuals are said to be in a status challenge. This is a highly emotional moment in which either the status between the two individuals bounces off each other, or the hierarchy changes. Simply put, status defines who's the boss at each moment during communication.

A holistic measurement of emotional communication based on the concept of status may be broken down into four non-verbal factors: mimic, gesture, posture, and action. Actors should be able to project a level of status on each of these factors independently.

A Picture Series Illustrating Increasing Status

A series of picture can be used to illustrate how actors can change their mimic, gesture, and posture to create changes in their overall status. Because these are pictures and not videos, the factor of action can only be implied and not represented. Such a series would begin with the first actor in the lowest possible status, logically a near-death situation. Into this scene steps another actor who assumes an ever-so-slightly higher status. When this is achieved, this second actor maintains his position while the first actor, whose status has just been slightly topped, assumes a new status again, ever so slightly greater. Continuing in this manner, the two actors, in attempts to maintain a higher status, will eventually result in aggressive behaviour to achieve the higher status or repulsion to end the status challenge. The exercise is also commonly played in the reverse order, ending with the inevitable and dramatic death of both actors. Through this exercise, actors can learn how finite changes on each of the factors of status may affect the overall projected status.

The Factors of Status

There are many factors of status, but there are only four non-verbal factors of status over which one has immediate control. Factors such as gender, health, age, income, attire, and more contribute to how people perceive emotional communication. However, when discussing the projection of emotional communication, we can eliminate factors that are not directly controlled through behaviour. Thus, the four non-verbal factors of emotional status—mimic, gesture, posture, and action—are the only ones that may be controlled in the mind. This is done by increasing one's conscious awareness of their emotional communication in terms of these four factors of status.

Mimic

Facial expression is expressed through mimic, the emotional expression projected through the face. The Facial Action Coding System (FACS) has done an excellent job of breaking down the various possible facial expressions by identifying the various muscles in the face which are used to make all facial expressions. Each specific muscle in the face is designed to cause a specific facial movement, called an action unit. Thus, the various basic emotions may be defined in terms of action units. An action unit is simply the contraction of a single facial muscle, most of which serve the sole purpose of expressing emotional facial expression. The FACS is essentially a nominal measurement of the various possible facial expression in terms of action units. In this study, the factors of status are equally weighted, however Karadag, Caliskan, and Yesil (2009) demonstrated that the factor of mimic might carry more emotional communication than gestures. Originally, I had disagreed with this idea and argued the emotion was more in the body than in the face, but the results of my dissertation illustrated that the face is the primary source of emotional projection.

Gesture

The factor of gesture is a measure of emotional communication of the appendages of individuals. As Bucci (2001) suggested, some gestures may be projected and perceived consciously or non-consciously. In addition, some gestures may have symbolic meaning while others do not. For example, the middle finger has a very specific meaning when extended out of the fist. In addition, the raising of the fist in general may be mapped to various meanings—or none at all. Gestures may be categorised on two levels, open/close and defending/inviting. The polarisation of status illustrates the element of defending or inviting. If individuals are more defending than inviting, they will have a low status on this factor. In many cases, this is a judgement call. If it is not obvious whether or not someone is defending or inviting, then one may defer to the intensity of the gesture in terms of open and closed.

Posture

Much research has been conducted to study the significance one's posture has on their emotional communication. Like the emotional expression projected through the face, emotion projected through one's posture often occurs non-consciously. Mehrabian (1968, 1969) found significant relationships between attitude and posture. Maslow (1973) found that the dominance of monkeys and their hierarchy could be significantly determined through the factor of posture. Dael et al. (2012) demonstrated the importance of posture in emotional communication. Meadors and Murry (2014) found that people's postures were indicative of their bias towards another person. In terms of status, the factor of posture is essentially a measure of size. The larger the individual projects oneself above his normal volume, the higher one's status on the posture factor. An individual whose posture makes them look smaller than their normal size will have a negative value of the posture factor.

Action

The action factor is a combined measurement of two elements: place in the environment and continual movement. An individual's placement in the immediate environment has a significant effect on their status. Business offices are purposefully constructed to take advantage of this. Thus, individuals who take action to obtain the vantage point in an immediate environment are awarded a higher status on the action factor than individuals whose position in the environment is less advantageous. As such, this factor considers the movement individuals make to occupy a specific place in the environment. In addition, the factor of action is also a measure of movement based on a unit of necessity. In short, relatively still individuals with no cause for action will have a higher emotional status than individuals who move significantly, although there is no distinct threat. However, if there is a distinct threat, individuals who move most effectively against this threat will have the higher status. Thus, stereotypical nervous movements will lower one's status, whereas quick reflexes out of necessity will raise one's status.

The Significance of the Action Factor of Status

A video that went viral a few years ago demonstrates how a factor of action can abruptly change the status relationship between two individuals. Even though some rumours have suggested the video was faked, it still illustrates how impressed humans are by quick and accurate actions of people. In this video, a female sports reporter was asking a baseball player some tough questions about his last performance. While he was responding, very much in the defensive, a foul ball was hit straight at the reporter's head. In the video, we hear the crack of the bat, followed by a distant and faint 'heads up'. The baseball player turns and catches the ball bare-handed right in front of the reporter's face. The reporter's high, penetrating, and almost aggressive status is immediately melted away and replaced with astonishment and admiration, while the baseball player nonchalantly threw the ball back with the instruction, 'Keep it on the field, boys,' and proceeded to answer the reporter's question, which suddenly did not seem to be as tough as it was only three seconds earlier (https://www.youtube.com/watch?v=DKMIlY6jHp0).

Now that the factors of status have been defined, we can discuss the dynamics of status. As previously stated, one's status is constantly changing from moment to moment. Even if one is standing perfectly still, the exertion to do this increases with time. After only a few moments, the struggle to remain perfectly still will be reflected in very small changes in status. A staring contest is a good example of this. In addition, a person's status is dichotomous; it is either high or low, but never completely neutral. Additionally, two individuals will never have exactly equal statuses. Like the same poles of a magnet, when the statuses of two people get too close, either they repel each other, or they very suddenly flip. In the performing arts, this is referred to as a status challenge. This is an exciting moment in any story when two strong characters meet head-to-head. It is less often seen in a film but frequently seen in reality when two weak characters challenge each other in terms of who has it worse.

Even non-verbally, such challenges take place. Here is an experiment you can try sometime: The next time you get in an empty elevator, stand in the very middle, assuming a high status, and ride up and down as people get in and out. Try to maintain a high status in the centre position no matter how crowded it gets; let the people move around you. Then do the complete opposite. Assume a low status, and as people get in and off the elevator, try not to be in anybody's way. You will find that regardless of your status, people will challenge your status with their mimic, posture, gestures, and action.

Although the term *status* is not generally used in psychology, the concept of status, as previously described, is a widely studied topic in scientific psychology. Many authors have used behaviour observation measurements that correspond directly to these factors of status (Dael, Mortillaro, and Scherer, 2012; Maslow, 1973), and a great number of emotional behaviour measurements have incorporated various aspects of the concept of status to some degree or another (Dael et al., 2012; Ekman, Friesen, and Hager, 2002; Maslow, 1973; Sayette et al., 2001). Damasio's (2000, 2006) somatic marker hypothesis is especially closely related to the concept of status.

The Somatic Marker Hypothesis

The somatic marker hypothesis suggests that somatic feelings mark the commencement of an emotional episode (Damasio, 2000, 2006), whereas Johnstone's (1981) description of status implied that abrupt changes in an individual's status might mark the commencement of an emotional episode. In addition, the somatic marker hypothesis and the concept of status both suggested that the evaluation of an emotionally provocative stimulus (EPS) takes place on a good versus bad categorical measurement. That is, upon the perception of an EPS, a cognitive appraisal of this EPS takes place. If this appraisal yields a good result, then a person's status will rise, and positive emotional feelings will ensue. If the appraisal yields a bad result, then a person's status will fall, and negative emotional feelings will ensue. If the appraisal yields neither a significantly good or bad result, a person's status will not change significantly, and no emotions will ensue.

If changes in people's status are significantly associated with changes in emotional facial expression, this would suggest that a change in their status, as well as the activation of specific emotional facial expressions, may serve as an indication of the commencement of an emotional episode. This may imply that the concept of status may play a significant role in the evaluation of an EPS. In addition, such findings would lend additional support to the somatic marker hypothesis and validate the idea that somatic feelings mark the commencement of an emotional episode.

In my dissertation, I tested a hypothesis that one's consciously projected emotional communication has a significant effect on the non-conscious projected communication of others. As it turns out, my data did not support this hypothesis. Despite my failed attempt to find evidence to confirm my belief, I stumbled onto something that my hypothesis neglected to address. Due to my experience as an improv actor, I was sure that emotion was primarily driven through somatic reflexes, as William James suggested in 1890, and devised an experiment to prove James and myself correct. In James's day, the debate that shook the world of psychology like the nature versus nurture debate does today was the question of the order of the emotional process. Do we feel an emotion and then become aware of it, or does the emotion first come into our conscious awareness and then into the body? Lazarus (1982, 1991) pointed out that metal effects are both necessary and sufficient to initiate an emotional episode. However, somatic effects are sufficient but not necessary to initiate an emotional episode. This is exactly what the data in my experiment showed.

James suggested that pre-existing non-conscious knowledge that frightening things could cause a bump in the night is sufficient to allow an emotional episode to ignite without first becoming aware of what it was exactly that caused the bump. This idea has been found to coincide with Lazarus (1982, 1991), who argued that the cognitive appraisal of an emotionally provoking stimulus is necessary as well as sufficient in order to initiate an emotional episode. However, knowledge of the nature of the EPS is also necessary but not sufficient in order to initiate an emotional episode. For example, suppose a child has not experienced or learned that stray dogs may be dangerous. In that case, the child may not demonstrate sufficient fear or respect when encountering a stray dog. In contrast, a child who has experienced how dangerous a stray dog may be could re-experience this fear merely by thinking of a stray dog, or at the sight of any dog without knowing if it is a stray.

Although it was not my intention, the experiment I conducted for my dissertation allows one to make implications about the human mind. The focus of my experiment was on emotional communication. I devised a measure of emotional communication based on the non-verbal components of status: mimic, gesture, posture, and action. The post hoc analysis revealed that the factor of action demonstrated low correlations to emotional communication. But this should have been expected because, after all, the subjects were essentially standing in a big box that served as a video studio, in which two cameras recorded the subject's face and body. So no movement was necessary.

Sad Eyebrows

Studies in facial expression have shown that specific muscles of the face, which are primarily controlled through the autonomic nervous system (ANS), are highly correlated with the basic emotions. You can test this yourself by trying to raise only the insides of your eyebrows, so that only the inner parts of the eyebrow rise in the middle over your nose. You will probably find that you cannot raise just the insides of your eyebrows without raising the entire arch. But if you think of something sad, you may find it easier to do. With some practice, it will become easier to do. The funny thing is when you are able to isolate and activate the inner eyebrows, you feel a slight sensation of sadness. This is because this little muscle in the middle of your forehead is primarily activated only in isolation through the limbic system in response to a sadness provoking stimulus. In the Facial Action Coding System (FACS), the isolated movement of the eyebrows is called AU1 and is indicative of sadness.

I wanted to test whether a person's status could influence the status of others. This is how I did it. The examiner randomly addressed and communicated with each subject in either a high or low status. The whole data collection process only took about one minute for each subject. The examiner asked the subject to stand on a fixed point and face forward. Then the examiner adjusted the camera to fit the subject's height. This action also served the purpose for the examiner to project the randomly determined status. When the cameras were set and rolling, the examiner asked the following question: Finden Sie sich schön? (Do you think you are beautiful?)

This question was specifically chosen to put the subject into a state of higher self-awareness. The question mentally puts one in front of a mirror. The reactions to this question were very interesting. The verbal reaction was recorded, and all subjects did react verbally and promptly. However, the verbal reaction was not the data I was after. Utilising the FACS, a binary scale of emotion or no emotion in the facial expression was categorically measured. The somatic, emotional expression was measured categorically based on status.

The data clearly showed that if emotion was projected through the body, it was very likely to be projected through the face. But the reverse was not true. When emotion was projected through the face, it was significantly less often also projected in the body. Thus, my hypothesis was completely wrong. And while I proposed to support James's theory of emotion, my data supported Cannon's theory of emotion.

Once again, we fall back to the concept of belief. I believed one thing, but the science demonstrated another. Immediately I considered measurement error and found a lot of it, but I am still reluctant to scrap my hypothesis totally. Nevertheless, I must concede that the mind seems to have a greater influence on our emotional processing than our emotional somatic feeling. It remains true that somatic processes have a significant influence on our emotional processing system, but much to my personal dismay, my study demonstrated that the mind has a greater influence on emotion than does the body. Nevertheless, I maintain that one can increase one's level of conscious awareness through the art of acting.

Increasing One's Awareness of Communication

With his iceberg diagram, Bartussek (2000) illustrated very well how Bucci's three levels of communication work together. Imagine two icebergs floating in the water next to each other. As I am sure you know, a much greater percentage of the iceberg's volume is underwater. Allow the water level to represent the boundary between conscious awareness and non-conscious unawareness. This is not a static straight line, because the icebergs bob up and down in the waves. Similarly, the border between consciousness and non-consciousness is not static, however if one could somehow decrease the density of the ice, the iceberg would float higher out of the water. Through various acting exercises, one can increase one's awareness over their status and thus raise one's conscious awareness of one's communication, particularly one's emotional communication.

Suppose the two icebergs are floating near each other. In that case, the distance between the tops of the icebergs will be greater than the distance between their bases underwater. This difference in distance reflects the speed of communication between two people. As was pointed out earlier, speech is a very slow and complex process. Emotional communication, in contrast, is incredibly fast, like a reflex. While the central nervous system controls verbal communication, emotional communication is significantly controlled by the autonomic nervous system, which is rooted in the brain stem and controls such functions as heartbeat, breathing, and reflexes. Emotional communication takes place so fast that one is seldom aware it is taking place at all. However, with very close friends, one may, at times, be seemingly in sync and able to communicate without words, in a 'are you thinking what I am thinking?' kind of manner. This is also the communication level between improvisation actors, team sports, and other such groups where people seem to know what the other person is doing and thinking without communicating it verbally.

The speed of the communication is dependent on the level of communication. Verbal speech is the slowest by far but carries the most information. Emotional communication takes place at the speed of a reflex because it is literally a reflex. Notice that this is true regardless of the level of awareness an individual possesses at the time of the communication. However, an individual's level of awareness does significantly influence the speed and overall quality of an individual's diagonal communications. *Diagonal communications* are communications that are either projected outside the speaker's or listener's conscious awareness.

Figure 2 Bartussek's (2000) Ice Berg Model of Communication

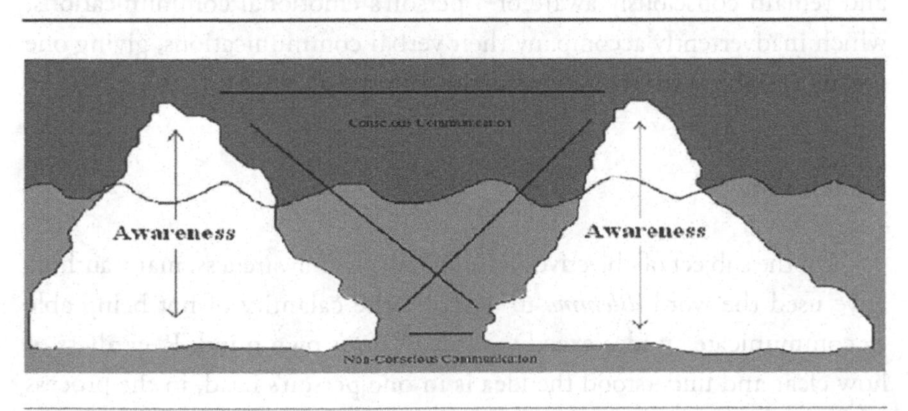

From Bewusst sein im Körper [Consciousness in Body] (p.16), by Walter Bartussek, 2000, Mainz, Germany, Matthias Grünwald Verlag,. Copyright 2000 by Walter Bartussek, Adapted with permission.

De Gelder (2006) referred to these diagonal lines of communication as incongruent sensitivity and stated they are a common cause of miscommunications and arguments. However, in these diagonal lines of communication, one can become a more efficient and productive communicator. When people are able to increase their level of conscious awareness, they will be able to send signals along with their verbal communication that listeners perceive non-consciously. This is essentially the principle behind the advertisement.

Bucci (2001) explained that interactions that may appear supersensory or supernatural may be accounted for through observable sensory means. Cues that are intentionally or unintentionally projected by one individual and intentionally or unintentionally perceived by another may or may not be expressed verbally in return; nevertheless, a communication transfer may still occur. While such incongruities cannot completely be eliminated, one might suggest that by increasing one's awareness of emotional communication, the degree and frequency of such incongruities could be reduced.

In addition, if one has obtained a greater awareness of emotional communication, one can use the diagonal communication lines to increase the productivity in their communication. While communicating verbally, one can also be consciously aware of the emotional communication one is sending with their verbal communication. One can perceive another person's verbal communication within the realm of conscious awareness and remain consciously aware of a person's emotional communications, which inadvertently accompany their verbal communications, giving one greater insight as to what the person is communicating.

Conclusion

On the subject of objective and subjective self-awareness, many authors have used the word *dilemma* to describe the calamity of not being able to communicate an idea exactly as it is in one's own mind. Regardless of how clear and understood the idea is in one person's head, in the process of communication, that idea will become distorted from how it was in the first person's mind to the next person. The next person has a totally different mind; therefore, the idea will be perceived in this mind, and this alone is cause for significant distortion of a communicated idea. The fact that one can become aware of this distortion is concrete evidence for the concept of a mind that cannot be reduced to neurochemical processes. While each brain consists of the same neurochemical processes, we know each mind to be uniquely different.

However, the very principle of reductionism is that one can always reduce a process to a lower level when evidence gets in the way. Thus, atheists often argue that the uniqueness of the mind is in the uniqueness of each individual's neurochemical processes. The problem with that argument is that the very practice of medicine is to group divergent processes. If it were assumed that each was unique, it would be pointless to group them. From a more theological viewpoint, Reinhold Niebuhr described the phenomenon as arising from the fact that human experience combines both 'nature' and 'spirit,' and man functions in both these dimensions simultaneously (May 1967, p. 11). Again, you, I, and everyone in the world will choose for themselves what they believe their mind is. Based on that, people can then decide what they want to do with their minds.

CHAPTER 4

Theory of Mind

Theory of mind (ToM) is a confusing term because it is both a theory and an abstract construct. An abstract construct is something that may be best defined through example. Love is an abstract construct because it clearly exists, but it is not tangible. It is not made of physical matter and thus exists only in our minds and not in the physical world. One cannot point to it and say, 'Oh, there is love. I've been looking for this,' and then proceed to physically put love in one's pocket as it exists in one's mind.

Humour is another example of an abstract construct. Although one may be very poor and have no possessions, one can always have a sense of humour. One may be very reluctant to admit not having a sense of humour; however, upon requiring physical proof of this humour, one would be unable to produce physical evidence of the presence of humour. In the same way, a ToM is an abstract construct. At about the age of five, children reach a point in their cognitive development in which they realise that other people have minds distinctly different from their own. Until a child's ToM develops, the child will not realise that other people want something different from what they themselves want.

Cheung (2010) defined ToM as the understanding that behaviours are motivated by internal mental states (e.g., desires, beliefs, and intentions), which has been the focus of intense developmental research over the past several decades. An important developmental milestone in children's ToM is false belief understanding or the recognition that actions are guided by beliefs even when they are not true. Research suggests that ToM follows a universal development sequence across cultures (Wellman and Liu, 2004; Wellman et al., 2006). That is, children come to understand simple desires and beliefs before false beliefs, which is then followed by a more sophisticated understanding of recursive mental states (thinking about someone else thinking about mental states). Interestingly, in comparison with the invariable developmental pattern, there appears to be more variability in the developmental timeline of the ToM. For instance, in typically developing children, false-belief understanding has been found to develop between three to five years of age (Wellman, Cross, and Watson, 2001).

When a child develops a ToM, this means the child is now able to realise other people may not share their wants and concerns. The entrance of this abstract construct is represented in the child's behaviour. Before the child's ToM had developed, the child may have flipped out if they lost a game because the child did not yet understand that in a game, all the players want to win. A child without a fully developed ToM would think, 'I want to win; therefore, everyone else wants me to win too.' The appearance of a ToM in a child's cognitive development is widely associated with a significant change in behaviour. A child with a fully developed ToM may no longer display inappropriate behaviour because of having lost a game because it now understands that the very nature of a game is the each of its participants wants to win; thus, the reaction in losing is improved. However, having a fully developed ToM, a child can then develop, express, and argue opinions. The ToM is the theory that a child, at some point in their cognitive development, has come to the realisation that their mind is distinctly different from everyone else's.

Liu (2005) suggested that having a ToM is essential in human communication, which involves considering the mental states of others and developing an appreciation of them. An understanding of concepts such as beliefs, desires, and emotions and their causal connections to behaviour is often referred to as having a 'theory of mind' (as cited in Wellman, 1990). Flavell (2004) defined the ToM development as an area of cognitive development research that investigates the nature and development of our understanding of the mental world, which is the inner world inhabited by beliefs, desires, emotions, thoughts, perceptions, intentions, and other mental states.

Some would argue that the mind is nothing more than the result of neurochemicals in the brain. This kind of reasoning is often referred to as reductionism or atomistic reasoning as opposed to holistic reasoning, which will be discussed in chapter 6. However, while one may be quick to reduce one's own mind to a mere sum of neurochemical processes in the brain when confronted with other people's minds, we are often not so quick to such simplification. Just this week, two mass shootings occurred in Atlanta and Boulder, and many have been discussing the reasons for these tragedies. But no one has said, 'Well, it's just how the shooter's neuroprocesses work.' I think deep down, we all somehow know that the mind is something more than the brain. Somehow, the whole is greater than the sum of the parts. This is what enables us to differentiate between sound and music, pixels and pictures, life and living.

Thus, it is the understanding that all humans have a mind. Our minds allow us to understand that different people can have different ideas about the same things. If one person likes baseball and another thinks it is boring, then it is our ToM that allows us to consider that the other simply has a different relation to the sport. As such, our ToM can reach boundaries when one tries to understand that some people believe that the earth is flat, do not believe that the holocaust has taken place, or other such ideas that are totally inconceivable to someone. At that point, we question the sanity of their mind rather than the effectiveness of their neurophysiology.

In seven points, Keskin (2005, p. 515) explained that an individual has a ToM if he ascribes mental states to himself and others. A system of inferences of this kind is properly viewed as a theory because such states are not directly observable, and the system can be used to make predictions about the behaviour of others.

1. Ideas and things are different: An idea of a horse and a horse, in reality, are different things because the former is mental and immaterial, and the latter is physical and material.
2. Reality and beliefs are different: Beliefs and reality may not be the same. For example, while the world is sphere-shaped in reality, one can choose to hold a false belief, such as believing the world is flat.
3. Desires and results are different: Planning and performing are two different things. No amount of mental activity of an action

can ever amount to the experience of that action. In other words, mental activities and deeds correspond to two different things.

4. Reality does not restrain fantasy: A person can imagine unreal, impracticable, or imaginary things. Moreover, human fantasy can and has become reality.
5. Mind is personal and individual: Because everyone has their unique personal mind, mental states or attitudes can differ across individuals. It is possible for me to perceive myself to be a good singer, while someone else can hold a different opinion.
6. Mind and body are not the same: The event of being locked up in a place does not restrict my thoughts. My thoughts can be free regardless of the physical situation I am in. Likewise, my mind can be exhausted even though my body is relaxed.
7. Opinions are not subject to reality: The way of thinking about reality versus thinking about the mind is only a difference of opinion. Our ToM makes it possible for us to form our own opinions and beliefs, independent from reality.

Having explained the ToM as an abstract construct, the theory behind the ToM is simply the theory that humans have a ToM. To make things more unnecessarily complicated, there are various ToM theories. One of them is curiously called the theory theory. It is not imperative that one be able to differentiate between the various theories because they differ mainly in their emphasis on how a ToM develops and its purpose. Some emphasise the development of a ToM with language development, and others do with objective self-awareness, emotional development, cognitive development, or play. Problems in these areas are often associated with autistic spectrum disorder; many studies on autism refer to the ToM as the cause, the result, or a symptom of autism. So, let us begin there.

Autistic Spectrum Disorder (ASD)

ASD is one of the greatest mysteries of neurology and psychology. Because it can be so terribly devastating to families, many people have very strong opinions about it. At the risk of opening up a can of worms that would confuse the focus of this book, please understand that this chapter is on the ToM, and this very short mentioning of autism concerns only its relationship to ToM.

In a previous article, I outlined the various aspects of ASD:

> *Autistic Spectrum Disorder* is a pervasive developmental disorder characterized by three categories of symptoms: qualitative impairment in social interaction, impairment in communication, and restricted repetitive and stereotyped patterns of behavior or interests (Sadock & Sadock, 2007). However, in addition to these behavioral characteristics, recent research, motivated to find a cause of ASD, has also discovered some physical characteristics. Through brain imaging, autopsy, and electroencephalographic studies, researchers have localized several specific physical characteristics associated with autism (Chan Sze, & Cheung, 2007; Courchesne et al., 1994; Courchesne et al., 2001). In particular, studies have shown that the amygdala may be particularly responsible for the cognitive processing of facial emotional expressions (Adolphs et al., 1999; Whalen et al., 1998). Neuroimaging research has established that neuroanatomical abnormalities often occur in autistic individuals, but no single type of reported abnormality is ubiquitous in autism. Such abnormalities have been found in the cerebral cortex, thalamus, basal ganglia, and brainstem, but only quite inconsistently (Courchesne, 2001). However, many studies have established relatively consistent evidence of a maldevelopment brain growth pattern in individuals with ASD (Courchesne, 2004; Hallahan et al., 2009; Williams & Boucher, 2008; Volker & Lopata, 2008).
>
> These studies have shown that in individuals with ASD, a brain overgrowth occurs during the first two to four years of life, which is then followed by abnormally slow, or event arrested growth (Courchesne, 2004; Hallahan et al., 2009; Volker & Lopata, 2008). This exceedingly rapid growth rate followed by growth arrest

> is most likely responsible for previous inconsistencies in brain size studies, in which individuals with ASD were compared to controls of the same chronicle age (Courchesne, 2004). However, it should be noted that Hallahan et al. (2009) presented evidence that the brain growth rate of individuals with Asperger's Syndrome may not follow this pattern. This could perhaps be a reason why the levels of functionality of individuals with Asperger's Syndrome are generally higher than that of those with an autistic disorder; however, further research must be done to confirm this (Kolb, 2009, p. 1).

Liu (2005) argued that the ToM is a developmental phenomenon, but without developmental neuroscience data, brain research is unable to provide complete insight into how a ToM develops. Thus, Liu examined the functional relationship between ToM development and brain development and found that children with autism tend to have a delayed ToM development. Children with autism perform significantly worse on ToM tasks than typically developing children and developmentally delayed children, even when mental age has been controlled for (as cited in Baron-Cohen, Leslie, and Frith, 1985; see Happe, 1995, for a meta-analysis of relevant research).

The children with autism performed poorly on the false-belief tasks, even though they performed at ceiling levels on the false-photograph tasks. The modularity interpretation of such specific deficits in the social domain is that autism is a neurodevelopmental disorder in which children with autism are born with a targeted impairment to their ToM module (Baron-Cohen, 1995; Leslie, 1994). Keskin (2005) also noted that several studies (e.g., Baron-Cohen, 1987; Baron-Cohen, Leslie, and Frith, 1986) have indicated autism may be related to an immature ToM. These authors stated that autism may be associated with a particular dysfunction regarding conceiving of mental circumstances. Children with autism display social deficiencies and difficulties engaging in pretend play. According to some researchers, it is because these children have an underdeveloped ToM (Baron-Cohen, 1988; Leslie, 1987; Wellman, 1992). Indeed, in accordance with Baron-Cohen (1988), though communication is possible without a ToM, it is not possible to participate in a conversation if one does not have a ToM. These findings beg the question, Is a poor ToM development responsible for autism or is autism responsible for a poor ToM development?

Thomson (2009) claimed that humans have ToM modules. Generally, people are not aware of these modules, and thus they experience them as a seamless part of the conscious mind. But they are hardly simple. People know without being taught that other people have minds like ours, with wishes, beliefs, desires, and passions. We can read the mental states of others with eye cues. At about the age of five, we have the capacity to know others might hold a different belief about something then we do. Perhaps we can most truly appreciate this capacity when we see its clinical absence, which is autism (Baron-Cohen, 1995). Similarly, Endres (2003) associated ToM development with children's ability to develop intimate and validating relationships in terms of social competence.

Proof of ToM

Indeed, ToM is a very interesting abstract construct, but how do we know it is a thing at all? Well, having a ToM enables a person to understand that other people have other minds with other ideas and beliefs. Scientific psychology has devised ways of determining whether a child has a ToM or not. One of the most common tests is the false belief test. To do this test, all you need is two dolls, a dollhouse or a playing area, and something that serves as a treasure.

First, I would simply play dolls with the child for a while in order to get the child interested in the dolls; the dolls are essentially my lab assistants. Then when the fun is at a maximum, so is the child's attention. At this point, I start the test. In-play, I will have already have introduced the dolls, Lacy and Barbie. I play Lacy, the child plays Barbie, and Lacy gives Barbie a tour of her clubhouse. Then after a short while, Lacy shows Barbie her treasure. It does not matter what it is, as long as it is small enough to hide in the play area. To start the test, I say, 'Watch this,' and I now play both dolls.

> Lacy: Hey, Barbie, do you want to see my treasure?
> Barbie: Sure, Lacy, where is it?
> Lacy: I keep it here under my bed, so Ken doesn't find it.

From under the toy bed, I bring forth a tiny marshmallow.
Lacy: We have to go to soccer practice now; I'll just put this back under the bed. Come on, let's go.
Exit Barbie and Lacy, and curtain.

Then I address the child: 'Watch this. I am going to play a trick on Lacy.' I take the marshmallow and replace the pillow that was under the covers at the head of the bed with it. Then I ask the child, as I give her the Lacy doll, 'Where will Lacy look for her marshmallow?' If the child has already developed a ToM, the child will play Lacy looking under the bed, wondering where her marshmallow is, and possibly even blaming Ken. In doing so, the child demonstrates the ability to realise that although she knows where the marshmallow is, Lacy cannot know that it has been moved. But if the child has not yet developed a ToM, then the child will play Lacy finding the marshmallow under the blanket where the pillow was.

Liu (2005, p. 52) pointed out that an understanding of false belief provides a rigorous demonstration that an individual grasps this important distinction between mind and world (as cited in Dennett, 1978). Moreover, Liu found that in twenty-four trials, children were asked false-belief questions, and in sixteen trials, children were asked true-belief questions. If the change in children's false-belief performance were steady and gradual, then within the age range in which this change occurs, some children should perform around chance. However, children's false-belief performance followed a clear bimodal distribution (Liu, 2005). The children, aged three to five, either got all of the questions right or got them all wrong. There was no evidence of a child getting some of them right and some wrong, as one would expect on essentially any other aptitude test. Thus it seems with ToM, you either have it or you don't.

Factors Involved in ToM Development

Taken together, existing research suggests that there is a strong relationship between the ToM and both child language and executive functioning (especially conflict inhibition). With respect to child language, both children's understanding of semantics and syntax relates to more advanced false-belief understanding. Interestingly, some evidence suggests that syntactic scores relate more strongly to ToM development relative to semantic understanding. Specifically, emerging evidence supports the notion that children's knowledge of sentential complements helps facilitate false-belief development. These patterns of results suggest that language is an important mechanism related to ToM development (Cheung, 2010, p. 37).

Language

One of the most important factors involved in the development of the ToM is a child's language development and skills (Pearson, 2013). Pearson found that deaf children born to non-deaf parents tend to develop a ToM significantly later than average, and bilingual children tend to develop a ToM significantly sooner than average. In addition to metalinguistic skills, the ToM has also been correlated with executive functioning skills, which has led to multiple hypotheses concerning ToM development (Pearson, 2013).

Social Skills

In addition to this, a child's social skills are also closely correlated with ToM development. However, it remains unclear whether social skills foster ToM development or whether ToM development fosters social skills.

Cognitive Development

Endres (2003) implied that the development of subjective self-awareness proceeds ToM development, suggesting that children behave as if the desire is part of the desired object, rather than a mental state (as cited in Bartsch and Wellman, 1995). Thus, children begin to understand that people can want different things only once they understand that desire is subjective.

Play

In the context of play, the importance of ToM development becomes very apparent. Endres (2003) illustrated that play might be closely associated with the ToM development. Keskin (2005) examined the relationship between ToM, symbolic transformations in pretend play and children's social competence and found a significant correlation between the ToM and children's role play. However, no significant correlation was found between the ToM and children's social competence, and no relationship was found between symbolic transformations in pretend play and social competence. That is, children who had scored low on the ToM tasks were still able to engage in more advanced ideational transformations (i.e., role attribution) when they interacted with a child who was more advanced in terms of the ToM.

Thus, peer contexts seem to affect children's symbolic transformations in pretend play and role play in particular. The findings suggest that along with peer context, role play, rather than pretend play in general, contributes to the development of a ToM. Thus, peer context seems to affect children's symbolic transformations in pretend play and role play in particular. The findings suggest that along with peer context, role play, rather than pretend play in general, contributes to the development of a ToM.

Research on play by psychologists and educators led to the consensus that play serves a developmental role. Moreover, play is related to children's social, cognitive, and emotional development. Play, for example, improves children's social development (Erikson, 1950) and their understanding of social rules and social roles (Berk, 1994; Vygotsky, 1978). Furthermore, play influences children's language/literacy development (Casby and Ruder, 1983) and their moral development (Walton, 1985). While many scholars have contributed to the body of knowledge on children's play, arguably, Piaget is one of the most important contributors. Piaget made a significant contribution to educational psychology's knowledge base and foundation (Mooney, 2000). More specifically, Piaget studied children's play and noted that their symbolic play behaviours satisfied children's egos.

Genetics

In addition to the previously mentioned factors, one must also return to the age-old question of nature versus nurture. However, in relation to ToM, the nature versus nurture question is probably more ambiguous than it is in any other aspect of development. Pearson (2013) stated that it is unclear whether a child's culture plays a significant role in the development of ToM. However, Cheung (2010, p. 20) found that the rate at which children develop a ToM (particularly false-belief understanding) may in part be influenced by family characteristics and experiences, citing evidence drawn from a behavioural genetic study that examined the relative effect of common genetic and environmental influences on ToM and language development in five-year-old identical and fraternal twins (Hughes et al., 2005).

ToM Theories

Flavell (2004), Liu (2005), and Keskin (2005) thoroughly outlined several different ToM theories, each of which offered explanations pertaining to the development of children's mentalistic understanding. The strangely named theory theory argues that our knowledge about the mind is not something to be determined by scientific means but rather is an informal, everyday framework or foundational theory based on philosophical understanding, in which a number of steps in children's progression towards the adult ToM have been described in terms of human desire (Gopik and Melzoff, 1997; Gopnik and Wellman, 1994; Perner, 1991; Wellman and Gelman, 1998). According to the theory theorists (Gopnik and Meltzoff, 1997; Gopnik and Wellman, 1992, 1994), our knowledge concerning the mental world is a theory which may never be confirmed, only believed. The mental world includes the realm of beliefs, wishes, objectives, thoughts, and more. The theory theory is sometimes called common-sense psychology (Forguson and Gopnik, 1988; Wellman, 1988). The theory theory asserts that our knowledge and understanding of the human mind is not something that can be known as fact, but only known in theory. Throughout our childhood development into adulthood, our everyday understanding of the human mind increases, but not our factual knowledge. The increased understanding that we perceive are merely fortifications of one's personal belief system (Gopnik and Wellman, 1994). According to Liu (2005), the theory theory account views our everyday folk psychology as a day, the naive theory of people and minds. According to this perspective, during development, children experience fundamental conceptual changes in their ToM (as cited in Gopnik and Wellman, 1994; Wellman, 1990; Wellman and Gelman, 1998).

The modularity theory postulated the development of ToM through neurological maturation of a succession of domain-specific and modular mechanisms for dealing with agents versus non-agent objects (Baron-Cohen, 1995; Leslie, 1994). Modularity theories suppose that young children do not necessarily attain a theory about mental representations (Flavell, 1999; Leslie and Roth, 1993). Leslie assumes that the acquisition of a theory occurs during the neurological maturation of a sequence of three domain-specific and modular mechanisms.

The simulation theory suggests that children become able to compute other people's mental states through a kind of role thinking or simulation process. Like theory theorists, simulation theorists also assume that experience plays a crucial formative role, in that it is through practice in role-taking that children improve their simulation abilities (Flavell, 2004). According to simulation theorists, children know their own mental states introspectively; because of this consciousness, they are able to assume others' mental states via role-taking, namely simulation (Harris, 1992). For instance, when children are asked to guess what another child would assume about the content of the candy box during the false belief task, they think about what they would say if they were in the position of the naïve child who knows only the appearance of the box (Flavell, 1999).

Created in the Image of God

Many researchers have approached the ToM from different perspectives. Some researchers perceive the ToM as a matter of developing a naive theory (Gopnik and Wellman, 1994), neurological maturation (Leslie, 1994b), simulation (Harris, 1992), and philosophical or social-cultural phenomena (Gauvain, 1998). Like simulation theorists (e.g., Harris, 1992), many researchers who focused on the ToM believe that examining children's play more specifically will help us identify the root of the ToM (Harris, 2000; Lillard, 1993, 1998).

ToM is a poorly worded concept. ToM is not merely a scientific theory but a milestone in childhood development. It is when an individual comes to their own subjective understanding that other people may have a significantly different understanding and perception of reality. Having a ToM is understanding that because other individuals may perceive the world differently, each person's mind is strictly unique and individual. Thus, it is ToM which essentially makes it possible for humans to feel empathy.

According to Christian theology, the difference between man and animals is that man is created in the image of God. The ToM may be evidence of that. Humans and all other animals are born with preprogrammed drives, instincts, and reflexes. This also includes emotions. But because animals lack verbal, symbolic communication ability, they cannot demonstrate that they have minds remotely like ours. In addition to this, humans but not animals have the ability to override their drives, instincts, reflexes, and emotions.

Like all other animals, humans can experience fear that triggers a flight, fright, or fight mode, which governs behaviour until the emotional episode is over. Thus humans can experience fear, which turns to anger in the fight modes and attack. However, humans alone have the cognitive ability to regain control over the emotional episode. This is done by becoming consciously aware of one's behaviour and communication. The concept of sin offers a third argument that humans are created in the image of God. Humans alone have the capability to understand what sin is and choose to commit it. Though an animal may experience rage and become ferocious and kill his kind or another, one could not deem this behaviour sinful. Such behaviour is indicative of an emotional episode which both humans and animals frequently have. I think it is even written in our laws that if a human kills another human during an emotional episode, then the penalty is significantly less than when the murder was an impulse from the person's mind. That is what makes the behaviour sinful. It is out of our understanding of sin that we have devised laws to govern and punish such behaviour. This is what it means to be created in the image of God.

Conclusion

It should be abundantly clear that the human mind is not a higher level of mind than all other animals. The human mind is a different kind of mind all together. Concrete evidence of this is given in that fact that only humans have a ToM, understand right from wrong, and have the ability to override their emotional impulses. To this affect, Barbour (1990) asked and discussed questions like the following: 'What is the place of religion in an age of science? How can one believe in God today? What view of God is consistent with the scientific understanding of the world? In what ways should our ideas about human nature be affected by the findings of contemporary science? How can the search for meaning and purpose in life be fulfilled in the kind of world disclosed by science?' In doing so, Barbour essentially asserts that the scientific method is the only means one should use to gain knowledge, because any knowledge not gained scientifically cannot be validated or tested for reliability and validity. The problem with that is that science can only address the question of how and not why. Thus, theories have arisen that propose how the universe and life could have come into existence, but the questions why and for what purpose are swept neatly under the carpet and ignored.

Theology has attributed the difference between humans and all other animals to humans having been made in the image of God. Humans and all other animals are driven by essentially the same drives, instincts, and reflexes, but humans alone have the ability to will their body against the influences of their fleshly desires if they so consciously and persistently decide. Humans alone can consciously choose how they wants to perceive any given situation (Frankl, 2006). Darwinian evolution suggests the reoccurring forms of appendages and the visual similarity between embryos of different species indicate that all living things originated from a single life form (Russell, 1916), which would have come to pass through a random chance of RNA molecules that merely obeyed their function and created random forms of DNA, one of which randomly came alive. The odds of this happening randomly have been calculated and statistically imply that life could not be a result of random chance. Nevertheless, not only are we alive, but we are alive and consciously contemplating our existence.

Thomson (2009) declared that Charles Darwin's theory of natural selection is the only workable explanation we have for the remarkable fact of our existence. He went on to list the vast diversity of plant and animal life, the compelling illusion of design in nature, and the architecture of the human mind as evidence. Thomson (2009) suggested that we are risen apes, not fallen angels, and that the human race and ethnicities hide this essential truth. Darwinian evolution asserts that the human species are descendants of a small group of hunter-gatherers who arose in Africa less than two hundred thousand years ago and conquered the world. Religion, then, is merely the remnants of mythological beliefs that have come about to explain phenomena that primitive societies could not understand and have since been kept alive by an institution for control and power over the people.

If one thinks purely scientifically and begins with the assumption that there is no God, then with the data from a few scant fossils, the theory of Darwinian evolution would be the result. Darwinian evolution asserts that each step towards a more complex organism came about perchance. Darwin observed that the beaks of finches have changed to adapt to the food supply. So that means complicated organs and systems can randomly mutate into existence in the same way. The result is what we see today, kingdoms of animals, in which the more closely related animals display more similar forms and structures. The fact that different kinds of animals share similarly formed structures is often taken as evidence of Darwinian evolution. However, intelligent design asserts that it makes sense various animals share the same structural forms. To do this would be an indication of an intelligent designer. After all, intelligent humans have been using the same designs since the beginnings of civilisation. But, despite all the amazing technology we have at our disposal today, the wheel is still round.

CHAPTER 5

Identity

An individual's identity is much more than an answer to the question, 'Who are you?' Numerous studies have been conducted to grasp the depth of this question and found that there is no end to the vastness of our identities. Even the most complete description of someone's identity will inherently leave something out. Bosma and Kunnen (2001) reviewed the extensive research on identity development from various fields of the social sciences, hoping to ascertain the determinants, factors, and mechanisms of identity development. Nevertheless, they and essentially all other studies begin with Erik Erikson's theory of psychosocial development and venture from there on any number of tangents of interest. Admittingly, you will find me doing the same.

Erikson's eight stages of development have become common knowledge in virtually all social sciences and fields that have to do with human behaviour. Despite having thoroughly outlined his model in my last book, I find it necessary to at least review them here because it is the material upon which more in-depth identity research is based, either because the researchers agree with it or criticise it. In this chapter, we will follow both Erikson's fans as well as his critics.

Although I have come across Erikson's model countless times, Capp (2004) told an anecdote about how Erikson came up with the idea of his model that was a pleasant surprise for me. In many of my past works, this one included, I have argued that the fields of psychology and the performing arts have the same subject matter: human behaviour. As such,

William Shakespeare was a diagnostic genius long before psychology was even a thing. Edgar (1935) noted that the characters in Shakespeare's plays were written to display specific psychological disorders and symptoms for which we now, six hundred years later, have listed in our modern diagnostic manuals. Shakespeare's line 'All the world is a stage' is widely known and understood, but do you know the following lines? The lines that follow are essentially Erikson's model of psychosocial development.

Shakespeare's Model of Development

All the world's a stage, And all the men and women merely players: They have their exits and their entrances; And one man in his time plays many parts, His acts being seven ages. At first, the infant, Mewling and puking in the nurse's arms. And then the whining school-boy, with his satchel and shining morning face, creeping like snail Unwillingly to school. And then the lover, Sighing like furnace, with a woeful ballad Made to his mistress' eyebrow. Then a soldier, Full of strange oaths and bearded like the pard, Jealous in honor, sudden and quick in quarrel, Seeking the bubble reputation Even in the cannon's mouth. And then the justice, In fair round belly with good capon lined, With eyes severe and beard of formal cut, Full of wise saws and modern instances; And so he plays his part. The sixth age shifts Into the lean and slipper'd pantaloon, With spectacles on nose and pouch on side, His youthful hose, well saved, a world too wide For his shrunk shank; and his big manly voice, Turning again toward childish treble, pipes And whistles in his sound. Last scene of all That ends this strange eventful history, Is second childishness and mere oblivion, Sans teeth, sans eyes, sans taste, sans everything (Shakespeare, As You Like It, act 2, scene 7).

Capps (2004) divulged that Erikson originally also had only seven stages, which were significantly based on Shakespeare's model. However, as Erikson was on his way to a conference, he had noticed that Shakespeare did not have a 'play stage' as Erikson did in his model. This meant that one of Shakespeare's stages of development was not represented in his own model. Thus, Erikson reflected upon these words: 'With spectacles on nose and pouch on side, his youthful hose, well saved, a world too wide for his shrunk shank; and his big manly voice, turning again toward childish treble, pipes and whistles in his sound.' From this, Erikson inserted the 'Generativity versus Stagnation' stage into his model on the way to a conference, where he then introduced his now very famous Eight Stages of Man.

1. Trust versus Mistrust (0–18 months)—Infants develop trust for those who meet their needs and mistrust those who do not. As previously stated, humans are born the most helpless and dependent creatures on Earth. However, this dependence serves the purpose of creating a fantastic bond between child and parent. In addition to this, the dependence of infants on their caregivers also serves to develop a mistrust of those who do not give them the same level of care. This assures that a child develops a healthy sense of stranger danger and is less likely to wander off as soon as the child gains the ability to walk.
2. Autonomy versus Shame and Doubt (18–36 months)—During this stage, children, still depending on others, begin to experience a sense of free will. This stage is often referred to as the terrible twos. Children in this stage have an exploratory impulse, which is quite the opposite of the previous stage. By this time, a child will have developed some skills and want to implement them independently, often frantically resisting assistance. Nevertheless, failure to perform desired tasks independently often leads to outbreaks of frustration.
3. Initiative versus Guilt (3–5 years)—With the momentum of the previous stage, a child begins to set goals, and activities become more purposeful. However, the adventurous instinct of the previous stage subsides, and the children are left to initiate challenges independently. This stage marks the beginning of socialization, which takes place in the framework of play.
4. Industry versus Inferiority (5–12 years)—Children acquire more fundamental knowledge and take pride in their work. It is at this time that the preliminary stages of identity development begin to take root. While children in this stage will not yet have

formed unique and well-structured identities, they will begin to do so through identification. It is not yet about who they are as a person but rather what they can do and with whom they are associated. They begin to express pride or disappointment in their achievements.

5. Identity versus Identity Confusion (12–21+ years)—It is at this stage that the process of a unique identity begins to develop. However, this is a very long process that continues throughout a lifetime. At various times in a person's life, identity can be seen as diffused, sought, or achieved. Identity achievement implies an individual has assessed their strengths and weaknesses and determined how they want to use their strengths to cope with their weaknesses. Identity achievement is not something that comes easily, nor is it a one-time achievement; it must be sought after time and time again, as life experiences and stress continually threaten to diffuse one's identity.
6. Intimacy versus Isolation (18–40+ years)—Intimacy implies the fusion of the identities of two people. Thus, the prerequisite for genuine and lasting intimacy is the achievement of an ego identity. Nevertheless, life experience and stress can rock the most established identities into diffusion. When this happens, intimate relationships can also crumble. Like identity, an intimate relationship is not a one-time achievement but rather something that starts in this stage of development and remains both a source of stress and strength throughout a lifetime.
7. Generativity versus Stagnation (40–65+ years)—Generativity is marked by productive creativity in terms of vocational and professional contribution to society. There comes a point in everyone's life in which they ask themselves for the first time, 'Was that it? Was that the pinnacle of my life's work, or is there more to come?' When this question sets in their mind, one essentially chooses to continue to grow and develop, or they shift life into neutral and coast.
8. Integrity versus Despair (65+ years)—The conflict of this stage is between the appreciation of previous life experiences or becoming bitter, resentful, and negative. From at least the age of five, everyone

> knows that they will someday die. This is the stage in which it is meant to happen. When we get to this point, having lived some sixty-five years or longer, how will we view death? Will we fight it off until our last breath, clinging to a lifelong since lived, or do we long to hear the words 'Well done, my good and faithful servant' (Matthew 25:23)?

Each of these stages is defined by the conflict or crisis individuals face in that corresponding period of their life. However, it is important to point out that this conflict or crisis is not something that can or should be avoided but rather a mechanism to induce change and growth (Bosma and Kunnen, 2001). Muuss (1996) likened Erikson's use of the term *crisis* with the Eastern philosophical meaning of opportunity. Sokol (2009) noted that Erikson (1968, p. 96) used the term *crisis* 'in a developmental sense to connote not a threat of catastrophe, but a turning point, a crucial period of increased vulnerability and heightened potential' (Erikson, 1968, p. 91–92) and explained his use of the term *conflict* like this: 'I shall present human growth from the point of view of the conflicts, inner and outer, which the vital personality weathers, re-emerging from each crisis with an increased sense of inner unity, with an increase of good judgment, and an increase in the capacity 'to do well' according to his own standards and to the standards of those who are significant to him' (as cited in Sokol 2009, p. 2). Paul explains that the hardship we face in life is not God's way of punishing us, but rather the hardships we face are there to help us develop spiritually:

> 'In your struggle against sin, you have not yet resisted to the point of shedding your blood. And have you completely forgotten this word of encouragement that addresses you as a father addresses his son? It says, 'My son, do not make light of the Lord's discipline, and do not lose heart when he rebukes you, because the Lord disciplines the one he loves, and he chastens everyone he accepts as his son.' Endure hardship as discipline; God is treating you as his children. For what children are not disciplined by their father? If you are not disciplined—and everyone

> undergoes discipline—then you are not legitimate, not true sons and daughters at all. Moreover, we have all had human fathers who disciplined us and we respected them for it. How much more should we submit to the Father of spirits and live! They disciplined us for a little while as they thought best; but God disciplines us for our good, in order that we may share in his holiness. No discipline seems pleasant at the time, but painful. Later on, however, it produces a harvest of righteousness and peace for those who have been trained by it. Therefore, strengthen your feeble arms and weak knees. 'Make level paths for your feet,' so that the lame may not be disabled, but rather healed.' (Hebrews 12:4–13)

In any Psych 101 textbook, you will find these eight stages described, along with a couple of paragraphs offering a few examples of typical behaviours that illustrate the defining conflicts. I did that as well in my last book. Or you can simply google Erikson's stages and find some classic examples. However, instead of doing that again here, I would like to turn our focus towards identity development as a whole. Much too often, people regard a development model of any kind as like stepping stones across a river of some skill set, be it Piaget's cognitive development, Kohlberg's moral development, or Freud's psychosexual development, just to name a few. In such models, the achievement of each stage is often viewed as a pass to the next stage on a one-way journey. While that may seem so in some of the mentioned developmental processes—like cognitive development, in which one's level of cognition does not readily slip back to previous stages then jump back and forth and all around—this does happen from time to time in some cases. Cognitively, at times we are very sharp, and at other times we fail to remember simple words or fail at simple math for some reason or another. Sometimes we feel a moral obligation to save the planet, the whales, and the children, and our hearts pour out love and generosity; at other times, we get angry and flip out because someone purposefully and intentionally made us late by braking in front of us, causing us not to make the red light, but they still got through in the yellow phase.

The fact of the matter is no developmental process is strictly a one-way street, however with respect to identity development, it is more like a canoe on the ocean with no land in sight. One chooses a direction and begins paddling while the wind blows you in different directions, and the unknown current takes you in another. Imagine that for a moment. Let us assume you have all the food and water you need to survive. Do you rely on your strength and paddle in the direction of your choice? Do you observe the wind and paddle in that direction? Or do you choose not to exert yourself and allow the wind and current to take you, hoping a ship will pass nearby? Although Erikson's model is very helpful and insightful, it is drastically oversimplified.

Muuss (1996) outlined a more complex version of Erikson's stages in which the primary eight stages of development occur on the diagonal of an 8×8 grid, consisting of additional horizontal and vertical development stages. In this more complex model, the fifth stage of identity development is set as a pivotal point in which all other stages work up to or continue from.

> The vertical sequence in the table above, beginning with 'Mutual Recognition vs. Autistic Isolation' and ascending until it coincides with 'Identity vs. Identity Confusion' in the diagonal sequence, demonstrates how each of the four preceding stages contributes significantly to the development of ego-identity or identity diffusion during adolescence. Thus, 'Mutual Recognition,' 'Will to Be Oneself,' 'Anticipation of Roles,' and 'Task Identification' are secondary outcomes of the earlier stages of psychosocial development that are essential contributing factors to the achievement of a syntonic identity in adolescence. On the other hand, failure in the earlier stages resulting in 'Autistic Isolation,' 'Self-Doubt,' 'Role Inhibition,' and a 'Sense of Futility' may contribute to a personal estrangement or identity confusion in adolescence. The horizontal sequence in Figure 3.1 beginning with 'Temporal Perspective versus Time Confusion,' depicts the derivatives or earlier relative achievements that now become part and parcel of the

struggle for identity. Erikson notes, 'It is necessary to emphasize ... [that] the early achievements must be ... renamed in terms of the later stages. Basic Trust, for example, is a good and a most fundamental thing to have, but its psychosocial quality becomes more differentiated as the ego comes into the possession of a more extensive apparatus, even as society challenges and guides such extension' (Muuss, 1996, pp., 46–47).

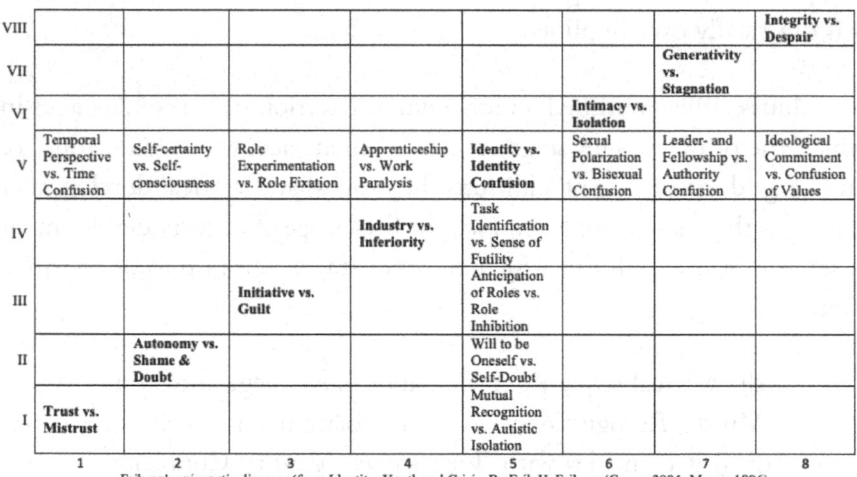

VIII								**Integrity vs. Despair**
VII							**Generativity vs. Stagnation**	
VI						**Intimacy vs. Isolation**		
V	Temporal Perspective vs. Time Confusion	Self-certainty vs. Self-consciousness	Role Experimentation vs. Role Fixation	Apprenticeship vs. Work Paralysis	**Identity vs. Identity Confusion**	Sexual Polarization vs. Bisexual Confusion	Leader- and Fellowship vs. Authority Confusion	Ideological Commitment vs. Confusion of Values
IV				**Industry vs. Inferiority**	Task Identification vs. Sense of Futility			
III			**Initiative vs. Guilt**		Anticipation of Roles vs. Role Inhibition			
II		**Autonomy vs. Shame & Doubt**			Will to be Oneself vs. Self-Doubt			
I	**Trust vs. Mistrust**				Mutual Recognition vs. Autistic Isolation			
	1	2	3	4	5	6	7	8

Erikson's epigenetic diagram (from Identity: Youth and Crisis. By Erik H. Erikson (Capps, 2004; Muuss, 1996).

Muuss's model recognises that the conflicts which define each stage of Erikson's model are by far not the only conflicts with which an individual is confronted at each of these stages of their lives. Other researchers agree and add that many other factors influence an individual's identity development.

Sokol (2009, p. 3) argued that the process of identity development begins much earlier than adolescence, suggesting that the 'seeds of identity are planted at a young age when the child recognises himself/herself as a unique being, separate from his/her parents. As maturation occurs, the child takes on characteristics and admired features of parents or significant others. Erikson referred to this process as identification'. During identification, which may begin in early childhood, a child builds a set of expectations about what he or she wishes to be and do, primarily based on the child's perception of their caregivers. At sometimes ridiculously young ages, a child may hear questions like, 'Are you going to be a great [insert occupation, activity, or any other defining attribute] like your [insert close family member]?' As the son of a professional football player, I know I heard this question so often that I got tired of hearing it. Imagine the look on people's faces had I been able to see into the future and replied, 'No, I am going to be in a wheelchair and use my head for something other than bashing people with it for a living.' But just as Sokol explained, a child eventually loses interest in merely adopting the roles and personality attributes of parents or significant others, and the process of identification ends while the process of identity formation begins.

While Erikson's fifth stage, occurring in adolescence, is most predominantly associated with identity development, most researchers would agree that each of these eight stages has a significant influence on the development of one's identity. Muuss (1996) explained that the core concept in Erikson's stages of psychosocial development is the acquisition of an ego-identity and the exploration of one's identity, which according to Erikson takes place primarily in adolescence. However, the true sense of personal identity is the psychological connection between childhood and adulthood. Thus, to develop a strong and healthy ego-identity, a child must receive consistent and meaningful recognition for their achievements. Erikson believed that identity development was fickle in that every element must arise at the appropriate time; otherwise, optimal identity development could be jeopardised. Each of Erikson's developmental stages is defined by a characteristic conflict that occurs in that stage.

Furthermore, individuals must experience both sides of the bipolar conflict to come to terms with it truly. Nevertheless, the defining crisis of each stage is never completely resolved and checked off, to never be dealt with again. That is, ego-identity is not something to be achieved but rather something to be sought after. For Erikson, identity development does not end with its formation (Hoare, 2002).

Identity development should be viewed as an ongoing process that captures various meaningful life experiences and makes one's subjective identity from them. Thus, identity development is both a normative period of adolescence and an evolving aspect of adulthood. In contrast to Erikson's extensive writings on the adolescent identity formation process, he did not offer detailed comments regarding identity's evolution throughout adult life (Kroger, 2007). As a result, Erikson has been criticised for extending his theory beyond adolescence without providing much detail. To complicate matters further, Erikson conveys contradictory messages speaking on identity development beyond adolescence. According to Erikson (1968), the final identity is fixed at the end of adolescence as identity concerns fade and as issues regarding intimacy occupy the mind and become the main focus. However, Erikson has also been recorded as saying that identity-defining issues of adolescence do not remain fixed; they retain flexibility for modification throughout the adulthood years due to new life experiences. Clearly these two statements appear contradictory, but the previous diagram illustrates why both of these statements may be true and not contradictory. Muuss's extension of Erikson's identity development model uses Erikson's fifth stage of development as the axis of chronological progression, illustrating that identity development occurs parallel to each of the other seven stages of development. And so in adolescence, all previously established aspects of one's identity converge and are sorted out, and an initial direction of continual identity development is fixed. However, from this initial direction, one can very often, if not usually, change direction throughout one's lifetime.

Sokol (2009) pointed out that identity-related issues continually emerge after adolescence throughout all stages of into adulthood. Kotre and Hall (1990) pointed out that during the later stages of life, and individual's conceptions of opposite-sex qualities, experience, and time change significantly. For example, studies have shown that men and women begin to embrace stereotypical qualities of the opposite sex (Huyck, 1990; James et al., 1995). As the reality that life is half over begins to sink in, adults tend to re-evaluate, redefine, and readjust vocational and social roles (Kroger, 2007). Additionally, more drastic changes in life circumstances such as career changes, divorce, empty nest, or death of a loved one can also force one to re-examine their identity (Waterman, 1993). Such changes are commonly associated with the term *midlife crisis* in which identity-related issues that were once resolved can resurface.

Nevertheless, because identity development seems to be a significant part of adolescence, many researchers tend to focus on this period of life. Waterman (1982) elaborated on the importance of Erikson's adolescent stage of identity development:

> The wholeness to be achieved at this stage I have called a sense of inner identity. The young person, in order to experience wholeness, must feel a progressive continuity between that which he has come to be during the long years of childhood and that which he promises to become in the anticipated future; between that which he conceives himself to be and that which he perceives others to see in him and to expect of him. Individually speaking, identity includes, but is more than, the sum of all the successive identifications of those earlier years when the child wanted to be, and often was forced to become, like the people he depended on. Identity is a unique product, which now meets a crisis to be solved only in new identifications with age mates and with leader figures outside of the family. (Erikson, 1968, p. 87)

Thus, while our childhood dreams of becoming a police officer, professional athlete, or whatever dreams we have based on our childhood perceptions of the world, there is no doubt that it is in adolescence in which these dreams begin to materialise. Optimally, adolescents undergo the identity-formation process. This process involves the ego's ability to synthesise and integrate important earlier identifications into a unique identity (Kroger, 2006). Nevertheless, the maturing adolescent identity development is also significantly influenced by their environment.

High School Daze

'Identity versus Role Confusion' marks the fifth in Erikson's eight-stage lifespan sequence of developmental tasks. This stage is significantly associated with adolescence because it is during this time that adolescents will seek to find some resolution between knowing who they are, who they are not, whom they want to become, and the confusion that comes from trying to figure out these things. There is no doubt that high school is extremely significant in an individual's identity development, and many studies have focused on the factors associated with high school and identity.

Lannegrand-Willems and Bosma (2006) aimed to study adolescent identity development in the school context and found that the school context played an important role in the student's identity development. As such, they determined that the role of the school experience as a personal resource in the development of identity. They used Erikson's (1968) theoretical framework of ego identity development and Marcia's (1966) exploration and commitment processes to form behavioural indications of ego identity.

Rich and Schachter (2012) also focused their research on high school identity climate, claiming that teachers not only teach but also serve as role models, fostering identity development. These researchers agreed that adolescence is the period most widely associated with identity development in an individual's life. However, they also criticised that Erikson's model neglected to sufficiently address the social, cultural, and historical resources that empower, constrain, shape, and maintain identity formation. As such, Rich and Schachter examined the contribution of three characteristics of school climate that were presumed to nurture adolescent identity development: teacher caring, teachers as role models, and a school program that cultivates the whole student rather than just academic learning. The authors suggested that students become confident in their ability to develop positive identities in the future, and they engage in exploration activities when secondary school students perceive that (a) their teachers care about them as persons, (b) their teachers are objects of identification who serve as positive role models, and (c) their school actively promotes a range of developmental domains and is not exclusively concerned with academics. Rich and Schachter concluded that while the relationship between the educational process and student identity development has not been a topic of extensive theory or research, there is good reason to believe that there are important linkages between them (Schachter and Rich, 2011). Identity development has been associated with adolescence; adolescents spend much of their time at school, and school is certainly one of the most important social institutions that adolescents experience. Additionally, identity development is often considered a product of the interaction between intrapersonal and interpersonal factors and the effects of social institutions (Kroger, 2007; Penuel and Wertsch, 1995; Sfard and Prusak, 2005).

Lemke (2008) pointed out the vast amount of influence the construct of 'good' and 'bad' have on our lives. It would seem that the curse of the forbidden fruit was not the gaining of the knowledge between 'good' and 'bad' but rather to be doomed to enforce the concept ourselves in our own lives.

> Schools work to make us over in their image of the good student or the good teacher. Families work to make us conform to their image of the good child, the good mother or father, the good brother or sister, the good boy, and the good girl. In doing this, each institution is embedded in its cultural and political-economic (i.e., ecological) relations to other institutions. It is not just families who are selling an image of the good son or daughter, but also Hollywood, the television networks, their owners and sponsors, magazine advertisers, fiction writers, journalists, and the like. The degree of convergence among these views of a particular identity is not simply a function of some miraculous invisible hand of shared or common culture. It is the product of interests and the domination of some interests over others. It is governed by an ideology that serves interests, and as Bourdieu (1990) argues regarding the limited autonomy of various social fields, such as the academy or the arts, much of the convergence is a product of the interests of those who dominate the dominant field of money-and-power. This view of identity asks us to imagine that identities are not purely matters of internal feeling states or personalized discourses. Identities are contested public terrain. As Foucault argues, modernism has found more and more ways to take the inner soul, which was private, if publicly accountable under older forms of Christianity, and make it into a more public terrain of identity, under surveillance and subject to control by outside interests. (Lemke 2008, p. 31)

In addition to this, Lannegrand-Willems and Bosma (2006) pointed out that a student's academic performance in school had no significant effect on the school's influence on student's identity development; however, students who were exceptionally talented in math tended to be more secure in their future academic paths.

Marcia's Identity Status Stages

Marcia (1966) also expanded on Erikson's model and devised a system that has been used to assess the progress of an individual's identity development. The identity control system responds to incongruence between social feedback and self-definitions and is particularly active during adolescence, in which exploration leads to the consolidation of self-perceptions into an identity (Kerpelman, Pittman, and Lamke, 1997). Marcia's status model differentiated the bipolar outcome of the identity crisis in adolescence described by Erikson. According to the status model, individuals can be classified into four statuses, achieved, foreclosed, diffused, and moratorium, which can be categorically measured in crisis, exploration, and commitment (Bosma and Kunnen, 2001). Marcia (1966, 1976, 1980, 1993) was amongst the first to operationalise Erikson's theory of ego identity development in adolescence. Marcia distinguished four identity statuses based on exploration and commitment.

The achieved status of identity development is marked by adolescents who have explored their options and have committed to a personally satisfying path of identity development. This individual has a good sense of who he is and who he is not; and, he has given a considerable amount of thought to the matter. A person who has become an identity achiever may live out their life continuing to develop faucets of their identity as they age and experience or they experience an event that shatters their identity. When that happens, a person can either get back on their feet mentally and restart the identity development process again or give up. For me, the is no option. Restarting the development process would begin with first coming to grips with whatever shattered the identity in the first place. Then one would begin the moratorium status again. And of course, that includes incorporating all the memories of pre- and post-adolescent memories, which may be related to the shattered identity. Thus, the second time around could be much more or much less difficult, depending strictly on the subjective lifetime experience and how an individual chooses to perceive the experiences.

The moratorium status of identity development is marked by adolescents, who are in the process of exploring available options but have yet to reach a final commitment. If you are reading this and over the age of twenty-five, you surely know by now that rushed decisions are most often, but not always, very bad decisions. A person who has entered the moratorium status may make life decisions that establish a secure identity and reach the achieved status. Or an individual could make bad decisions or simply have bad luck. If an individual becomes stagnant in the moratorium status, they could go with whatever option is on the table that they have been looking at for years. If they do this, one of two things is likely to happen. They could hit the jackpot and reach the achieved status, later wondering why it took them so long to find themselves. Or they become unhappy with the rash decision and fall into the foreclosed status, pondering the what-ifs of their life. But if they continue not to decide at all, they are likely to stop the search for their identity and regress to the diffused status of identity. Under the stressors of life, one could argue that taking a step back and re-evaluating one's life situation from time to time may lead to better life choices. But sometimes you also just have to go for it. In any case, when it comes to life choices, not having made a choice can be the worst decision. The sad fact is that sometimes people give up and fall into the diffused status of identity development or make a hasty decision and find themselves in the foreclosed status of identity development.

The foreclosed status of identity development is marked by adolescents who have committed to a path of identity development; however, they have done so in an ineffective manner. A person in the foreclosure status may find that the premature or ineffective choice proved to be a good choice after all. Or one could realise that they need to return to the moratorium status and put forth more effort in the process of their identity development. In the midst of all of this life stress, it is important to remember that it is not the things that happen to us in our lives that causes stress, but rather it is how we choose to perceive all the things that happen to us in our lives that causes stress. The commitment to a path of identity development is indeed a heavy one. If the choice of path becomes so terribly dissatisfying, then one's identity can shatter like the reflection in the mirror. It is as if one wakes up and no longer wants to be the reflection in one's mind mirror. When that happens, it can be a horrible experience, but it can also be a blessing. From within the foreclosed status of identity development, one can decide to re-enter the moratorium status but do so with more determination and with more life experience than previously. Or in the face of familiar defeat, one could give up and enter the diffused status stage of identity development.

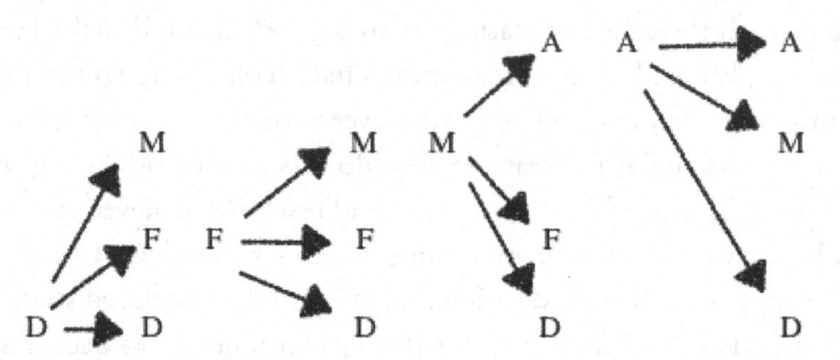

A model of the sequential patterns of ego identitiy development (Waterman, 1982, p. 343). D= diffusion; F=foreclosure; M=moratorium; A=achievement

The diffused identity development status is marked by adolescents who have neither explored their options nor committed to any options. A person in the identity diffusion status may begin to explore their identity, dive too quickly into the next best identity, or continue pushing the issue off mentally. Simply put, the choices we make lead to the status of our identity development.

Bosma and Kunnen's (2001, p. 42) illustrated how individuals can progress from one status of identity development to another throughout their life. Of course, the goal is to achieve a secure identity, but such is life that each of these stages will inevitably be reached by nearly every human during the course of their long lives. Waterman (1999) and Berzonsky and Adams (1999) tend to dismiss the idea that the four statuses can be ranked in order from the least secure identity to the most secure identity. That is, none of these stages is categorically better than another, and one does not simply advance through the ranks like on a one way street to achieved identity security. The path to achieved identity status is a rocky developmental process.

Kerpelman, Pittman, and Lamke (1997) concluded by stating that the developmental theory indicates what develops, and the identity control theory assesses the hows of the identity development process and offers a lens for viewing and understanding the identity processes while emphasising the importance of personal standard derived from social exploration and commitments. As such, the identity control theory may provide a framework for explaining the psychosocial processes that underline the development of identities and may promote understanding of the connections between interpersonal relationships and identity development.

The Factors of Identity

Outlined thus far are only the most popular ways in which scientific psychology has viewed identity development. Still, others have argued that many other aspects of identity development must be taken into consideration. It has been stated repeatedly that identity development occurs primarily during the adolescent years; it surely does. However, some authors have argued that identity development begins long before and continues long after. Kerpelman, Pittman, and Lamke (1997) explored the following questions: 'What triggers identity exploration?' (which begins long before adolescence), 'What occurs during consolidation?' (which occurs shortly after adolescence), and 'What leads to the initiation of identity devaluation?' (which occurs long after adolescence). To cover all of this would be to write a book on identity development. Thus, I will only point out a few aspects of identity development that occur before and after adolescence.

Before Adolescence

We already discussed that the identification phase, in which small children identify themselves with their perceptions of their parents' identity, begins longs before adolescence, but it is nevertheless a significant part of the process. YouTube is full of videos in which small children are displayed performing behaviours that they associate with their parents.

Indeed, many people who have achieved greatness in a particular discipline have begun practicing this discipline because they observed their parents participating in the discipline. This begs the question, Would they have reached such greatness or even acquired an interest in the discipline if their parents did not first partake? The answer to this question brings us back to the nature versus nurture debate, which I discussed in chapter 1. Thus, I will leave it at that.

Waterman (1982) maintained that aspects such as gender, sexual orientation, religious beliefs, and political ideology may play an important role in adolescents' identity development. By the time a child is in kindergarten, they are aware if they are a boy or a girl. Regardless, whether they are dressed in a skirt or pants, given dolls or trucks as toys, have long or short hair, when the teacher says, 'Boys on this side, girls on that side,' by the age of four a child will know to which side they are directed. Although sexual orientation is not my field of expertise, I have read that this also begins before adolescence. Chapter 1 of this book was dedicated to the fact that religious beliefs begin long before adolescence. I would even argue that political orientation begins before adolescence as well, at least in the framework of identification. My five-year-old daughter, who has never lived in the United States, recognises who Donald Trump is and has an opinion of him, even if her opinion is primarily based on my opinion of him. Furthermore, long before adolescence, American children are taught to pledge allegiance to the American flag, illustrating my point.

Gumperz's (1982) work on identity development focused on the influence our speech has on our identity development. Clearly, speech begins long before adolescence, and even if a child is unaware of how their accent, vocabulary, articulation, and the many other linguistic aspects will later define them, the stage is set long before (as cited in Caldas-Coulthard and Alves, 2008). It is curiously interesting that a child learns a language long before they know what a language is. My children have been raised bilingual from birth, but they did not begin to recognise that for themselves until about the age of five. Until then, they spoke English or German, but they did not know if they were speaking English or German. In any case, being raised bilingual has had a significant impact on the development of their identity.

Finally, a child is born into an ethnic group based solely on their DNA.

The feedback they get from the environment based on their ethnicity will surely significantly affect their identity development long before adolescence. The whole discussion on the Black Lives Matter movement is evidence of that fact, regardless of where you stand in the discussion. The very fact that it is a discussion is irrefutable evidence that ethnicity significantly influences identity development.

After Adolescence

After adolescence comes a period of identity consolidation during which previously established identity characteristics are challenged and tested. One could even argue that it is not high school, which is most significant for identity development, but rather college. During consolidation, which takes place after high school, more major life-changing decisions are frequently made. Because a significantly lower percentage of individuals attend college than high school, studies supporting this notion may be questioned in terms of reliability and validity. Nevertheless, Waterman (1982) maintained that identity development continues in and throughout adult life. Similarly, Kerpelman, Pittman, and Lamke (1997) stated that the outcome of identity consolidation is what truly leads to the formation of identity, pushing the time of the process into early adulthood. Lemke (2008) pushed the timeline back even further, claiming that events such as the death of loved ones, divorce, loss of employment, remarriage, the birth of children, and other such significant events that generally happen later in life may prove to be the finalising test of who we are. Suggesting who we are in good times is a less accurate description than who we are in hard times. Perhaps Lemke (2008, p. 38) sums it up best:

> If you are asked, as we so often are, 'what do you do?', how do you feel about any particular reply that you give? How adequate a representation of your identity do you feel any of the stereotypical, culturally named, institutionally sanctioned options available to you really are? In multi-ethnic New York, there is a common social question: 'Lemke, so what kind of name is that?', which is part of the effort to simplify social relationships by

> fitting each person to one of a small number of ethnic-religious groups, mainly those that have been or are of political consequence in the city's alliances of interest. I can claim several such identities, but none of them are ones that I feel much identification with. It is taboo to ask people about their sexuality beyond some overt markers of gender, but I would feel equally unsatisfied with any possible conventional answers. We do not usually ask people more simply, 'Who are you?' in any sense other than asking for their name, but if it was asked, and you were to try to name your identity or identities, could you do so in any way that was satisfying to you? Imagine some answers of the sort: 'I'm an educator, 'I'm a teacher, 'I'm an American,' 'I'm a mother, 'I'm a lesbian,' 'I'm a hacker,' 'I'm a Goth kid,' 'I'm a researcher, 'I'm a physicist, 'I'm a theoretician,' 'I'm a Catholic, 'I'm a liberal, 'I'm Jewish,' 'I'm a twin,' 'I'm a woman'... and think not so much about how each leaves out a lot that you also are, but about how good a fit you feel with any of these generic identities? How much more would you want to say to qualify such an answer? How would you get closer to saying who you feel you are? What do you feel your identity is in terms of nationality, occupation, sexuality, cultural disposition, religion, ethnicity, and so forth? How much of your identification with these categories is based on the need to find allies against prejudice or opponents? Or to gain acceptance in social circles or institutions? Or to increase your status? Or not to offend your family or colleagues? Or not to have to deal with unresolved ambivalences in your own feelings?

Lemke (2008) concluded by pointing out that despite all we have learned about the process of identity development, we certainly do not know all there is to know about it. The following remains to be established:

- How agency and positionality play off one another.

- How the multiplicity of identity mirrors the diversity of communities.
- How changing opportunities for making identities are connected to changing institutional and social configurations.
- How identities are made across multiple timescales and in the spaces created by the conflicting demands of institutions.
- How identities are grounded in embodied experience, fear, and desire.

Bosma and Kunnen (2001) suggested that historical changes in the social and cultural context, such as increased freedom of choice, the emergence of an inner self, and the loss of main value bases, have led to changes in the nature of identity, and they claimed that the identity status approach has focused too heavily on statuses as an intrapersonal attribute, whose development is solely affected by individual factors and this has been at the cost of paying attention to contextual factors. Bosma and Kunnen distinguished the proximal and distal factors and explained that distal factors concern the historical/cultural macro context. Studies have shown that the distribution of statuses in samples of late adolescents is related to changes in economic and cultural conditions, providing evidence that the historical (macro) context is associated with different patterns of development in adolescence. However, history and culture can affect people only by utilising concrete proximal environmental factors, which may affect or interact with personal factors. Lemke (2008) pointed out that the term *identity* is often associated with constructs such as soul, psyche, persona, personality, selfhood, subject, and agency, and he emphasised the multiplicity of identity as a construct, noting that individuals act differently with children and with peers, formal and informal situations, in professional or private settings.

You Are Your Heart's Desire

To review, having put forth significant thought, we can choose to believe that God created us and did so for a specific purpose. This purpose will then have a significant effect on our identity. Thus, we also believe that God knows us, our specific identity, as we know ourselves and more. As the research has pointed out, identity development is coupled with crises and conflicts. And again, one could choose to conceive of this as only problems delivered by a cruel world or as milestones of challenges to which we are enticed to aspire to greater heights undefeated by any circumstances. For if you believe God is for you, who can be against you?

Who we are, simply put, is what we want, our heart's desire. Reiss (2000) defined a basic desire as a desire valued intrinsically rather than its effect on something else. That is, it should serve an end rather than a mean. Furthermore, each basic desire is separate and unrelated from other desires. An individual's basic desires have explanatory significance for understanding their lives, perspectives, and experience. Reiss identified sixteen basic desires:

1. Power—the desire to influence others.
2. Independence—the desire for self-reliance.
3. Curiosity—the desire for knowledge.
4. Acceptance—the desire for inclusion.
5. Order—the desire for organization.
6. Saving—the desire to collect goods.
7. Honour—the desire to be loyal to one's parents and heritage.
8. Idealism—the desire for social justice.
9. Social Contact—the desire for companionship.
10. Family—the desire to raise one's children.
11. Status—the desire for social standing.
12. Vengeance—the desire to get even.
13. Romance—the desire for sex and beauty.
14. Eating—the desire to consume food.
15. Physical activity—the desire for exercise.
16. Tranquillity—the desire for emotional calm.

Reiss's sixteen basic desires could be used to assess one's Basic Desire Profile by simply rating oneself in a three-point Likert scale (–, 0, +) for each of the sixteen basic desires. Reiss suggested that each individual has a unique desire profile and that this desire profile greatly influences one's ability to communicate with other individuals according to their profile. Our basic desires come to shine through our emotional communication.

This is where the concept of status, as defined in chapter 2, comes into play. For a while, I may not have a complementary desire profile with someone; I am first able to recognise this instantly and adjust my status (body language) to foster communication and communicate effectively.

Reiss discussed his theory of compatibility, which suggests that couples with similar desire profiles have higher compatibility, and that does seem to have face validity. However, I strongly disagree with the author's suggestion that a person's desire profile illustrates an individual's priorities that one may follow to find long-lasting, deep happiness and fulfilment. Satisfying your most important desires can help you experience life as meaningful, bringing a sense of deep satisfaction beyond pleasure and pain. However—and perhaps I am self-hugging—I believe this is where spirituality comes into play. For it is not fulfilling one's own desire that brings this level of happiness, but fulfilling God's plan for our lives and becoming exactly the person He created us to be.

You Are Your Testimony—Story of Our Lives

It is common practice that individuals may address an audience and give their testimony. From a Christian theological background, a testimony is the story of how an individual came to know God. However, I suggest that if one were to question all the people that have ever given a testimony, each person would claim that while the story was about how this person came to know God, it is really a story about how well God knows that person. While sharing testimony is a theological concept, scientific psychology has examined people's narratives, which is essentially the same thing.

McLean and Syed (2015) claimed that children learn storytelling skills beginning in very early childhood during their development. These skills eventually allow them to understand their identity in terms of an autobiographical self or the self through time (Fivush, Haden, and Reese, 2006). Children's thinking about themselves becomes increasingly complex as they move into and through adolescence into adulthood as they construct a personal life story or narrative identity (Habermas and Reese, 2015).

McLean and Syed (2015) also suggested that when individuals speak of themselves in the narrative, they are more likely to find an association between themselves and society. In addition, time and sequencing narratives dictate a temporal and sequential order to the telling of events, foster detailed memory and reflective understanding of events and experiences. As such, narratives bring the dynamics of time and sequence to similar existing concepts in the form of representations or schemas about the expectations for behaviour, cognition, emotions, and values of a particular social group (Dovidio et al., 2010). McLean and Syed argued that narratives provide a uniform metaphor for understanding the individual and the structure by representing individual and structural factors in one's life story. Additionally, adopting a narrative to represent individual and structural factors inherently resists the pitfall of conceptualising and measuring either in static terms.

Thus, whereas Christian theology teaches that sharing one's testimony fosters spiritual development, scientific psychology determined that creating a master narrative fosters mind development. The term *narrative*, by definition, implies subjectivity, malleability, and flexibility (Hammack, 2011; Sarbin, 1986), which are characteristics critical for understanding the dynamics of identity development. McLean and Pasupathi (2012, p. 14) explained that 'people use narration as a way of exploring potential identity commitments. In doing so, they can also try out those identities and commitments in social contexts.' Lemke (2008, p. 27) illustrates this nicely.

> We are what we fear; we are what we desire. 'Who are we?' is the basic question of identity. Who by natural gifts and weaknesses; who by membership and affiliation; who by social positioning, by financial, social, and cultural capital; who by what we have and what we lack, what we desire and what we fear? Values and ambitions, search, and avoidance are clearly grounded in fear and desire.

Our longer-timescale identities could then be defined as our soul, which will be the topic of my next book. Just as Lemke (2008) explained that our identity results from how we perceive our past experiences over a lifetime, I will propose that the human soul is the result of how we want our future experiences to be. In each moment, we act in response to our environment, and through our behaviour, we contribute to the events, producing the conditions and affordances of actions by ourselves and others in the next moments to come. At the same time, how we act in response to momentary events depends on both relatively automated and relatively volitional processes of identity maintenance, which operate continuously throughout our life span development (Lemke, 2008). The testimony and the master narrative of any individual will consist of the trials and tribulation that the individual conquered, continue to struggle with, or have conquered us. Lemke (2008, p. 35) pointed out,

> We are far more likely to live as part of multiple families through divorce, remarriage, foster care, and so forth, both in our youth and throughout our lives. Because of social mobility, we are much more likely to move around from school to school in our youth and community to community throughout our lives. We no longer expect to spend our lives working in one company or university or even pursuing one career or line of work. We are even more likely to shop around from church to church, if not change religious affiliation more than once during our lives. We are exposed through mass media and communications and travel to a wide range of social institutions and their norms and cultures. While most of these institutions of all kinds show a certain convergence of culture because of their common domination by dominant interests and their common historical heritage, there are inevitably also contradictions and conflicts among them. The more institutions we visit in our lives, the more likely we are to encounter and recognize these internal contradictions and conflicts, thereby acquiring at least some independent freedom of vision regarding possible values and identities.

Born Again, the Pursuit of a Deeper Identity: The Soul

The heart, which is the human emotional processing system; the body, which is the fleshy mass; the mind, which comprises the cognitive processes; and the soul, which is the intersection of the previous three components, are the four components of the human being. Each of these four components interacts and influences behaviour through each other. Thus, each component is connected to the others. The connection between the mind and the body takes place at the level of neuroplasticity. The connection between the mind and the heart takes place in the limbic system. The connection between the heart and the body takes place in the framework of passionate activities. The connection between the soul and the heart, body, and mind collectively takes place through the process of identity development. An individual's soul is the identity of the person they long to become.

Thus, defining the soul in this manner draws associations to Freud's definition of ego, which supports the notion that our identity is who we are, but our soul is whom we want to become. As such, one's core beliefs, serving as a lens through which reality is perceived, may significantly influence the development of the soul. One may think of the soul as something given to us at birth by the Creator of life, or one could choose to perceive the soul reduced to neurology alone. Either way, the soul is something that develops during and through a lifetime of experience. In fact, it is this property of continuity that serves as proof that something like a soul exists (Van Inwagen, 1997). Compare yourself now to who you were when you were two years old. You do not have the same body, you do not the same mind, and your emotional processes have also completely change. The only thing about you then and you now that is remotely the same is your soul.

We humans, being aware of our existence, have the cognitive capability to make plans about the future. We are aware of where we are now, both figuratively and literally, and we think about where we want to be in the future. Throughout our lifetime, our identity develops like the roots of a tree, turning into a foundation of our choosing. The roots meet resistance in some places and may halt in others. But when a tree falls in a storm, if its roots are still in the ground, the tree will continue to grow, though in a different direction.

> I am the true vine, and my Father is the gardener. He cuts off every branch in me that bears no fruit, while every branch that does bear fruit he prunes so that it will be even more fruitful. You are already clean because of the word I have spoken to you. Remain in me, as I also remain in you. No branch can bear fruit by itself; it must remain in the vine. Neither can you bear fruit unless you remain in me. 'I am the vine; you are the branches. If you remain in me and I in you, you will bear much fruit; apart from me, you can do nothing (John 15:1–5).

Conclusion

One's behaviour today will influence where one will be tomorrow. This occurs naturally. But as humans, we also have the power to plan for our future, and above all, we have the power to adapt to any situation with which we are confronted. If we see our lives as fulfilling a purpose, then we will perceive our experiences for what they are: challenges from which valuable knowledge can be learned.

In any developmental process, time is a decisive factor. So it is also with identity. I believe very few would claim to have gotten it right the very first time. From a theological perspective, our identity may be perceived, as indeed I do, as predestination. The topic of predestination is another can of worms that would distract us from our current topic, but it would be interesting to consider how the concepts of development and predestination work together. A study on testimonies and master narratives may offer some insight. A testimony and a master narrative are the stories and consecutive thought processes of a person's experience over time. This story essentially explains why a person has the core belief they have. If one chooses to take God out of the story, one calls it a master narrative, and it was designed to serve the same exact purpose: a thorough explanation of one's core believes. Such a story takes time to experience and reflect upon over many years.

For this reason, I found it a particularly interesting idea to put each of Erikson's eight stages of psychosocial development, in which some stages last only a few years, while others a few decades, into equal ten-year periods. When we do this, it becomes apparent that we do not go through these eight stages only once but repeat them on various levels, with the spiritual being the highest. Waterman (1982) also supported this notion, citing Erikson's reference to William James, that some individuals seem to experience a second birth in that they go through the psychosocial developmental processes twice. The idea of rebirth is of course associated with the teaching of Jesus. In John 3:1–21, Jesus teaches Nicodemus that people must be born again. The Bible teaches that when we make God our heart's desire, we can trust in Him that He has created us with a specific purpose. When we choose to submit to Him and follow and strive to become the person He created us to be, with that, we essentially give him our soul and become like-minded with God.

CHAPTER 6

The Relational Mind—The Gestalt School of Thought

The German word *gestalt* has a much deeper meaning than is often depicted in English literature, and it is often inadequately translated. *Gestalt* refers to 'an unrecognizable and/or not clearly defined' form, indicating a tone of mystery. If you think you see someone or something rummaging around in your backyard in the dark, in English we would say, 'I think I saw something,' which would beg the follow-up question, 'What did you see?' But in German, one could say, 'Ich habe da einen Gestalt gesehen,' and there would be no follow-up question because the term *gestalt* would clarify that the object could not be more accurately described or identified. Similarly, the word is often used in the verb form, describing 'an unrecognizable and/or not clearly defined' action. Had we lived in Germany as I, at twelve years old, took our lawnmower apart to harvest its engine for a go-kart, my mom might have yelled, 'Was gestaltest du da?' instead of, 'What are you doing?' Thus, the term *gestalt* implies that there is certainly something there, but it is unclear what it is or what it is doing. And the only way to obtain a better idea of what is or what is going on is to turn on the lights and take a closer look.

Behrens (1998) tells the story of how the concept of gestalt psychology was discovered. During a train ride in 1910, Wertheimer discovered that when stationary flashing lights were sequenced in a certain way, they seemed to depict a single light in motion. This became known as the phi phenomenon and is the basic principle of motion pictures (Boeree, 2008). Wertheimer decided to investigate the phenomenon more in-depth, and with the help of Kurt Koffka and Wolfgang Köhler, he published a work in 1912 entitled *Experimental Studies of the Perception of Movement*. Later, Koffka and Köhler expanded on the idea. Since then, the gestalt school of thought has become a framework of logic which does not categorically assume that life, nature, and the universe can be reduced by physics alone, but rather that the whole can be greater than the sum of the parts. That is, though music is sound, sound is not necessarily music. The alternative is called reductionism, aka atomism. This school of thought assumes that complex systems can be broken down into simpler systems. As such, to the reductionist, the mind is nothing more than chemical processes taking place on a molecular level in the brain. To the reductionist, a complete set of disassembled car parts is the same as a car.

Although Wertheimer is typically accredited with the discovery of gestalt psychology, its concepts are actually rooted in a number of older philosophers and psychologists (Boeree, 2008). Ernst Mach introduced the concept of space and time forms, which explained how and why we perceive in terms of categories. For example, we recognise a tree as a tree regardless of its size, shape, kind, and time of perception. The spark of the idea came from Christian von Ehrenfels in 1890, as he realised that a melody could be recognised in any musical key. This meant that we did not recognise a melody based on the notes of which it consisted. Instead, we recognise the relationship between the notes.

This was the first clue pointing to the relational mind. That is, our minds perceive, process, and remember in terms of relations. Our perception is based on the relationship between objects and not the objects strictly in and of themselves. The idea is more counterintuitive than it may first seem. An example may help to illustrate the founding principle. Look up from this book and glace for a moment on any object. What did you see? Whatever it was, I could argue that you did not see that, but rather the contrast between that object and the rest of the perspective background. If the object looked just like the rest of the background, then you would not have been able to see the object. This is essentially the principle behind camouflage. We perceive an object in our mind when our eye can define a gestalt (form) which contrasts from all other perceptual input. As such, we do not actually perceive an object; rather, we perceive the contrast between objects.

Furthermore, our understanding and cognitive processes are also based on relationships. I am listening to a song right now, but try as I might, I could not describe this song to you so you might gain an understanding of the song without mentioning any relations or association to the song. If I want you to understand what I hear, I have to communicate in terms of relations, associations, and categories. Even the term *song* is categorically different from the terms *sound* and *noise*. But if I say I am listening to classical music, you start to get an idea of what I am hearing. If then I continue the description by mentioning the instruments used, your understanding of what I am hearing increases. Spanish guitar, orchestra, string quartet—these words have relational meanings in that each of these music genres has a defined meaning.

Finally, studies on memory have clearly demonstrated that we remember things in terms of relation and association. In fact, after having made this discovery, some individuals have demonstrated incredible feats of memory by employing a technique in which elements to be memorised were systematically coupled with a previously well-known association called a mnemonic. While the principles of gestalt psychology were discovered and defined in terms of perceptions, many psychologists have demonstrated that the relational attribute of the mind is not limited to perception alone but manifests itself in behaviour and thought processes.

Principal Laws of Gestalt Perception

Boeree (2008) outlined the principal laws of gestalt, which are based on the observation that our experience of our environment is not merely the sum of our sensations. An illusion is when we see more than is actually there; a hallucination is when we think we see something that is not there at all. To be clear, the principal laws of gestalt may be likened with illusion but not with hallucination. As such, an illusion is when we see the effect of an event as a whole, which is not contained in the sum of the parts. The underlining principle of gestalt psychology is that not only do we have the ability to experience a structure as a whole as well as individual sensation, but also we have a strong tendency to fill in the gaps to perceive a whole rather than parts. Incidentally, Wage et al. (2013) also thoroughly outlined gestalt principles and concepts with many examples and studies.

The law of prägnanz (conciseness succinctness) says that we are innately driven to experience things in as good a gestalt as possible. This is what gives us the ability to see various objects in cloud formations and share the images by pointing out the parts until the other person says, 'Oh, yeah, now I see it.' It would seem that our minds do not like empty blanks, and so they tend to fill in the blanks through logic and past experience. I have heard it said that this is the reason for the 'earworm'. We experience a song as an earworm and cannot stop thinking about the sound. But when we try to sing it out loud or only in our minds, we find that we do not know the text in its entirety. Thus, the song occupies our mind as it tries to fill in the blanks. The cure of an earworm is quite simple. All one has to do is listen to the song one time in its entirety, and then the mind will be satisfied, at least for the moment.

The law of closure says that if something is missing from an otherwise complete figure, we will fill in the missing part. This is what makes proofreading so difficult, and this is what makes a lot of close-up magic tricks possible. In one such trick, I would put a dime on my right elbow for everyone to see very clearly. Then as I turn my body to make sure that everyone can clearly see the dime on my elbow, I move just a little too swiftly so that the dime falls off. This is made to look like an accident, but it is really what makes the whole trick work. I bend over and pick up the dime with my right hand. Now, you may not have thought about this, but it is impossible to put a dime on your right elbow with your right hand, so when I seemingly transfer the dime to my left hand and seemingly put it back on my elbow, this movement causes the audience to see the dime on my elbow again, because it makes sense in their minds, and that is where they saw the dime before. Of course, I actually keep the dime in my right hand and put the dime in my ear as I say, 'OK, you can all see the dime on my elbow.' Curiously, by telling the audience they see it just where they saw it previously, the audience can be convinced they see it even though it is not there. One does not even have to be sneaky about it or have much dexterity. It is sufficient to merely go through the same exact motion as previously, before the coin fell. Then I drop my arm, pretend to catch the dime with my right hand, and proceed to show that the dime has disappeared. Bringing back the coin is even more fun. This time, I take an invisible dime out of the air and place it on my right elbow. I give everyone a good look at the invisible dime on my elbow. Now, all I have to do is take the dime back out of my ear, go through the same catching motion as before, and voila, I present the dime in my hand.

The law of similarity says that we will tend to group similar items and see them as forming a gestalt within a larger form. The mind simply likes to see things in groups, and thus, we tend to put things in groups. In your silverware drawer, the chances are that you have your spoons, forks, and butter knives in separate groups. You may think that you do this to find each utensil more quickly, but I would argue that that is not the case. In a pile of spoons, forks, and knives, your eye can locate any one member of these three categories just as quickly. Here we see a figure made up of 11 Os and 110 Xs. If the Os were scattered about the form, then one may be less likely to see two groups of Xs, but as they are displayed here, one cannot help but see two groups.

OXXXXXXXXXX
XOXXXXXXXXX
XXOXXXXXXXX
XXXOXXXXXXX
XXXXOXXXXXX
XXXXXOXXXXX
XXXXXXOXXXX
XXXXXXXOXXX
XXXXXXXXOXX
XXXXXXXXXOX
XXXXXXXXXXO

****

****

****

The law of proximity says that things that are closer together are seen as belonging together. In an instant, one sees three rows of asterisks rather than fourteen columns of asterixis. In our minds, things that are closer together belong together. We will later discuss that all of these principles go far beyond illusionary visual phenomena, but the law of proximity is very much present in human social interaction. When two people are seen together, one may begin to speculate whether they are a couple. In a high school cafeteria, students build groups, and neighbouring groups are seen as more closely related to each other than groups that are farther apart. If you see someone standing next to a five-dollar bill on the ground, or a piece of trash, or whatever, you would think it belongs to the person standing the closest to it, although the wind could have blown it close to that person, or the person could have just happened to stop and stand next to it.

[ ][ ][ ]

The law of symmetry says that things facing each other belong together. Here we see three pairs of brackets, instead of two pairs of brackets, back to back. The law of symmetry also has social connotations. Two people standing facing each other at a bus stop are thought to be acquaintances, whereas two people standing side by side at a bus stop are thought to be strangers.

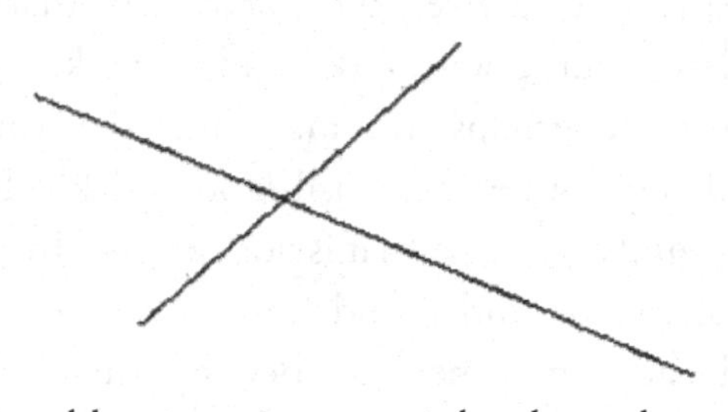

The law of continuity says we like to see lines continuing through intersections, and here, one is inclined to see two intersecting lines rather than four individual lines. This law becomes apparent when one is following road directions and is told to continue straight through an intersection but then finds oneself on a road with a different name. The question that comes to mind is, 'How did I get on this road when I didn't make a turn?'

The law of figure-ground says we can focus on either foreground or the background, but not both at the same time. The classic example of this is the 'Vase, Face' illusion in which the observer either sees a black vase or two white faces in profile. But try as one might, one cannot perceive both images simultaneously. Instead, one's attention is only able to oscillate back and forth between the two gestalts. If one were to examine the individual sensations associated with the perception of the vase-profile image, the process of sensory integration would be the same in the perception of the vase as in the perception of the profiles; nevertheless, the two perceptions are very different. As such, something must be lost in the process of decomposing the two main percepts into their distinct elements (Green, 1997).

In his classic work *The Analysis of Sensations*, Ernst Mach (1890) investigated the connection between perception and cognition. He argued that all concepts, material or mental, were reducible to all sensations on an atomic level. He applied this reductionist point of view to all complex sensations and viewed them as simple sets of atomic sensations in the mosaic of perception. As such, only the atomic elements are 'real' (Cat, 2007).

Both from a theological as well as from a psychological perspective, it has been said that humans were created for relationships. Psychologically, this means that humans get lonely, and theologically, it means that God created humans to be in a relationship with Him. While I could argue that both of these perspectives hold true, my emphasis in this chapter will be on the relational mind. That is, our minds operate in terms of relationships. What later became known as gestalt psychology began as simple studies on the perception of optical illusions.

Observe the three boxes: On the left is a grey box, in the middle is a black box, and on the right is a white box. Each of the boxes contains a circle. Each of these circles appears to be of a slightly but discerningly different shade of grey. You may not be surprised to learn that each circle is indeed the exact same shade of grey. If you wish, you can confirm this by punching three holes in a piece of paper so that each of the holes falls within each of the circles while the squares are covered up. Remove the three-holed paper, and the circles are again three different shades of grey.

The simple reason for this is that the different coloured squares influence the perception of the colour of the circles. Against a white background, the circle seems dark grey, as it truly is. But against a slightly darker background, the circle seems to be lighter, and, against a still darker background, the circle seems lighter still.

Such optical illusions are quite fun and well-known. However, the interesting fact is that not only does our sensory perception work like this, but our entire cognition works on this same principle of relations. Our mind is relational and grows by building more and more associations. Here is another fun experiment. Think of any random word. One, two, three. By now, you will have had a fair many ideas in your mind before you landed on and decided on your random word. If it was *tree*, you probably thought of a specific tree, or a season, or of being outside, or some other associated detail. Try as we might, we cannot think of any one thing in a total absence of anything else. When I used to work as an improv actor, we would warm up by playing word association games, and we tried to quicken our minds to hop from one association to the next as fast as possible before we went on stage. This served to cure us from overthinking and trying to be funny, because a good improv actor is an associative actor.

Gestalt Psychology

The gestalt movement initially grew out of the question: If perception is composed of 'bundles' of sensory elements, what elements make up the perception of time and space (Green, 1997)? Gestalt psychology began as a theory of perception, but since then, it has become much more. Köhler (1940, p. 55) argued that a theory of perception should be used as a field theory in which 'the neural functions and processes with which the perceptual facts are associated in each case are located in a continuous medium; and that the events in one part of this medium influence the events in other regions in a way that depends directly on the properties of both in their relation to each other'. The only way that one is able to recognise a gestalt is because its form or manner differs significantly from the commonly known background. This concept is deeply rooted in psychology in that we recognise things, even abstract concepts, not only based on what they are but also based on what they are not. It is the relationship between things that defines them; nothing exists in and of itself, but rather everything exists with respect to something else (Köhler 1969).

Green (1997) suggested that gestalt psychology proposes to integrate the facts of inanimate nature and mind into a single scientific structure. In doing so, it incorporates the concepts of order and purpose into physical science. Concerning the concept of order, Koffka (1935, p. 16) wrote, 'In inorganic nature you find nothing but the interplay of blind mechanical forces, but when you come to life you find order, and that means a new agency that directs the workings of inorganic nature, giving aim and direction and thereby order to its blind impulses.' Concerning the aspect of purpose, Green (1997, p. 3) argued, 'Without incorporating the meaning of experience and behaviour, Koffka believed that science would doom itself to trivialities in its investigation of human beings.'

The gestalt school of thought suggests that we perceive in terms of relationships and that the whole is greater than the sum of the parts. The opposite side of this is called materialism, reductionism, or atomist, which believes that everything in the mind can be reduced to neurochemical processes. Koffka (1935) defined materialism in this way: 'This materialistic solution is astonishingly simple. It says: The whole problem is illusory. There are no three kinds of substance or modes of existence, matter, life, and mind; there is only one, and that is matter, composed of blindly whirling atoms which, because of their great numbers and the long time at their disposal, form all sorts of combinations, and among them those we call animals and human beings.' Personally, this would be like viewing a magnificent photograph and denying its significance with the argument that it is only made up of meaningless pixels.

Gestalt Therapy

Henle (1978), who is a self-proclaimed gestalt psychologist, examined the relations between gestalt psychology and gestalt therapy, which was established as a therapeutic method by Fritz Perls. Henle concluded that gestalt psychology and gestalt therapy had little more than the word Gestalt in their name in common. According to Henle (1978, p. 26), Perls dismissed the mind-body dichotomy as a superstition: 'We do not have a body, he maintains, "we are a body, we are somebody.... Thoughts and actions are made of the same stuff.... If mental and physical activities are of the same order, we can observe both as manifestations of the same thing: man's being.... Reality is nothing more but the sum of all awareness as you experience here and now."' According to Henle (1978, p. 27), the only common concept between gestalt psychology and gestalt therapy is the concept of closure, which Perls often referred to as unfinished situation: 'Our life is basically practically nothing but an infinite number of unfinished situations—incomplete gestalts,' writes Perls. 'No sooner have we finished one situation than another comes up.' The neurotic 'individual somehow interrupts the ongoing processes of life and saddles himself with so many unfinished situations that he cannot satisfactorily get on with the process of living.' These unfinished situations from the past compel him to repeat them in everyday life.' Henle (1978, p. 29) stated, 'Gestalt psychology is most developed in perception and cognition, while gestalt therapy is concerned with personality, psychopathology, and psychotherapy. Comparison of approaches to such different areas is often difficult. Nevertheless, in the present case, additional issues invite comparison. As it happens, none of them is trivial.'

The Applications of the Gestalt School of Thought

Boeree (2008) pointed out that the gestalt principles are not restricted to perception alone and offered examples of how the above laws confirm memory, learning, mathematics, and problem-solving. Koffka (1922) found the concepts of sensation, association, and attention in every psychological system. Ideas based on gestalt are insightful and continue to grow in various fields of science. For example, Read, Vanman, and Miller (1997) demonstrated that mathematics and physics have lent significant support to gestalt concepts. Rock and Palmer (1990) outlined the diversity of the gestalt principles and added two more. In addition to this, they also demonstrated how these concepts may be found in biology. In the field of child development, gestalt concepts are very important. Rhyne (2001) stated that children are natural gestaltist, and their art has meaningful associations in their lives, which can be harnessed to foster therapy. Moreover, art in itself is an associative process that follows the principles of gestalt. And finally, Klapp and Jagacinski (2011) pointed out that each of the four major principles of gestalt psychology—holism, constancy, mutual exclusivity, and grouping—can be applied to motor action.

As such, the principles of gestalt psychology are not limited to the field of psychology. Cat (2007) pointed out that Koffka extended these ideas to motor action and included functional concepts such as tasks as ways in which experiences can be organised and brought under law-like relations. Cat asserted that a framework was needed for unifying the different narrow 'schools' of psychology: behaviourism, gestalt theory, psychoanalysis, associationism, and humanistic psychology. 'The real challenge, thinks Köhler, appears for evolutionary theory. If we accept the radically different status of values and reject their place in nature, the ensuing dualism destroys the "hope of unity of knowledge" (Köhler 1944, 372). … We can see that fundamental issues rest on the issue of psychophysical isomorphism. From the philosophical point of view, Köhler would readily describe it as the mind-body problem' (Cat, 2007, p. 158).

Isomorphism

These laws of gestalt have led to the deeper concept of isomorphism, which literally means the same form. The concept of isomorphism attempts to describe the border between the brain, consisting of matter, and the mind, which is not made up of matter. The reductionist would argue that everything that goes on in the mind is actually only happening in the brain. As such, the mind is merely a by-product of the physical brain. However, if this were true, then one would have to equate sound with music. Other authors have investigated how gestalt principles may be used to better understand the various mental processes that occur in the brain that can be transposed in the mind. Koffka (1922, p. 1) claimed, 'The Gestalt-Theory is more than a theory of perception; it is even more than a mere psychological theory. Yet it originated in a study of perception, and the investigation of this topic has furnished the better part of the experimental work which has been done.'

Koffka (1922, p. 3) explained, 'What the stimulus is to the sensation, the residuum is to the image.' Let us break down this vocabulary so that it is easier to understand. A stimulus is that what our senses are able and designed to perceive. They can be light, sound, smell, texture and temperature, taste, and acceleration. Our bodies are equipped with organs that can convert or interpret such stimuli into sensations. This process occurs through the interaction of the sensory organs: eyes, ears, nose, tongue, skin, and the peripheral vestibular apparatus consisting of the saccule, utricle, and semicircular canals. The light bouncing off an object reaches my eye. Being sensitive to light, my eye converts the light into neurological data that can be transported via the optic nerve. At this point, although the eye has detected light, I will not have seen anything until the brain processes this information. Only then do I experience the sensation of sight and see the object. But where do I see the object? Not in the brain but in the mind. How do we know this?

While the object from which the light bounced off is in the physical world, the residuum of this is in our mind, not in the physical world. Furthermore, when two people perceive the same object, although the neurochemical processes involved in creating a mental process are the same, each person will have a distinct mental image of the object. Each person's mental image will be created in relation to various other past experiences. Right now, I see an image of Simone Biles. If any of you see the same image, the image created in your mind will be distinctly different from mine, although our brains are doing the exact same thing. Thus, the images we see are created by the eye and the brain, but it is in the mind that images and all other sensations have meaning and are truly seen.

Because each separate sensation-element leaves behind it a separate residuum, we have a vast number of these residua in our memory, each of which may be separately aroused, thus providing a certain independence of the original arrangement in which the sensations were experienced. This leads to the theory of the association mixtures, which asserts that in the process of creating mental images based on sensory input, sensation, association, and attention are all significantly involved in influencing the resulting mental perception in the mind.

To this effect, *sensation* is defined as the separate, but not inseparable, bundle of elements that make up one's consciousness. This has been introduced as the 'bundle hypothesis' for this conception; psychology's first task is to find out their number and properties. Our six sense organs register sensations from our environment in terms of intensity and quality; however, the clarity or degree of consciousness depends on our associations and attention.

It is through our associations to an image that gives the image meaning. Our sensory organs take in much more data than we could ever know, but most of that data never becomes a mental image because there are no associations to it in the mind. Only when a sensor triggers an association, which is essentially a memory of the past experience, will it attract the mind's attention. Association is the primary factor governing the coming and the going of our ideas. If we perceive something of no relevance to us, our minds dismiss the sensation, and no mental image is created. Thus at every moment, lasting associations are working, reinforcing, and inhibiting each other.

As clear and simple as association and sensation appear to be, attention is much more obscure. Whenever there is an effect that cannot be explained by sensation or association, attention appears to be the factor or cause. 'If the expected sensation does not follow when it's appropriate stimulus is applied, attention to other contents must have caused it to pass unnoticed, or if a sensation does not properly correspond to the stimulus applied, the attention must have been inadequate, thus leading us to make a false judgment' (Koffka, 1922, pp. 3–4). Thus, before a mental image comes to mind, one will have had to have a corresponding sensation. This sensation will have to have a corresponding association. And all of this will have had to have engaged a significant level of attention.

Finally, I want to again point out that while the term *image* is often used to describe visual sensations, it is applicable to each of the six senses.

The sensations that result from smells, tastes, sounds, touch, and movement can and do lead to mental images in the same manner.

Gestalt and Motor Processes

A motor gestalt, like a perceptual gestalt, is holistic because it is processed as a single unit. When one begins a motor action, this action must be completed before a new action with the same muscles can begin. As such, if one is in the process of taking a step, the foot that is in the air at that time must land where it was programmed to land. Otherwise, the balance will be significantly compromised. A motor gestalt can be represented independently of specific muscular effectors, thereby allowing motor constancy. For example, the act of increasing speed in a car is performed by applying pressure with the right foot to the gas pedal in a car and rotating the right wrist down on a motorcycle. However, those accustomed to driving both a car and a motorcycle do not need to remind themselves whether to activate their wrist or foot due to gestalt-like grouping of muscle actions.

Similar to the law of pragnanz, the neuroprocessing of an action is limited to one motor gestalt. When one sees a box and wants to pick it up, the brain will decide how heavy the box is and apply the appropriate amount of strength to lift the box. If the brain is deceived and the box is heavier than expected, then the attempt will fail, and the brain will have to recalculate the necessary strength needed for the second attempt. The gestalt principle of grouping in motor cortex functioning leads to stream segregation in visual and auditory perception; this segregation is present in motor activity and is dependent on the temporal rate. Complicated juggling patterns seem mesmerising for the audience, but to a skilled juggler, these complicated movements are sorted into groups, which significantly simplifies the patterns. The principle of grouping in respect to motion action is a question of integration versus streaming. That is, complex movements can be merged into one unit of movement (streaming), or separate units of movements can be integrated to appear as one movement. This phenomenon of movement groupings can best be illustrated through the difference between juggling and sleight of hand magic. To juggle, one has to group the many motor actions into a single gestalt. To do sleight of hand magic tricks, one has to isolate many motor actions into separate gestalts. That is, a juggler's motor actions do not consist of individual throws and catches, but the maintenance of a single throwing and catching pattern. In contrast, a sleight of hand illusionists breaks down a complex motor action into isolated movements. The best way to understand this is to learn how to juggle three balls and learn how to do the basic sleight of hand magic. You can search YouTube for the 'The French Drop' and '3 Ball Cascade' to quickly learn the difference between grouping and isolating motor gestalts.

Balance in the neuromotor sense and the philosophy of life sense is another good example of how the concept of gestalt exceeds the boundaries of perception. As such, balance exercises are a good tool for achieving this state of mind because one is generally not aware of their balance until it is gone. Holism suggests that a gestalt is more than the sum of its parts. This is equally true for movement. Take for example an individual's ability to walk on a balance beam ten centimetres wide positioned on the floor. The required neurological function remains the same when the beam is ten metres in the air as it is when the beam is on the ground, however the gestalt principle of mutual exclusivity, suggesting that one cannot assume two perspectives simultaneously, becomes vividly apparent. This is why it is much more difficult to walk on top of a ten-metre-high wall that is only five centimetres wide than to walk on a five-centimetre-wide board on the ground, although the motor skill required to perform these tasks are the same. Similarly, the principle of abstractness suggests that a perceived object actually remains the same regardless of its position in space, although the object may be perceived to be quite different. This phenomenon is equally observable in terms of motor action, to which our previous example also applies.

Conclusion

The primary goal of gestalt psychology is to provide a theory which maps perceptions to thoughts (Cat, 2007). Kazdin (2000) suggested that gestalt psychology attempts to connect consciousness and behaviour by presenting a holistic view. The theory of isomorphism attempts to do this. Kohler also postulated the concept of isomorphism, which means there is a kind of a mental map of the objects in the environment, and this mental map helps in learning by insight. This means that in the mind of individuals, there is a map which, according to him, is the explanation of the things around him. In other words, the map is the individual's perception of the world around him (Kazdin, 2000).

Kohler's main contribution in the gestalt school of thought is his discovery of learning by insight through trial and error (Kazdin, 2000). As I discussed in chapter 2, humans are born with reflexes, instincts, and drives that jump-start the learning process. But these innate processes only get the learning behaviour started by establishing the first stimulus-response associations. Pertaining to learning, Koffka (1922, p. 8) explained, 'If an animal is confronted with two stimuli and is trained to react positively to the one and negatively to the other, what has it learned? The traditional theory would reply: the animal has formed a connection between the one sensation corresponding to the first stimulus and the positive reaction and likewise between the other sensation and the negative reaction; our theory, however, would say that the animal has learned to react to a certain structure.' The structure he refers to is the basic principle of action and consequence, which is the basic principle behind trial and error.

When we face a problem and do not know how to solve it, and the problem persists, we will try anything. That is, we act upon the problem. These actions will then lead to a consequence. Most of the time, we do not get it right the first time. But the next time we are faced with the same problem or even a similar one, we remember our previous actions and the associated consequences. Then we make changes to our actions and evaluate the new results. If at first, we do not succeed, we try and try again. This process's efficiency relies on the quality of our associations between past experience and present problems. Thus, not only do we perceive the world in terms of relations and association, but we also learn and think in terms of associations and relations.

Philosophers of mind maintain that scientific psychology should be naturalistic because psychological processes are part of the natural world, and thus they are subject to natural-scientific investigation (Epstein and Hatfield, 1994). However, methodological naturalism asserts that scientific psychology should be reduced to only elements that can be measured with reliability and validity (Epstein and Hatfield, 1994). Even if the consciousness of the mind were purely physiological, a simple result of neurochemical processes, this would not change the fact that we perceive our minds through our consciousness and that we are not conscious of the neurochemical processes that belong to physiology. That is, even if consciousness is merely a result of neurochemical processes, there remains a distinct border between the brain and the mind. This border is what we often refer to as consciousness.

CHAPTER 7

Consciousness

Scientific psychology has generated numerous definitions of consciousness. Panagariya (2018) defined *consciousness* as the subjective, phenomenal experience of external and internal worlds and the sense of awareness of the 'subjective self'. Thus, consciousness may be closely associated with the concepts of identity and subjective self-awareness, which have been previously discussed. Shani (2010) suggested that consciousness gave birth to humanity and marks the divergence of man from animals in Darwinian evolution. Avoiding the philosophic and theological rhetoric, other authors have attempted to define consciousness in terms of cognitive behaviours. Russell (2008) listed several ways consciousness could be described through memory, ideas, or core belief. In addition to this, many constructs such as desires, pleasure, and pain may be described as mental constructs, about which one may or may not be conscious. Isay (2009) suggested that it is our consciousness that makes autonomy possible. Being aware of our surroundings is one thing, and all animals can do that. But humans are aware of this awareness. We can make plans far into the future and retrieve memories far from that past. Humans' level of consciousness far exceeds animalistic drives, instincts, and reflexes, as well as emotional and cognitive processes.

The Nature of Consciousness

You have probably heard the famous statement from René Descartes, 'I think; therefore I am.' But what does that mean? And is it even true? When Descartes posed this question, he was contemplating existence. Previously, I suggested 'I believe, therefore I am' would be a more accurate description of consciousness because consciousness believes that our senses produce accurate mental images of our environment in real-time.

The existence of consciousness is theoretically unprovable, but it is nevertheless a fundamental assumption about the world in which we live. Each of us experiences it, and only the most sceptical of philosophers would question the validity and reliability of our consciousness. However, Descartes argued that the proof of consciousness lies in the fact that we are able to discuss, question, and reflect upon our existence. The ability to do this is evidence that humans can achieve a significantly higher level of consciousness than all other animals. Whereas consciousness is not exclusively possessed by human beings, it is widely understood that the consciousness of animals is significantly different from that of humans; however, many would argue that this difference is one of degree rather than kind (Isay, 2009). Contrary to atheist scientists, who assume that there is no intelligent design, I argue that the difference in the level of consciousness between humans and other animals is so large that it may be considered a different kind of consciousness, rather than merely a different degree of consciousness. The significance of the difference lies in the ability to know and understand right from wrong and have the conscious free will to choose one over the other.

Understanding, Knowledge, and Experience

While sensory integration is the spark that fuels the intellect, it is not a very accurate means of gaining knowledge of our environment because it is easily and readily deceived. For simple observations, it is sufficient. For example, through sensory integration, one can measure the length of a table with a tape measure. However, if we attempt to calculate the value of pi (π) in the same way, by measuring the circumference of a circle and radius of a circle, and then dividing the circumference by the radius, one would be lucky to come up with a value between 3.1 and 3.2. Even with very precise tools, we still cannot measure as accurately as we can deduce through rational, logical thought. Through our cognition, we can perceive things that cannot otherwise be comprehended. Such is the case with the concept of consciousness (Oderberg, 2008).

The term *consciousness* is understood and used in various ways, but the central theme in all definitions of the word is experience. Consciousness is why we experience anything, and we experience nothing without consciousness (Tegmark, 2015).

Cognition

According to Meinong (1899), there are three elements involved in the thought of an object: the act, the content, and the object. The act thinking is the same regardless of what I am thinking. Depending on the content of the thought, be it something emotional, structural, mathematical, et cetera, the thought may take place in a different part of my brain, but wherever it is taking place, the neurons there are doing the same thing as the neurons in other parts of my brain.

The content of a thought is simply what I am thinking about. I can think of people, places, things, and many other things. However, while the act of thinking always takes place in the here and now, the content of the thought may be from the past, present, or future. Furthermore, while the thought is always real, in that I am really thinking, the content of the thought may be something imaginary. That is, I can have real thoughts of unicorns. Also, the content of the thought is not the same as the object of the thought. The content must exist in my mind when the thinking process occurs, whereas the object need not be present, material, or real.

Thus, the content of a thought exists when the act of thinking occurs, regardless of whether the object of the thought truly exists. However, there can be no thought content without an object of that thought. That means whenever you are asked, 'What are you thinking about?' To respond 'nothing' is technically incorrect. The correct response would be, I' am not thinking.' While it is possible not to be thinking, it is impossible to think about nothing. The object of any thought will have at one time come into the mind from the environment through sensory integrations. Once this is done, the object of a thought can be a mental image such as a memory. Still, this mental image is different from the content of the thought. For example, right now, I am thinking about the mental image I have of my eleven-year-old daughter right after her birth. Although the mental image is always the same, the content of the thought differs. The content of this image is usually that of happy memories of a joyous day, but right now, the content of the same memory serves the simple purpose of offering an example. Later, the same memory may bring about still different content.

Levels of Consciousness

The very fact that we can be awake and conscious, but at the same time non-conscious (unaware) of things going on in our minds, bodies, and environment, illustrates the idea of levels of consciousness. When we awake from a good night's sleep, we regain consciousness relatively quickly, in that we suddenly become aware that we are no longer sleeping, but we might not become so quickly aware of where we are, what time of day it is, or what we have planned for the day. After a cup of coffee, we usually get such basics sorted out and can go about our day. Maybe we turn on the news or read the paper and find out some things about the world outside our immediate environment. In doing so, our level of consciousness may be said to reach a level of global awareness. Then we see the clock and think of work, family, and anything else that interests us. Throughout the day, our thoughts bounce around from one thing to another, jumping from association to association and doing so on various levels of consciousness.

Edelman's theory of consciousness has found appreciation because it explicitly lists the requirement of consciousness. If an organism displays these four requirements, then that organism could be described as being fully conscious. If an organism displays fewer requirements, then it could be described as having a lower level of consciousness.

According to Edelman's theory of consciousness, Stapp (2004) outlined the four components that make up consciousness: perceptual categorization, values, memory, and learning. Perceptual categorization refers to the particular patterns of neural activity from the sense organs. Values refer to the neural pathways dedicated to fulfilling the physiological needs of the organism. Memory refers to the continual creation of new patterns of neural activity, which creates new categories. And learning refers to behavioural changes governed by values. Thus, according to Edelman's theory, an organism is fully conscious when it perceives sensory input from the environment, uses this input to survive, remembers how it did this, and learns to improve the process.

Mind/Body Dualism

The concept of mind/body dualism is one upon which I will significantly expand in my next book on the human soul. In the introduction of this book, I briefly outlined my model of the human being, which was represented by three intersecting circles. In this model, a person's heart, body, and mind are represented by three intersecting circles. The soul is then represented by the area where all three circles intersect. In this diagram, the concept of mind/body dualism is represented by the area where the mind and the body intersect.

This intersection of mind and body is an example of one concept in which science and theology significantly disagree. Most scientists conform to a concept called materialism, aka. reductionism. Materialism asserts that an immaterial object, such as the human mind or soul, cannot act upon a material object, such as the brain. Thus, materialists argue that the mind and the soul are merely illusions generated through consciousness. In their attempts to deny anything that cannot be observed and measured scientifically, materialists argue that consciousness, behaviour, personality, and all other mental concepts can and should only be explained in terms of material neurophysiology.

Although only a handful of researchers question the validity of materialism, materialism does not explain consciousness, nor does it attempt to do so. However, the concept of dualism offers a plausible explanation of consciousness (Dilley, 2004). While dualism recognises the significance of neurophysiology, it argues that after having completely dissected the human brain and accurately determined the function of each part of the brain, the part of the brain responsible for consciousness experience is yet to be discovered. This is not due to having not yet discovered all brain parts; it has been mapped out extremely thoroughly.

The difficulty of explaining consciousness is not only in the problem of mental awareness or functioning but much more in the subjective character of experience. Two people sitting side by side on a roller coaster are having the same phenomenological experience, and if we look at their brains during this experience, the same parts of the brains will be active, the same neurochemicals will be involved, and the neurons will be doing the same thing in each of their brains, but two people will not have the same consciousness experience. Countless experiments have been conducted in which subjects were given various sensory stimulation in terms of sight, sound, taste, smell, touch, and motion while functional brain images were observed and measured. Such studies have demonstrated that while it is possible, through brain imaging, to determine if a person is seeing, hearing, tasting, touching, smelling, or moving, we cannot know what these sensations mean to them in terms of experience. The reason for this is something that has become known as *qualia*. Dennett (1988), who coined the term *qualia*, later stated that he regretted having given a specific name to such a broad concept (Dennett, 2020). Nevertheless, qualia may best be described as a unit of experience.

In the Pixar movie *Inside Out*, which fairly accurately describes how emotional processes work, there is a scene where the Characters Joy and Sadness wandered through the character's memories, which were stacked like bricks forming a maze of memories. In this cartoon model of the brain, each little brick, which built the maze of memories, may be as good a depiction of qualia as any other. But the simple fact of the matter is that we cannot see qualia in the human brain. And while two people may have the same memory of an event, they will not have the same qualia. This is sometimes referred to as the 'qualitative gap', or 'impassable chasm' between mental states and brain processes that no one knows how to bridge from the materialist side (Dilley, 2004).

Theories of Consciousness

Velmans (2007) outlined some of the many various theories concerning consciousness. These theories range from the idea that only humans are conscious to the idea that all matter is to some degree conscious. Initially, it may sound ridiculous that matter could in any way be conscious but remember Luke 19:40 stated that 'even the stones will cry out'. Thus, the idea, derived from quantum mechanics, that consciousness may be generated by the interaction between matter and energy (Tegmark, 2015) is not at all in conflict with Christian theology. Theories of consciousness may be classified into discontinuity theories and continuity theories. Discontinuity theories argue that consciousness emerged when material forms reached a given stage of evolution but propose different criteria for the stage at which this occurred. That is, at some point, humans were suddenly conscious, just as we are now. Such theories differ in the point in the timeline in which consciousness suddenly appeared. And they differ in the mechanisms that supposedly turn the consciousness from off to on, be it the acquisition of language, theory of mind acquisition, learning potential, the neocortex, a critical brain size, or complexity.

Continuity theories argue that matter evolved from simple atoms to complex organic molecules that came to life consciousness co-evolved. Thus, continuity theories do not have to explain what suddenly triggered consciousness as discontinuity theories attempt to do. For example, James (1890, p. 149) argued, 'If evolution is to work smoothly, consciousness in some shape must have been present at the very origin of things.' Similarly, Velmans (2007) argued that consciousness emerged as carbon-based life forms developed into creatures with sensory systems, through which they were able to perceive their environment and thus essentially gained the ability to experience. As such, one could argue, and some do, that plants experience and are at least to some degree conscious because they react in response to the sun, as sunflowers demonstrate in that they move to face the sun throughout the day (Atamian et al., 2016). But if it remains utterly inconceivable that plants may experience, it should be less deniable that lower animal life forms may. Oderberg (2008) stated that even the lower animals have sensory receptors that take in information from their environment, interpret it to guide and drive behaviour, amplify it where necessary, filter out noise, and communicate it to conspecifics.

While these theories are frequently coupled with the idea of Darwinian evolution, the Christian theologist need not turn a deaf ear to them or any other scientific theory out of fear of becoming a fallen child of darkness. Instead, we can take this idea, compare it with the Holy Scriptures, and see if a conflict exists. When we do this, we find that both the discontinuity and continuity theories of consciousness are represented in Christian theology. The discontinuity theory corresponds with the story of Adam and Eve, who immediately after eating from the Tree of Knowledge suddenly became self-conscious of their nakedness. However, the idea of walking with God, getting to know Him better and better through our spiritual growth, and gaining an increased understanding of the purpose for which He has created us reflects the continuity theory of progressively developing consciousness. Even the bizarre idea of matter obtaining consciousness is represented in the Bible. Ecclesiastes 3:20, Psalm 103:14, and Genesis 3:19 clearly state that we were made from dust, became conscious, and have the potential to grow in this consciousness. Thus, once more science seems to be knocking on heaven's door.

Thus far, I have discussed the two different kinds of theories of consciousness that address the nature of consciousness and how consciousness came to be. But such theories tell us very little about what consciousness is and how it works. In this short section, I will very briefly review three such theories that seem to have received the most attention in the study of consciousness.

The Multiple Drafts Model

In his iconic work, *Consciousness Explained*, Daniel Dennett investigated the nature of consciousness and developed his multiple drafts model. This model is based on the idea that throughout their waking lives, people seem to find themselves as the subject of a unified stream of experience that presents each of us as the subject of our lives (Schneider, 2007). Dennett referred to this live stream of experience as the Cartesian theater. Schneider (2007) focused on three features of this perspective. First of all, the thing that makes a theater, a theater, is the stage. The stage of the Cartesian theater is what each of us individually and subjectively would call our lives. While we are conscious of the events that take place on the stage, backstage could be associated with our subconsciousness. And the sound, lighting, and special effects operated from the Technik could be associated with our sensory integration and perception. The director of this production is often referred to as our 'mind's eye'. This is where the events of the Cartesian Theater are perceived and directed. Qualia, then, could be described as the director's opinion of any particular scene. As a former actor, play writer, and director, this metaphor resonates with me, for a similar conflict of will exists between what the director would like to see on stage and what actually takes place on stage.

Global Workspace Theory

Other theories of consciousness include the global workspace (GW) theory of consciousness and the closely related global neuronal workspace theory of consciousness. Similar to the multiple drafts model, the GW theory has also been categorised as a kind of theater model, but according to the GW theory, consciousness is a highly distributed activity in the cortex, so there is no single location in the brain where consciousness comes together (Schneider, 2007). According to the GW theory, consciousness serves the purpose of facilitating the information exchange between the various parts of the brain, unlike other organs in the human body that seem to have a single primary function. The brain is an organ that has many parts, and each part has a primary function. Thus, for the brain to function properly as a whole, the various parts of the brain must communicate with each other effectively. It is common knowledge that the sight function of the brain is located in the back of the head. That is essentially where we see something. But simply seeing something does not do us much good if the information is not shared with the other brain parts.

Imagine going to the auto mechanic for new brake pads, and he just handed them to you over the counter, still in the box. You have new brake pads, but they do you no good in your hands. So you say, 'Could you please put them on the car?' Then, he puts them on top of the car. 'Install them in the car!' And he fastens them with the seat belt in the back seat. Essentially, the GW theory asserts that our consciousness assures that we do not continually have a '*Who's on First*' Abbott and Costello routine bouncing around between the various brain parts and their functions. Many find the GW theory to be a promising informational theory of consciousness, however those sympathetic to problems involving qualia may argue that while it might be a promising scientific theory of the information processing involved in consciousness, it does not address the question of qualia (Schneider, 2007).

Integrated Information Theory

The integrated information theory takes a totally different perspective based on mathematics rather than psychology. It is based on the fact that the brain is an amazing data storage device. While a computer can compute much more efficiently than the human brain, the human brain has the capacity to store about one million gigabytes of data. Tegmark (2015) explained that the reason for this is the wiring. In the way a computer is wired, one byte of data takes up one byte of data space; however, the human brain stores data much more effectively through integration. Let me give you an example: Read and think about the word *breakdown*. By now, you will probably have many mental images in your mind, with various associations. You probably have mental images of car breakdowns, mental breakdowns, people who were involved, associated emotions, events, memories, reminders, and countless other thoughts. Just one word like that causes a rippling effect in your mind. And these ripples are likely to cause other associations that cause ripples, that cause other associations and ripples. According to the integrated information theory, these ripples and consequential associations are essentially our consciousness. The cool thing is that by perceiving consciousness in this matter, it may be possible to measure consciousness using the laws of entropy and quantum mechanics.

Let me explain how this might be possible without getting into the complicated math. First, we have to assume that the brain is a closed system of energy. That is, thoughts, ideas, mental images, and other such mind-stuff do not simply ooze in and out the brain randomly. Second, we must give the GW theory some credibility and assume that the communication between the various functioning brain parts is indeed associated with consciousness. Then we can use functional brain imaging to measure brain activity while exposing a subject to sensory input. That is, we give them something to see, hear, smell, touch, or taste, or we put them on a roller coaster. Then we can see what part of their brain lights up first, which parts light up after that, and so on. We measure the energy created by these ripples of brain activity, and then we have essentially measured consciousness according to the integrated information theory.

Nevertheless, and much to the disappointment of materialists, none of this will tell us anything about qualia.

Language

Thus far, the only possible way to get any sort of measurement of a subject's qualia is to ask them and communicate with them. Thus, many authors and theories have suggested that consciousness and language go hand in hand. Velmans cited several authors and their ideas. For example, Popper and Eccles (1976) argued that only through language can humans communicate sufficiently well with each other and demonstrate their consciousness. Jaynes (1990) stated that language is a necessary condition for consciousness even firmer.

Similarly, Humphrey (1983) addressed the concept of consciousness via the concept of the theory of mind, which is known to be strongly associated with language. Velmans's (2007) research made it clear that the higher cognitive functions of humans are manifestations of experience, often in the form of verbal thoughts, commonly referred to as 'inner speech'. Thus, without language and the ability to reason, such 'inner speech' thoughts would no longer be a part of what we experience. Still, just to cover all sides of the issue, it should be pointed out that there is no empirical scientific evidence to support the theory that language, the ability to reason, and a theory of mind are absolutely necessary conditions for consciousness. The simple fact is that consciousness is solely and strictly subjective. I know I am conscious, but I can do nothing more than to take your word for it that you are conscious. And you and I both have no idea if any other object, plant, or animal is conscious because they can neither confirm nor deny it through explicit verbal communication. Velmans (2007) went so far as to point out that we cannot even be sure if babies or severely demented or autistic individuals are conscious.

> Consciousness in humans appears to be regulated by global arousal systems, modulated by attentional systems that decide which representations (of the external world, body and mind/brain itself) are to receive focal attention. Neural representations, arousal systems, and mechanisms

> governing attention are found in many other animals (Jerison, 1985). Other animals have sense organs that detect environmental information and perceptual and cognitive processes that analyze and organize that information. Many animals are also able to communicate and live in complex emotional and social worlds (Dawkins, 1998; Panksepp, 2007). Overall, the precise mix of sensory, perceptual, cognitive, and social processes found in each species is likely to be species-specific. Given this, it might be reasonable to suppose that only humans can have full *human* consciousness. But it is equally reasonable to suppose that some non-human animals have unique, non-human forms of consciousness. (as cited in Velmans, 2007, pp. 274–275)

Emotional Processing

All living animals are bestowed with primal instincts, drives, and reflexes. In addition to this, vertebrates are bestowed with what is referred to as the reptilian brain, which drives that autonomic nervous system (ANS). The ANS can access the skeletal muscles in vertebrates to respond in a fight, freight, or flight modus. When the skeletal muscles are driven through the ANS, the muscles are able to respond much quicker than when the muscles are driven through the central nervous system (CNS). The limbic system is positioned directly between the ANS and the CNS, which enables the basic emotions. Experts disagree on how many basic emotions there are. Fear, anger, joy, sadness, and disgust are on everybody's list, but some include surprise, contempt, anticipation, or trust. Based on their behaviour, it could be determined that the lowest vertebrates certainly can display and experience fear and anger. The more complex the CNS is in a vertebrate, the more basic emotions it will have.

Under humans, primates are said to have a far greater cognitive capacity for emotion than all other animals. This idea is often used to support Darwinian evolution. However, the statement is very misleading because many animals other than primates have also been observed displaying emotional behaviour. Therefore, the similarities in features and emotional capacity cannot imply an ancestorial relationship because many animals not sharing similar physical features do share a similar emotional capacity. Dogs, dolphins, horses, and many other animals with which humans have had significant contact display sadness, joy, surprise, anticipation, and trust. If you have a pet, I am sure you would agree. Thus, one could conclude that humans, like all other higher vertebrates, display and experience at least basic emotions. Atheist scientists would have us believe that animals have the same emotions as humans, but our emotional pallet is much more complex.

Many claim that the difference in consciousness between animals and humans is one of degree, not of kind. But I disagree because humans alone have the ability to consciously override their instincts and evaluate their emotional behaviour in terms of right and wrong. This ability represents a totally different kind of consciousness that no other living creature has. Because humans are able to judge between right and wrong, they are the only animal that has a concept of sin, which is willingly doing that which one knows to be wrong.

Free Will and Sin

Baumeister et al. (2009) stated that belief in free will is widespread and intuitive. The concept of free will is the cornerstone of theology and law; however, in science, a movement was started that attempted to discredit the concept of free will as an illusion while at the same time establishing that disbelief in free will is associated with poor health and anti-social behaviour. Still, many scientists accept materialism as a necessary assumption rather than a proven fact.

The idea that free will is only an illusion originated from the experiments of Benjamin Libet. He found that neurons preparing for motor actions began firing 200–500 milliseconds before subjects consciously decided to perform the action (Andersen, 2006). Libet interpreted this to mean that the conscious decision to perform an action was not causally efficacious of that action because the action was already initiated by a neuron before the decision or urge to move was reported. Thus, Libet concluded that we do not consciously initiate action, so free will is merely an illusion. As a result of these findings, the atheist scientific community made great efforts to promote these findings and conducted similar studies to support Libet's findings.

In his book *The Illusion of Conscious Will*, Wegner (2002) cites various studies that have been interpreted to suggest that non-conscious rather than conscious neuro-processes are linked to the causality of behavior. Wegner's arguments are primarily based on the Libet experiments and the discovery that action and consciousness occur on separate neural pathways. As I read these studies, I realised quickly that the motivation to promote this idea of illusory free will was not to promote science but rather an attempt to denounce God. I would not go so far as to say that it was all a hoax, Libet's findings were accurate, but the conclusion was totally manipulative. Andersen (2006) pointed out that the movement to renounce free will is based on two pillars. The first points out that neurons activating a behaviour occur before the conscious decision to perform the behaviour. The second shows the experience of conscious will and behaviour seem to take place on separate processing pathways.

Actually, these two arguments have the same basis, and they are also not completely new findings. What Libet found was merely a new, more sophisticated way of measuring classical conditioning. Classical conditioning is something we all experience and have probably heard of before. Let me explain how it works with an example. The light switch for my bathroom is on the right side, just outside the bathroom door. As I walked into the bathroom, I would hit the switch to turn on the light, and I would hit it again as I left, but about two years ago, the light in my bathroom broke. I never got around to fixing it because there was already another lamp in the bathroom that no one ever used or needed. The funny thing is when I go into the bathroom, I still hit the switch as I go in, which does nothing, and I hit it again as I go out, and it still does nothing. This is classical conditioning. My arm is so used to performing this action as I pass through this door that unless I consciously think about the situation and consciously remember that the light switch is broken, I will non-consciously hit the switch as I go in and out of the bathroom. This implies that even when the light was working, I was not turning the light switch on because of my conscious free will but rather due to classical conditioning.

In such experiments as Libet's, subjects are carefully explained what they are to do in the experiment, and if precise motor action is involved in which reaction time is significant, then the subject is often given a trial run or two. This alone will activate a so-called readiness potential so that motor neurons can react faster. After a few repetitions, the neurons begin firing before we become consciously aware of the action we are performing. It is a good thing we have this system. Otherwise, we would be so slow if we had to be consciously aware of every little single motor action. I am experiencing this right now as I am typing this. I am a pretty good typer, so I do not have to think to push every single letter key. Instead, I can think in words and phrases, and so my brain is prepared to type the last letter of a word before I consciously begin writing the word. But this certainly does not mean I am writing this book outside my conscious free will.

Fortunately, since the 'free will is an illusion' campaign became a thing, other psychologists have pointed out the flaws in the validity of Libet's experiments. Andersen (2006) also pointed out that it has been long since understood that the neural pathways governing conscious experience are different from those that govern behaviour. As such, humans are indeed consciously aware of much less than our sensory integration has to offer. The purpose of conscious awareness is not to evoke free will by causally influencing other unconscious causes involved in automated behaviour (Andersen, 2006). If that were the case, it would be like having an airbag deployed by the push of a button, which would not be very useful.

Our conscious awareness is a very slow system and can focus only on a very limited number of things at a time. Thus, the effect of our conscious will on our behaviour is not directed at the unconscious components of behaviour but rather at the outer world and the results of our behaviour (Andersen, 2006). Viktor Frankl famously said, 'Between stimulus and response there is a space, In that space is our power to choose our response. In our response lies our growth and our freedom.' Still, some would like to suggest that behaviour is an automated system that leaves no room for free human choice, in that we are creatures of habit, subject to our drives, instincts, and reflexes. These automated processes are then grouped into tendencies, which later become habits and eventually addictions over which we seemingly have no control. At that point, it may seem like 'everything that happens is the unavoidable product of prior causes. The universe resembles a giant machine, grinding along exactly as it must. There is no difference between the categories of possible and actual in this view: Everything that happened was inevitable, and nothing else was ever possible. The subjective impression that when you make a choice you really can choose any of several options is an illusion, because forces outside your consciousness are in motion to determine what you will choose, even if you do not know until the last minute what that choice will be' (Baumeister, 2008, p. 14). Based on this, atheist scientists attempted to make a case for the illusion of free will in the same way they claim Darwinian evolution is a fact. The really terrible thing is that atheist scientists continue to promote the hoax that free will is an illusion, although follow-up studies have found that promoting this idea has been found to increase poor health and antisocial behaviour. The only explanation for this is sin. If one can convince themselves that they have no free will, they can drink, smoke, do drugs, and do everything that makes them feel good, and they can do it without remorse or responsibility. If free will were only an illusion, humans could no longer be held accountable for their actions. A murderer could argue, 'I did not pull the trigger; the neurons in my motor cortex did it 500 milliseconds before I became consciously aware of my actions.'

If free will were the illusion scientific atheists preach, humans would be free to do what they love most: rationalise and justify sinful behaviour. The only thing that this warmed up and stirred stew of leftover information is meant to do is attack the Christian's argument that, because of free will, humans are the only animals that are capable of sin. No other animal can commit sin. Some may argue that chimpanzees have been known to wage war against and murder rival groups (De Waal, 2005), and dolphins have been known to torment other aquatic species (Crespo-Picazo et al., 2021). Nevertheless, one must admit that these animals do not have the capacity to judge their own behaviour in terms of right and wrong. Thus, even horrific animalistic behaviours are still only animalistic behaviours. Humans have the same animalistic nature. We get angry and lash out, scared and ready to fight, and when this happens, we are also capable of horrific animalistic behaviour, but we have a different kind of consciousness. Even during an emotional override of the CNS, we are able to become consciously aware of our emotional state and judge our intended behaviours in terms of right or wrong before we carry them out. Moreover, we even set laws in our societies to make sure everyone does indeed judge their intended behaviours before they carry them out. Regardless of whether or not one believes in God, one cannot deny the ability to judge between right and wrong. Exactly this is what it means to be created in God's image.

Conclusion

Regarding the nature of consciousness, there is no way to deem one model more accurate than another because there is no way to identify the place or time in the brain in which mental events enter into consciousness. In my humble opinion, consciousness is what happens when the heart, body, mind, and soul come together. Consciousness is something that we know so much and so little about at the same time. Ask anyone at all, regardless of age, mental state, or even language, 'Are you conscious?' If they respond in any way, then you know the answer is yes; if they do not respond in any way at all, then you know the answer is no. We all know what consciousness is and can recognise it in anyone and ourselves. Scientific psychology knows the destruction of the cerebral cortex leaves people permanently unconscious, but the complete removal of the cerebellum does not affect consciousness at all. We know that neurons in the cerebral cortex remain active while sleeping, but consciousness fades at certain times during sleep. However, while we dream, we can experience consciousness, although we are oblivious to our environment. And we know that different parts of the cortex influence different aspects of consciousness: damage to certain parts of the cortex can impair the experience of colour, while damage in another area may distort the perception of shapes. Increasingly sophisticated neuroscientific tools are uncovering increasingly distinct aspects of the neural correlates of consciousness, but when we are pressed with the question, 'So, what is consciousness exactly?' we really do not know.

> Our lack of understanding is manifested most clearly when scientists are asked questions about consciousness in 'difficult' cases. For example, is a person with akinetic mutism—awake with eyes open but mute, immobile, and nearly unresponsive—conscious or not? How much consciousness is there during sleepwalking or psychomotor seizures? Are newborn babies conscious, and to what

> extent? Are animals conscious? If so, are some animals more conscious than others? Can they feel pain? Does a bat feel space the same way we do? Can bees experience colors, or merely react to them? Can a conscious artifact be constructed with non-neural ingredients? I believe it is fair to say that no consciousness expert, if there is such a job description, can be confident about the correct answer to such questions. (Tonoi, 2008, p. 217)

Although there is no observable evidence of the human consciousness, we still have to conclude that it does indeed exist. Furthermore, as it was previously stated, the difference in consciousness between our supposedly closest ancestors, the primates, is greater than the difference in consciousness between the amoeba and the primates, because although all animals, including humans, are driven through drives (Gaylin, 1990), instinct, and reflexes as well as a complex emotional processing system, humans alone can judge their intended behaviour in terms of right and wrong. On a psychological level, this is what it means to be a child of God.

CHAPTER 8

Development of Mind and Behaviour

Development is the field of psychology that interests me the most. Development in all fields of science interests me. However, it frustrates me how many authors, either knowingly and with the intent to deceive, or simply out of ignorance, use the word *evolution* when they are really talking about development. This occurs very often in biology. One can read about how a caterpillar evolves into a butterfly. But the very idea of a caterpillar evolving into a butterfly contradicts the definition of Darwinian evolution, which asserts that there is no design involved. If there is no design involved, then there can be no goal involved. And if there is no goal involved, a caterpillar cannot evolve into a butterfly because the butterfly would be the goal. If a caterpillar would develop into something totally unexpected by random chance, then we could talk about evolution. But as it is, a caterpillar develops into a butterfly. As such, one could define *development* as a process towards a goal.

When we speak of child development—cognitive, emotional, social, and more—then we do so with a goal in mind. For this reason, scientific psychology has formed various models of development that are generally broken up into stages and describe the abilities and behaviours that should be achieved in each stage. The final stage then serves as a goal of that particular developmental process. Thus, it should be readily accepted that development implies movement towards a goal. If that is the case, what might this movement look like? I would suggest that the oxymoron *cognitive behaviour* is actually a fitting description. The term is an oxymoron because behaviour is generally defined as any manipulation of our environment, and cognition is thus not deemed a behaviour. Nevertheless, allow me to define cognitive behaviour as a person's thought patterns and typical thinking habits.

The cognitive behaviour of someone is something that no one else can observe or measure by any means. Science has developed fancy gadgets that can show which parts of the brain are active and working in a person during any various controlled stimulus, but no one can really know how someone thinks, what thoughts and ideas are bouncing around in their head, and what a person does with these thoughts and ideas. The best one can do is observe their behaviour, make inferences, and ask questions. After having done this with many people, we can build hypotheses and theories; this is what we call scientific psychology. However, when we discuss cognitive behaviour, one can only speak and understand subjectively. I can tell you how I think, what ideas I have in my head, how I formulate and process them, and how I allow them to affect my behaviour. I can do this through a testimony or main narrative. All you can do is hear my words and observe my behaviour. But you cannot gain access to the mental images in my mind.

Although experts on emotional facial recognition can express some insight on what emotions a person might be feeling at any particular moment, no one can know what anyone else is thinking. As of yet, human thoughts are impermeable, and it will be a very long time until reality catches up with Hollywood film fantasy. Nevertheless, many find comfort in their belief that God knows each of us so completely that He even knows our thoughts. Some may claim that this comfort only comes from the belief and not the fact, much in the same way the placebo effect has been found to be effective. However, the fact that the Holy Scriptures describe cognitive behaviour in the same way that scientific psychology does lends significant support to the belief that God is real.

Popular TV evangelist Joyce Meyer wrote a book entitled *The Battlefield of the Mind*, and it addresses the topic of cognitive behaviour and illustrates with examples from scripture how God demonstrates that He knows what we are thinking and offers very good advice as to how we should be thinking. Any psychologist would agree to everything Meyer pointed out if they did not know it came from the Bible. Meyer was so thorough in her extrapolation of good and bad cognitive behaviour examples that to list them all here would be to rewrite her book. Therefore, allow me to point out that both the Bible and scientific psychology have the same concept of cognitive behaviour in three major points.

Strength in Weakness, Not Despite of It

First, studies hardly need to prove that one's thoughts and emotions are intricately connected so that each has a great effect on the other. We know that bad thoughts can lead to bad feelings, and bad feelings can lead to bad thoughts. But we also know that good thoughts can lead to good feelings, and good feelings can lead to good thoughts. In psychology, this is commonly referred to as the placebo effect. Much of the work of a psychological counsellor is to bestow upon the client a positive outlook on life. But one does not need a psychologist to understand that when one is in a very bad life situation for any reason, sitting around and doing nothing because one believes that nothing will help is not at all helpful. Anyone who was in a bad situation and got out of it did so because they believed it was in some way possible to get out of it.

What we are talking about here is hope. To define it in mathematical terms, hope is the product of our heart and mind. That is, a very strong mind can still yield a significant amount of hope despite a weaker heart, and a very strong heart can still yield a significant amount of hope despite a weaker mind.

Hebrews 6:19 teaches that hope is the anchor of the soul. As such, when working with suicidal patients, Frankl (2006) was known to ask a surprisingly provocative question. He would ask them, 'Why have you not yet succeeded in killing yourself?' As provocative and controversial as the question may be, Frankl argued that the answer to this question is the last fibre of hope to which the patient is still holding on. And if there is still hope, no matter how little, there is hope of improvement. The Bible takes this even a step further and differs in the power of positivity in this way. Where optimism is finding hope despite a bad situation, the Bible teaches us that hope is found through bad situations. Thus, Paul wrote:

> Therefore, since we have been justified through faith, we have peace with God through our Lord Jesus Christ, through whom we have gained access by faith into this grace in which we now stand. And we boast in the hope of the glory of God. Not only so, but we also glory in our sufferings because we know that suffering produces perseverance, perseverance, character, and character hope. And hope does not put us to shame because God's love has been poured out into our hearts through the Holy Spirit, who has been given to us. (Romans 5:1–5)

'We glory in our suffering'? At first glance, this may sound masochistic and crazy. Why on heaven and earth should we glory in our suffering? OK, I understand that what doesn't kill us makes us stronger, but glory in our suffering? I did not understand this at all when I was younger. I chalked this verse up to something that was to be taken metaphorically rather than literally. But now I am fifty years old, and my body is wasting away due to muscle dystrophy, which has taken from me a promising athletic career, an exciting career as a performing artist, and a fulfilling career as a psychological counsellor for children with developmental disorders. This has left me physically incapable of doing anything else but sit in a chair and read and write. But now, knowing that God made me for that very purpose, I'd rather be in a wheelchair doing God's will than having not suffered anything in life and being outside of God's will.

Only much later did I come to realise that each of my previous careers prepared me for the next, and all of them have built up to what I am today. As an athlete, I learned what it meant to work hard, be dedicated, be disciplined, and push myself to the limit and beyond. These are the prerequisites of a performing artist, although a performing artist does not have a team or a coach to encourage and train them. To become a professional juggler, I trained just as hard, but I had to do it all by myself. As an athlete, I competed against other people and had a good chance of winning; as a juggler, I competed against gravity and had no chance of winning. Take the best juggler in the world and give him one more ball, and he will fail just like everyone else. The performing artist takes on the impossible quest of displaying perfection under the careful attention of an audience. This is the prerequisite of working with children. They catch every little mistake, don't they? But unlike a performing artist who can play off the mistake and simply continue the routine with no harm done to anyone but their own pride, a mistake in the behavioural therapy of children can impede behavioural development drastically. In my work with children with developmental disorders, my previously acquired clown skills were invaluable. My clown skills of being able to make inanimate objects appear, disappear, and seemingly come to life became a means through which I was able to build interpersonal and therapeutic relationships with children. But finally, my body became too weak to do this also, so now instead of doing this myself as one person, through the ministry I can teach many others how to make these connections for others, for their families, and themselves, and in the process, I have come to know God so much more than ever before.

Am I glad to be sick? Of course not. Do I wish to be healthy? Of course I do. But am I more fulfilled and blessed, and am I mentally and emotionally stronger? Yes, definitely, because it is through these hardships that my strengths have flourished, not despite of them, but rather because of them. While positive thinking tells us to remain strong despite our weaknesses, God makes us strong through our weaknesses.

Our Actions Are a Result of Our Minds and Hearts

Second, the Bible and scientific psychology agree that it is our minds that generally control our behaviour, but the heart (our emotional processes) can override the mind and take control at any time, if only for a brief moment. The fact that our actions and behaviours are controlled in the mind and not in the brain is an interesting and fun little experiment that we can do right now, by making an imperative statement which I would like to ask you to follow simply. We will discuss it momentarily. The imperative statement is this: Turn the page.

How did you do that? How did you get your arm, hand, and fingers to complete this bodily movement? Although the task was completed within the realm of full consciousness, you did not consciously activate your motor cortex to do it. You did not at all consider the many various neurochemical processes required to complete this behaviour, nor did you consciously activate these processes. But to do what you just did, the motor cortex had to be activated. So how were these processes activated? Since every action must have a cause, what caused your motor cortex to become activated? The only plausible answer is your mind. You simply willed your arm to reach out, and you willed your hand and fingers to grasp the corner of the page, hold on to it, move it to the left, and then let go. Out of your mind, not out of your brain, you simply willed your arm and hands to perform the task, and your appendages obeyed this will without any conscious awareness of how this process takes place in the brain. It simply happened as a result of the will of your mind. The mind controls the body, although the mind is not a part of the body.

Thus, we can conclude that it is through our minds that we control our behaviours. That is unless our autonomic nervous system decides to take over. If something startling happens, a motor reflex may be initiated. When this happens, the impulse comes from the brain stem enabling a much faster response. Similarly, upon the perception of an emotionally provocative stimulus, the limbic system may initiate an emotional episode, which may lead to a fight, flight, or fright response or other emotional behaviours controlled by the limbic system rather than the mind. As such, the heart and the mind together create a behaviour-controlling system that can disrupt each other or help each other. When an individual's emotional processing system has a negative effect on one's behaviour, this is referred to as a mood disorder. While everyone experiences some degree of anxiety and depression at some time in their lives, some people suffer intensely and for a longer period of time. When this happens, a simple mood disorder can become a very serious psychological problem.

Some have brought forth ideas that life may be easier, more productive, and overall better if humans did not have these disturbing emotions. Hollywood has played around with the idea of making emotions illegal in the movie Equilibrium; created the admirable Vulcans from Star Trek, an alien species that so effectively suppress their emotions that they prosper through intelligence and rational thought; and created the Jedi from Star Wars, who need to rid themselves of fear lest they fall susceptible to the dark side. Indeed, emotions can cause problems when they continually override rational thought processes. But they can also be very helpful when they do what God created them to do, which is to initiate specific behaviours to help us react to critical situations quickly. Each of the basic emotions has a specific purpose. Joy prompts behaviours that help us experience more pleasure. Anger prompts us to face problems. Disgust prompts us to avoid harmful elements. Fear prompts us to avoid harmful situations. Sadness prompts us to accept a loss so we can move on. Surprise prompts us to recognise new information.

Thus, both the heart and the mind can regulate our behaviour, and each can significantly affect the other for the good or the bad. For example, if someone is plagued with the negative thought 'No one likes me', they will be less likely to try to make friends, and so they make fewer friends. This will confirm their negative thoughts, feelings of resentment and spite will surface, and eventually they will become unfriendly. Similarly, if someone is plagued with the feeling of sadness, then he or she will be less likely to demonstrate behaviours that bring pleasure. As the sadness persists, they will eventually accept it as lost and become lonely. Eventually, the mind will induce thoughts that explain the emotional state, and one may eventually conclude that one is simply unlikable.

However, when we set both our hearts and our minds individually on God, each of the two separate systems can work as a backup for the other.

> Since then, you have been raised with Christ, set your hearts on things above, where Christ is, seated at the right hand of God. Set your minds on things above, not on earthly things. For you died, and your life is now hidden with Christ in God. (Colossians 3:1–3)

When they are working together and properly, the two systems are one dual self-cleansing system. For example, an individual is plagued with the negative thought 'No one likes me'. If this individual has their heart focused on God, as Colossians 3:1–3 instructs, then one will still feel the love of God, which can help one recognise the negative thought and expel it. Similarly, if one is plagued by negative emotions but still has their mindset on God, then Bible verses can be brought to mind that can expel the negative feelings.

The Mind's Reboot Switch

The reboot switch is the third point on which scientific psychology and Christian psychology agree concerning the human mind. Life stress is an inevitable, non-stop avalanche that will bury each one of us if we do not renew our minds from time to time and forget about all the terrible things that have happened.

> Do not conform to the pattern of this world, but be transformed by the renewing of your mind. Then you will be able to test and approve what God's will is—his good, pleasing and perfect will. (Romans 12:2)

In my personal and professional opinion, knowing and understanding God's plan is the key to happiness. Regardless of how bad the circumstances are, if one is able to say, 'I know this is God's will for my life,' then one will not only be able to stand strong against any hardships—and one will even do it joyfully.

While constructs such as angels and demons have been given no relevance in the field of scientific psychology, these supernatural influences are deeply rooted in theology. Very often I am asked by a fellow Christian, 'What percent of psychological problems are the work of the devil?' My answer is, 'Indirectly, all of them, and directly, many that have been deem incurable by science.' However, that is the difference between clinical psychology and counselling psychology. In clinical psychology, the focus lies in the pathology, figuring out what is wrong. In counselling psychology, the focus is on behaviour, emotion, and cognition, as well as figuring out how to improve it. I do not claim to know much about personality disorders and schizophrenia, forms of which have been deemed chronic and progressive. Psychological disorders of this magnitude can cause patients to lose such control of their executive cognitive functions that they are no longer able to grasp reality. Thus, they create a reality of their own. Such patients display behaviour in which one may question whether they have control of their own minds or are under some unknown external force. Of course, science cannot even consider the possibility that something supernatural might be going on. Thus, science can do no more but observe, measure, and conduct experiments.

My clinical field of interest is in what psychologists call mood disorders. These consist primarily of two kinds, anxiety and depression. As both a psychologist and theologian, I suggest that the devil and his demons need not directly come into direct, mind-controlling contact with a person to inflict such harm. Our human nature is one of sin, so we do quite well messing things up from the start all on our own. Life is a struggle; that is a fact, whether one believes in kobolds, demons, karma, or that the world itself is against us. However, to develop means to struggle. Some choose to believe that our struggle is not only against flesh and blood. Christian theology, based on the Holy Scriptures, asserts that the devil and his demons are indeed real. If you do not believe in the devil and demons, you would still probably agree that this world is an immense struggle. The only difference would be that you would have a different explanation as to why life stress exists and ultimately leads to anxiety and depression.

Based on the Holy Scriptures, Meyer (1995) illustrated how, through careful strategy and cunning deceit, Satan attempts to set up strongholds in our minds. A stronghold is an area in which we are held in bondage due to a certain way of thinking. For example, suppose an individual believes they are incapable of achieving a goal. In that case, they will have a more difficult time being successful than if they did believe they were capable. Throughout her book, Meyer describes human behaviours that would correspond to mood disorders in psychology. Unfortunately, here is where psychology and theology differ significantly. A theologist would tell a person struggling with a mood disorder that they need to believe in Jesus, whereas a psychologist would tell them that they need to believe in themselves. However, the Bible teaches us something totally different.

> Blessed are the poor in spirit, for theirs is the kingdom of heaven.
> Blessed are those who mourn, for they will be comforted.
> Blessed are the meek, for they will inherit the earth.

> Blessed are those who hunger and thirst for righteousness, for they will be filled.
> Blessed are the merciful, for they will be shown mercy.
> Blessed are the pure in heart, for they will see God.
> Blessed are the peacemakers, for they will be called children of God.
> Blessed are those who are persecuted because of righteousness, for theirs is the kingdom of heaven.
> Blessed are you when people insult you, persecute you and falsely say all kinds of evil against you because of me. Rejoice and be glad, because great is your reward in heaven, for in the same way they persecuted the prophets who were before you. (Matthew 5:3–11)

When I read the Beatitudes, I understand that Jesus was calling out to those who suffer under psychological distress, those who are coping with a loss, those who have mentally quit, the suppressed, and those who are trying to help but struggle in the process. It is of both my professional and personal belief that such individuals do not need Freud, Erikson, Piaget, or William James; rather, they first need Jesus. They need to set their core belief on God first and then, with that foundation, turn to psychology. Psychology and theology disagree significantly about from where the power to develop comes. When one is poor in spirit, mourning, unmotivated, unsatisfied, oppressed, inflicted, and constantly fighting inside and out, then one does not need a psychologist. One needs to surrender to God and admit that the power to continue to develop is in Him, not in us.

One cannot have a positive life and a negative mind, which is well founded in the widely proven placebo effect. Positive minds produce positive lives, and negative minds produce negative lives. Positive thoughts are always full of faith and hope, and negative thoughts are always full of fear and doubt. Furthermore, if we know that psychosomatic illnesses are physical illnesses due to mental causes, then one should also understand that psychosomatic healing is equally possible. These are statements with which I believe theologians and scientific psychologists agree.

Similarly, the human attribute of persistence has merit in both psychology and theology. Meyer explained that the mind must be continually renewed to follow after the Spirit and not the flesh. Woefully, the default mode of human behaviour is sin, rooted in the flesh in which our basic desires, our drive, and our instinctual behaviour. As such, we must purposely choose to do right and avoid doing wrong. In Deuteronomy 30:19, the Lord told His people that He had set before them life and death and urged them to choose life. And in Proverbs 18:21, we are told death and life are in the power of the tongue, and they who indulge in it shall eat the fruit of it. Thus, our thoughts become our words and actions, just as scientific psychology has also discovered. Still, sin is unavoidable. Those who believe in God know that all have sinned and fallen show of the glory of God (Romans 3:23), and those who do not believe in God know that nobody's perfect. However, from this agreement between believers and non-believers emerges a very significant discrepancy that is illustrated in Romans 8:1–5.

> Therefore, there is now no condemnation for those who are in Christ Jesus because through Christ Jesus the law of the Spirit who gives life has set you free from the law of sin and death. For what the law was powerless to do because it was weakened by the flesh, God did by sending his own Son in the likeness of sinful flesh to be a sin offering. And so he condemned sin in the flesh, in order that the righteous requirement of the law might be fully met in us, who do not live according to the flesh but according to the Spirit. Those who live according to the flesh have their minds set on what the flesh desires; but those who live in accordance with the Spirit have their minds set on what the Spirit desires. The mind governed by the flesh is death, but the mind governed by the Spirit is life and peace. The mind governed by the flesh is hostile to God; it does not submit to God's law, nor can it do so. Those who are in the realm of the flesh cannot please God.

But as I pointed out in chapter 2, these instincts are also what give humans the capacity and inclination to grasp hold of beliefs. In chapter 1, it was explained that belief is a choice; we choose our beliefs, and these beliefs serve as the lens through which all we experience is filtered. In chapter 5, I said that how we perceive our lifelong experience forms the basis of our identity and our soul in terms of the identity of the person we want to become.

Scientific Psychological studies on Cognitive Behaviour

The cognitive experiential self-theory may be understood as comprising two systems that give rise to two types of thought processing: the rational and the intuitive systems. King et al. (2007) used the term *experiential system* instead of *intuitive processing*, but both terms reflect the nature of the process to access memories of experience to better navigate the present. While operating holistically in the heart, body, mind, and soul of an individual, these two systems run separately. The two systems can share control of behaviour management, compete for behaviour management, suddenly take over behaviour management, or shut down, leaving the other to manage behaviour. In many ways, it is not entirely like a hybrid car running on gas and electricity. Both systems have their advantages and disadvantages. As we are experiencing our environment throughout our day, these two very different systems of thought manage our behaviour cognitively.

The intuitive system of thought is set as the default mode of thought, and it is present and active at birth. It is through this system that we learn the first lessons in life. When a newborn baby is hungry, it cries. Initially, it cries because of the hunger, but then very quickly, it intuitively learns that someone comes and gives it attention whenever it cries. And so it begins to cry for any number of reasons, or only to get attention. In this manner, intuition can develop and improve as one collects more and more experiences in the form of *if this behaviour, then then this result* (Epstein, 1990, 1993, 1998).

Furthermore, the intuitive system of thought is closely associated with the limbic system, which drives our emotional processing (Damasio, 2000, 2006). Similar to how our emotions are designed to prompt behaviours, our intuitive thought system is designed to prompt decisions. Together with our emotional processing system, our intuitive thought is responsible for 'gut decisions'. And although Damasio demonstrated through a gambling experiment that our 'gut decisions' are pretty good, the intuitive system is resistant to change, prone to broad generalisations, and significantly influenced by emotion. Finally, our intuitive system of thought operates significantly outside of our conscious awareness and often fails to solve problems with logical solutions.

Conversely, the rational thought system is not present at birth and begins to develop much later in childhood, though slowly. Based on logic, our rational thought system is slow and intentional, as it continually second-guesses our intuitive thought system. The rational system of thought contemplates and reflects on memories of past experiences with logic rather than instinct and operates primarily within one's conscious awareness, and it has been shown to relate to the application of probabilities and logic in problem-solving tasks (Cacioppo and Petty, 1982).

During our daily lives, the intuitive and the rational systems of thought work together by essentially working against each other. Intuitive thought jumps to conclusions prompting behaviour based on instinct, while the rational system of thought second-guesses behaviour based on logic. Intuitive judgements are made outside of conscious awareness, and reflective judgements are made with conscious awareness. To me, it makes perfect sense that God created humans in the default modes to believe in Him and that atheists have to choose to rationalise that there is no God consciously.

Intuitive Belief in God versus Rational Atheism

Cacioppo and Petty (1982) found that people's belief in God and the supernatural is significantly related to the tendency of an individual's primary manner of thinking: rational or intuitive experiential systems. Thus, these authors may suggest that people who believe in God and the supernatural do so because they have past experiences that support this belief, and they do not question it rationally but simply believe it intuitively. Many other studies on cognitive thinking styles have come to similar conclusions.

As previously discussed, scientific data support the statement that individuals with a greater tendency to rational thinking seem more likely not to believe in God's existence than individuals who demonstrate a greater tendency for intuitive thinking styles. King et al. (2007, p. 905) examined the relationship between the experiential system and positive effect in predicting superstitious beliefs and sympathetic magic. These authors found that people's belief in God and the supernatural is significantly related to the tendency of an individual's primary manner of thinking: rational or experiential systems. While this is often portrayed to support Darwinian evolution, for reasons discussed in chapter 1, it actually supports the theory of intelligent design.

Gervais (2012) applied a dual-process model of cognitive processing to examine the cognitive underpinnings of religious belief. He tested the hypothesis that analytic processing promotes religious disbelief and found that individual differences in the tendency to override initially flawed intuitions in reasoning analytically were associated with increased religious disbelief. Four additional experiments provided evidence of causation, as subtle manipulations are known to trigger analytic processing also encouraged religious disbelief. Combined, these studies indicated that analytic processing is one factor that promotes religious disbelief. Thus, a novel visual prime that triggers analytic thinking also encourages disbelief in God.

Gervais (2012) suggested that God made humans with both intuitive and analytical thinking capabilities. Furthermore, it would seem that the default thinking mode, intuitive thinking, is supportive in believing in God, whereas analytical thinking is supportive in disbelief. Again, this coincides with the teachings of the Bible (Proverbs 3:5-6). Similarly, Shenva, Rand, and Green (2012) questioned whether belief in God is intuitive, a natural (by-)product of the human mind given its cognitive structure and social context. If it is, then the extent to which one believes in God may be influenced by one's more general tendency to rely on intuition versus reflection and logic. Studies support this hypothesis and link intuitive cognitive style to belief in God.

One study showed that individual differences in cognitive style predict belief in God. Participants completed the Cognitive Reflection Test (CRT; Frederick, 2005), which employs math problems that, although easily solvable, have intuitively compelling incorrect answers. Participants who gave more intuitive answers on the CRT reported a stronger belief in

God. This effect was not mediated by education level, income, political orientation, or other demographic variables.

Here is an example of one such test question: A bat and a ball cost $1.10 in total. The bat costs $1.00 more than the ball. How much does the ball cost? (Hutson, 2013). Intuitively, one may think that the ball costs 10 cents, but this is wrong. If you do the math carefully, it becomes obvious that the ball costs five cents and the bat 1.05. Tricky questions like this one make up the CRT. Hutson (2013) administered this test to believers and non-believers and found that non-believers scored significantly higher than believers. Another study demonstrated that the correlation between CRT scores and belief in God also holds when cognitive ability (IQ) and aspects of personality were controlled. Moreover, both studies demonstrated that intuitive CRT responses predicted the degree to which individuals reported having strengthened their belief in God since childhood, but not their familial religiosity during childhood, suggesting a causal relationship between cognitive style and change in belief over time. And a third study revealed a causal relationship over the short term: Experimentally inducing a mindset that favours intuition over reflection increases self-reported belief in God (Hutson, 2013).

Some like to interpret this data to mean that people who believe in God are simply stupid, but this is a very false conclusion. In fact, the same studies admitted that humans have such superior intelligence compared to other animals because of the human ability to think intuitively. These findings correspond with the teaching of the Bible, in that we should think like children, who first develop an intuitive mode of thought (Matthew 18:3). As Blaise Pascal put it, 'It is the heart which perceives God and not the reason. That is what faith is: God perceived by the heart, not by the reason.'

The phenomenon of blind sight is a perfect example of this. The concept of blind sight is not what one may initially believe it to mean. It has less to do with visual impairment and more to do with consciousness. Blindsight experiments are basically conducted in the following manner. Individuals are presented with a two-by-two grid on a computer screen, in which a small dot randomly and extremely briefly appears in one of the four sectors of the grid. The dot appears and disappears so fast that one cannot actually see the dot. Nevertheless, individuals are able to guess in which of the four grids the dot appeared with an accuracy significantly greater the 25 per cent chance.

Pennycook et al. (2012) asked, Why do some people hold very strong religious beliefs while others are quite dubious of them? Answers to this question will almost certainly involve many factors at many levels, including affective, experiential, family, institutional, developmental, and cultural variables, amongst others. However, the rather ambiguous connection between intuition and the supernatural does link cognitive theories of religiosity with decades of decision-making literature that suggests intuition plays a fundamental role in reasoning processes. 'Our data are consistent with the idea that two people who share the same cognitive ability, education, political ideology, sex, age and level of religious engagement can acquire very different sets of beliefs about the world if they differ in their propensity to think analytically' (Pennycook et al., 2012, p. 335).

> Intuition understands things in relation to God. It proceeds from an adequate idea of the formal essence of certain attributes of God to the adequate knowledge of the (formal) essence of things. But that does not mean that it has access to a transcendent realm beyond the reach of reason. Intuitive knowledge is not a form of non-rational mystical insight into the real natures of things. Nevertheless, it is undeniable that intuitive thought processes are present at birth while rational thought processes need to develop over a lifetime. And even when rational thought processes have developed, the intuitive thought process is generally the default mode in everyday life. Intuitive knowledge is clearly meant to conjure up continuities with older beliefs in the power of a divine presence in human life and in a human capacity to transcend the frailty and vulnerability of bodily existence (Lloyd, 1996, pp. 109–10).

Mind and Behaviour

Thomson (2009) reasoned that all behaviour results from underlying psychological mechanisms; all mechanisms are the product of causal processes that shaped them and the environment in which they were formed. According to Thomson, natural selection is the only organic process we know that designs and maintains functional mechanisms.

Skinner's concept of behaviourism underlines the idea of dualism, in that it rejects subjective mental phenomena, which is inaccessible to observation, and concentrates only on behaviour, which is observable. However, Ryle (1949) claimed that mental concepts are really statements of dispositions to behave in particular ways; therefore, mental concepts can be translated in concepts referring to observable behaviour (Barbour, 1990).

Both scientific psychology and Christian theology suggest that our actions are a direct result of our thoughts. If we have a negative mind, we will have a negative life; if, in contrast, we renew our mind according to God's Word, we will, as Romans 12:2 promises, prove out in our experience 'the good and acceptable and perfect will of God for our lives' (Meyer, 1995).

Conclusion

So what is the human mind really? That is a difficult question to answer. The human mind is not something that is tangible, pointed out, and localised based on empirical data. Nevertheless, it is something that can hardly be refuted.

The mind is something abstract, not tangible, whereas the body, including the brain, is tangible. The brain and the mind seem to coexist independently and influence each other while at the same time remaining completely distinct from each other. How can that be possible? Something similar goes on within our brains as our emotional thought processes take over our behavioural processes. These processes are believed to be driven by the limbic system, which is a lower, more primitive level of functioning than the cognitive system. We would like to believe that our cognitive system is in charge most of the time, and it probably is. Nevertheless, when the limbic system kicks in, one's cognitive thought processes are overridden and driven by emotional processes.

This distinction is clearly understood in the court of law, which commonly punishes crimes that result from sudden emotional outbursts of behaviour less harshly than premeditated crimes. A premeditated crime is a crime that one knowingly and intentionally commits. However, crimes of passion are crimes that one commits without rational thought. It is still a crime, and people need to be held accountable for their actions. But in addition to our rational thought processes, humans have drives, instincts, and reflexes like all other animals. Thus, we can and do become animalistic at times.

Lloyd (1996) explained that there are two vantage points from which Spinoza considered minds and bodies. On the one hand, we have thought and extension, which is essentially our behaviour as a whole. From this vantage point, we view our physical somatic behaviour from its origin: the mind. The second vantage point is from the mind towards the brain. This is illustrated by the simple observation that ideas in our minds correspond to objects we perceive through our senses. As such, we have relations between ideas and objects, which hold across these different attributes. 'The relation of mind to body is thus framed both by Spinoza's doctrine of the sameness of substance thinking and substance extended, and by the relation between ideas and their objects. In medieval thought that relation had also often been articulated as a kind of sameness—as a unity of the object, considered as known, and the act of intellect in knowing. In bringing that doctrine together with his own doctrine of the uniqueness of substance, Spinoza once more gives a new twist to an old theme' (Lloyd, 1996, p. 63).

Pinker (1997) claimed that we are our minds, and the mind is what the brain does (as cited in Thomson, 2009). Like our other organs and all other living matter, the brain has been shaped by Darwinian natural selection. Biologically, the brain has evolved over time to aid the maximum reproduction of the genes that built it. It was designed to make decisions about how to enhance reproductive success, no more and no less (Gazzaniga, 1998, as cited in Thomson, 2009).

Panagariya (2018) pointed out that the neurophysiology of the human brain is represented by the triune brain model, which portrays the human brain into three consecutive developing brain functioning levels: the reptilian cortex, paleocortex, and neocortex. The most primitive level is the reptilian cortex; it is the area that invokes involuntary systems such as fight, flight, and freight reflexes, and reproductive and aggressive behaviour. The paleocortex (aka emotional brain) deals more with love, hate, fear, pleasure, and emotions like sexual feelings, jealousy, and social attachment. The amygdala of the paleo cortex seems to be the supposed flip-flop switch, shunting between the reptilian brain and the neocortex. The neocortex is commonly believed to be the most recently developed part of the cerebral cortex that deals with cognitive skills, logical thinking, and abstruse thinking related to spiritualism and philosophy.

Panagariya (2018) posed the question, Is it the brain that resides in a human mind, or is the mind that resides in a human brain? The human brain and the human mind are two inseparable, internal, and intertwined aspects of the central nervous system. The human brain has been described as being made up of varied cortices and subconical structures, but none of these or any know combination of these is known to make up what we have come to understand as the human mind.

MacLean (1946, p. 3) examined and critically discussed the concepts of ToM, labelling them 'confused', and pointed out that the philosophical problem is that of relating incompatible theses, and especially of discovering what is involved in 'mind' and 'substance' since these produce a fantastic set of 'conclusions'. He argued that while 'substance' and 'thing' are used as equal categorical terms, they are nevertheless not synonymous. MacLean proposes that 'mind', 'soul', and 'self' are synonymous in some of the uses of the words but maintains that 'mind' and 'soul' are not truly the same; the attribute of substance complicates the issue even more.

All of the authors cited in this section addressed things that were a mystery of science years ago in association with the concept of mind, in that we cannot know which substances are responsible for which actions. The things that appear to be responsible for a specific action may be composed of various substances, one or more of which may be the true cause of the action. However, regardless of how well the nature of the substance is known, its relation to the cause of actions may still be a mystery.

'Thoughts are ontologically distinct from things thought about. That is, the "horse" I think about is distinctly different in substance from the "horse" about which I am thinking' (MacLean, 1946, p. 155). It is an age-old debate pertaining to that which truly exists, the substance, or the idea. I believe it was Kant who argued it is the idea of something that truly exists and not the material object. The proof goes like this. Suppose all pawns from every chessboard in the whole world were to disappear at once. What would happen? Chess players all over the world would first wonder what happened to their pawns, and someone would get rich fast making and selling pawns to all the baffled chess players. But now imagine that the idea of the pawn was to be erased from everybody's mind. What would happen then? Chess players all over the world would wonder what these extra pieces were, and they would set them aside and play the game without the pawns. Only after a while would someone realise that chess is stupid, because the rooks simply capture each other on the first move. Then someone might propose to invent a new piece that stands in a row in front of the back line. This piece could become what was previously known as the pawn. But it would require the birth of an idea, rather than the formation of a physical object.

CHAPTER 9

The Mind of Jesus of Nazareth

Finally, I come to the chapter which addresses the question that inspired me to write these books: What made Jesus of Nazareth so different? When discussing the person of Jesus, one cannot address this matter from a scientific perspective or mode of thinking. Scientific thinking requires one to be able to examine data through controlled experiments and make conclusions based on observation. Matters of historical nature cannot be examined in this way. With scientific data, one cannot prove where they were twenty-four hours ago and what they did. They could present historical evidence in the form of pictures, videos, and statements from witnesses, but these are not scientific data because they cannot be repeated, examined, and observed in a controlled experiment.

Nevertheless, based on historical data, both of a religious and secular nature, one cannot dispute that a man named Jesus of Nazareth once lived. The only thing that can be debated is the impact and relevance Jesus has on our individual lives today. Those who believe that Jesus was the Christ, who died for the sins of the world and made possible the reconciliation to God the creator of life and the universe, base this conclusion on the Gospels presented in the Holy Bible. Others may only believe that Jesus of Nazareth was an influential man whose life became the standard of time upon which our calendar is based.

Whether Jesus walked on water, was born of a virgin, or performed any of the miracles described in the Bible is essentially irrelevant. The only historical event that truly matters is that He was put to death and came back to life. If that is true—and the historical evidence supports this claim abundantly—then surely he has the power to perform a few lesser miracles. Some choose to believe on blind faith alone and never give the matter a second thought. Others, viewing this as an outright impossibility because such a thing has never been observed or replicated in a controlled environment, dismiss the Gospels of Christ as a fairy tale and never give the matter a second thought. Then there is a whole spectrum of people whose belief lies somewhere in between and fluctuates over the course of their life and even throughout their day. Some people have put a great amount of effort into forming this belief, others less. Nevertheless, after all the debating, reading, and writing is done, the question is not, 'Is Jesus Christ Lord?' The only question that matters to you is, 'Is Jesus Christ your Lord?' Ultimately, it does not matter to anyone else what you believe; it matters only to you what you believe. As for me, I believe. I have spent a considerable amount of time forming and critically examining my belief, and still, I have no conclusive proof. But that is exactly what the gospel is about: Choosing to believe in God and surrender one's life to follow God's teaching, not because of any amount of proof but ultimately on faith alone: 'For it is by Grace you have been saved, through faith' (Ephesians 2:8).

While the claim that Jesus was an influential personality cannot be disputed, because this is a book based on science, I cannot offer any scientific evidence or cite any studies pertaining to the mind of Jesus Christ. Thus from this point on, I am writing as a believer. For the record, this is what I believe: I believe in God, the Father Almighty, the Creator of heaven and earth. I believe in Jesus Christ, his only Son, our Lord. He was conceived by the power of the Holy Spirit and born of the Virgin Mary. He suffered under Pontius Pilate, was crucified, died, and was buried. He descended to the dead. On the third day, He rose again. He ascended into heaven and is seated at the right hand of the Father. He will come again to judge the living and the dead. I believe in the Holy Spirit, who unites the people of God, which is the Church. I believe in the forgiveness of sins, the resurrection of the body, and the life everlasting.

Jesus, Fully Man and Fully God

According to the Holy Scriptures, Jesus was not merely a man but God incarnate. That is, Jesus was both completely human and, at the same time, fully God. But how is this possible, and how can this belief not collide with my understanding of scientific psychology? The Holy Trinity is a concept that is often made much more complicated than it actually is. Many scientific atheists enjoy ridiculing the idea that God could be three parts and at the same time one part. The fact that they do this illustrates how their belief is laced with animosity towards God, because the underlying concept of the Trinity is well established in science.

The proof of this is quite elementary. What is the chemical formula for water? H_2O. What is the chemical formula for ice? H_2O. And what is the chemical formula for steam? H_2O. Three distinct properties and states of matter, but the substance is one in the same. If I want to cool something, I use ice; if I want to heat it, I use steam; and if I want to wash it, I use water. In the same way, God the Father, God the Son, and God the Holy Spirit are one God, but each has their own specific properties and attributes. A lot of people do not understand completely is that Jesus existed long before He was born. The attributes, personality, character, and all the things that came to be in the mind of the human Jesus of Nazareth were already present in the attributes of God the Son before Jesus was born as a human. The Gospel of John illustrates that Jesus existed in the Holy Trinity before time began and that He played a significant role in the creation.

> In the beginning was the Word, and the Word was with God, and the Word was God. He was with God in the beginning. Through him all things were made; without him nothing was made that has been made. In him was life, and that life was the light of all mankind. The light shines in the darkness, and the darkness has not overcome it. There was a man sent from God whose name was John. He came as a witness to testify concerning that light, so that through him all might believe. He himself was not the light; he came only as a witness to the light. The true light that gives light to everyone was coming into the

> world. He was in the world, and though the world was made through him, the world did not recognize him. He came to that which was his own, but his own did not receive him. Yet to all who did receive him, to those who believed in his name, he gave the right to become children of God—children born not of natural descent, nor of human decision or a husband's will, but born of God. The Word became flesh and made his dwelling among us. We have seen his glory, the glory of the one and only Son, who came from the Father, full of grace and truth. (John 1:1–14)

Many other verses support the idea that Jesus was played a role in the creation (Colossians 1:16; 1 Corinthians 8:6; Hebrews 1:2). And many other verses illustrate Jesus's deity (John 10:30; Philippians 2:5–6; John 1:18; Colossians 2:9–10). I am well aware that many dispute Jesus's deity and still claim to be Christian believers. As much as I would like to dispute that now, this would diverge from the current topic of the mind of Jesus. Rather than getting into that discussion, allow me to pose the question in this manner: How could Jesus's Godliness be manifested in His human body? The answer to this is His mind. Jesus, having retained all of who He was in the Holy Trinity, literally had the mind of God, and so He was God but in human form. Nevertheless, 'being in very nature God, [He] did not consider equality with God something to be used to his own advantage; rather, he made himself nothing by taking the very nature of a servant, being made in human likeness. And being found in appearance as a man, he humbled himself by becoming obedient to death—even death on a cross!' (Philippians 2:6–8).

Jesus's conception and birth are also matters of significant debate that would exceed the framework of this book. And given the enormous historical evidence of Jesus's existence, such a debate is irrelevant. We know Jesus lived; thus, He was conceived and born. How that happened is not relevant for this topic. What is relevant and needs to be pointed out is that Jesus was fully man, having been conceived in some way that twenty-three pairs of chromosomes grew into a foetus in his mother's womb; was born; and went through the same stages of childhood development as all of us.

The only difference was this whereas each of us grew up to be the person God created us to be, Jesus grew up to become the person He always was. In that way, He was fully human and at the same time fully God. His deity lay in His identity, in His mind, which was the mind of God.

The *mind of God* is a term that is frequently found in the Bible. But what does that mean? Matthew 24:36 illustrates that Jesus did not have all of the knowledge that God the Father had. When He was asked when the world as we know it now would end, Jesus replied, 'But about that day or hour no one knows, not even the angels in heaven, nor the Son, but only the Father.' While some could use this to argue that Jesus's mind was not one and the same as the mind of God the Father, the fact that Jesus is not omniscient like God the Father only illustrates the difference in the attributes of the three persons of the Trinity. Being omniscient is an attribute of God the Father and of God the Spirit. That Jesus was neither of these does not lessen His Godliness because God the Son had different attributes: the attributes of a humble, obedient servant full of love. That is who He was before He was born a man, and that is whom He became as a man. God is all-loving, and this attribute is expressed through the person of Jesus.

Despite His godliness, because he was fully human, Jesus had to learn to walk, talk, read, and more. Jesus had to go through all the developmental processes that all humans go through; otherwise, He would not be fully human. He was not awarded any shortcuts. He was not born with the knowledge of the Holy Scriptures preprogrammed in His brain; He had to learn them just as all humans do. Perhaps he had above-average intelligence, but still He had only human intelligence. In fact, the mind of Jesus and His cognitive development only differed from all other humans in one way. Whereas all other humans grow up to become the people God created them to be, Jesus grew up to become the person He had always been. His identity, His personality, attitude, and all of the things that make each human mind unique were preprogrammed on His blank slate. But, He still had to discover all of these mental attributes through His cognitive development, just like the rest of us.

As was previously pointed out in chapter 2, a significant amount of who we are—our personality, our identity, our attitude, our likes and dislikes—is embedded in our DNA. This must be true for Jesus as well.

As such, if Jesus was truly the Son of God, then His attributes, personality, and identity, which were present at the time of creation, must have been embedded in his DNA at the time of His conception, just as our attributes, personality, and everything that contributes to our identity is embedded in our DNA. As such, Jesus's deity, His Godliness, lay in His human mind, in His identity. The scriptures illustrate that Jesus existed as a part of the Holy Trinity before He was born as a man. Thus, His identity as a part of the Holy Trinity, that is, who He was before He was born a man, had to be the same as His identity as a man.

But if Jesus existed as a part of the Holy Trinity, before time and creation, and He was later conceived in human form, then during the course of development, at some point He would have come to realise who he was, much in the same way all of us have come to realise who we are. As such, the baby Jesus, not yet having developed a ToM, will not have been much different from any other baby. This may explain why the Bible does not speak very much of His early childhood. There will have been nothing relevant to report. What, then, of His later childhood development? Being fully human, Jesus would have had to go through all the various stages of the various developmental processes. As such, he must have acted out at times in accordance with the previously described developmental stages. Whose children have not written on the walls, cut their own hair (or the hair of others), or thrown things in the toilette? Aside from wandering off and having gone missing for three days, the Bible does not report on such child development incidences. However, other ancient documents, which have not been included in the Bible, tell stories of Jesus's childhood development that coincide with childlike behaviours of someone coming to the realisation that He is the Son of God. Such anecdotal stories about Jesus's childhood can be found in the Quran and Gnostic scriptures. However, because I am not adequately familiar with these documents, I do not wish to reiterate these stories here and will later only refer to the one biblical story of Jesus's childhood.

Nevertheless, as an expert on child development, I would suggest that Jesus's development from a child to a young adult was certainly a struggle for Him, as it was for all of us. The Bible illustrates that Jesus's teaching was not readily accepted in his hometown. In addition to this, James, the brother of Jesus, did not seem to have much to do with Jesus or His teaching until after His death and resurrection. This may be a reflection of Jesus's childhood development, which given His identity would likely have been perceived as an abnormal childhood development.

How could have Jesus's childhood development not have been abnormal? Matthew 24:36 points out that Jesus was not omniscient. However, before His crucifixion, he spoke of His coming death three times in the Gospel of Mark (8:31, 9:31, 10:32–34). Therefore, during the course of His identity development, sometime between early adolescence and early adulthood, Jesus would have come to the realisation that He was the Messiah and destined to suffer a terrible death on the cross in payment for the sins of the world, and then after that, He would have to fight His way out of Hell and come back to life. This is not knowledge would have had to been preprogramed onto His blank slate. It is safe to say that His mother will have told him the circumstances surrounding His birth, just as each of us do with each of our children. And we know that even in His childhood, He became extremely familiar with what we now call the Old Testament. Thus, sometime during His childhood development, he would have put two and two together and realised He, Himself, was the Messiah He was reading about.

Therefore, He will have known about His own death and the circumstances surrounding it because exactly that was His identity, in that He was the Messiah. However, one can only speculate at what time Jesus came to know His identity as the Christ, the Lamb of God, whose death will be taken as payment for the sins of the world. I would suggest that Jesus likely achieved full development of His identity as the Messiah, including knowledge of his horrific death, at a relatively young age.

Luke 2:41–52 tells of the story of when Jesus, as a child, failed to follow his parents' home after a festival. I think all parents have experienced this. I do not know anything more terrifying then the moment that someone realises that their child has gone missing. When Jesus went missing, I can imagine that the course of events was something like this:

Every year, Joseph, Mary, and the whole extended family went to Jerusalem for the Passover festival. This was the event of the year, requiring lots of preparation for the long trip to Jerusalem, three days of partying, and the long trip back home. If you have ever been on such an event, you know it can be loads of fun, but when it is over, one just wants to get out of there as fast as possible and get home. So when it came time for Joseph and Mary to start the long trip home, they were busy packing up all their stuff and shuffling the kids into the camel wagons. And as discussions about who is riding with whom ensued, they may have not heard Jesus say, 'I have to go back to the temple and check something out.'

Meanwhile, exhausted from the vacation, yet happy that everyone had a good time, the camel caravan begins their long journey home. While Simon, Joseph, and their sisters are singing '100 Bottles of Beer on the Wall', and the younger ones are asking every ten minutes, 'Are we almost there yet?' Mary gets that strange feeling that mothers get when something is wrong and asks, 'Where's Jesus? James, did you see Jesus? James?'

James, having just fallen asleep in the overpacked camel-drawn wagon, replies, 'Come on! Am I my brother's keeper?' To which Mary stoutly replies, 'James, if I've told you once, I've told you a thousand times: stop quoting Cain!' James replies unconcerned, 'Chill, Mom. He's probably riding with Aunt Lizzy.'

Then Mary asks Judas, 'Judas, did you see Jesus get on the camel with John?'

'You mean that weird hairy kid? No. And, I told you to call me Jude!'

'Those two deserve each other,' interjected one of the sisters, and all the kids begin laughing. 'James bet him a denarius that he wouldn't eat a locust, and he ate a whole bucket of them!'

As the kids continued to swap stories of the weird cousin, the did not notice the panic that was beginning to boil in the front seat of the camel, until Joseph slams on the breaks and screams, 'Everyone, be quiet!', as he brings the camel to a screeching stop.

Luckily, Mary's sister and her husband are not far behind them and are able to wave them down. By now, Mary is in full panic mode. 'Is Jesus riding with you?' Elizabeth, Mary, and Joseph begin retracing their steps mentally as Zechariah, Aunt Lizzy's husband, listens in silence. Finally, Mary breaks down totally, Joseph tries to consul her, and Liz smacks Zechariah and says, 'Say something!' But before he can pronounce his carefully formulated thought, John, who had been camel sick from eating too many candy-covered locusts, eventually speaks up. 'Last I saw, He was reading Isaiah 53 and seemed upset about something.'

Mary, Joseph, Liz, and Zech's eye's lock as if they are communicating through telepathy. Just as Zech was about to say something, Joseph rattles off the plan. 'Zech, you and Mary take one of the camels back to Jerusalem. Liz and I will get the kids home, and as soon as we get there, I'll hurry back and meet you at the temple.'

In any case, Jesus had gone missing. He had been hanging out at the temple and talking scripture with the priests. He was twelve years old at the time of this event, old enough to know how to read. Moreover, twice in this chapter of Luke, directly before and directly after this story, it was written that Jesus grew in wisdom. Thus, He most likely had an innate capacity for reading and learning scripture. His knowledge would have had to have been acquired through learning, because only the capacity to learn and gain knowledge is programmed in human DNA, not knowledge directly. In any case, He had acquired an impressive understanding of scripture at an early age. While He was still talking shop with the priests, His panicked parents show up and react as all parents do in such a situation: 'Son, why have You treated us like this? Your father and I have been anxiously searching for You.'

Jesus replies nonchalantly, 'Why were you searching for Me? Didn't you know I had to be in My Father's house?' The passage goes on to explain that Jesus's parents did not understand what he was saying to them, but after this incident, Jesus's behaviour was obedient to them (Luke 2:46–51). From a psychotherapeutic perspective, this is a very interesting exchange. We all know the circumstances of Jesus's birth: angels, wise men, a bright star, and a dramatic escape to Egypt. Mary went through all of that, and it must have been clear to her that Jesus was very special. But every mother thinks that about their child. And so, after twelve years of cleaning up after the kid, and having had a quite a few other children, her focus on Jesus will not have been the same as it was at the time of His birth. I am not saying she forgot that she gave birth to the Messiah. I am simply saying that since then, she's had many other things to worry about, and now her oldest son has gone missing. So of course she wasn't thinking, 'Oh, no problem. He'll be fine. After all, He is the Messiah.' She was worried sick and angry at the same time, just as any mother would be. So it would seem that since the dramatic birth, Mary had a very typical mother-son relationship with Jesus, and the fact that He was the Messiah was probably not a very frequent discussion topic in the family.

Being a normal human, Jesus will not have had any memories of His birth. He will have certainly heard the story from His parents many times, just as we tell the story of their births to our children. So by the age of eight, Jesus will have heard about the wise men showing up, the star, and the escape to Egypt—and surely His brothers will have often reminded Him that He was born in a barn. It is safe to say that He knows the circumstances of His birth quite well. And in His reading of the scriptures, He will have come across a few parallels between His birth and what was written about the birth of the Messiah. Imagine you find an old birth certificate with your name on it, the name of your mother, but a different name listed as your father. There is an address for this father, it is a church, and you happen to be just around the corner. Of course you are going to check it out, and you may not even ask your parents' permission first. So Jesus was talking to the priests, and I suspect that they were talking about the prophecies concerning the Messiah. The priests will have confirmed Jesus's suspicions that the Messiah He had been reading so much about is in fact Himself. Then, Mary comes busting in like a Maury Povich paternity test scene:

> 'What are you doing here?' Mary demanded.
> Jesus retorted, 'Didn't you know I'd be at My Father's house?'

Perplexed and probably a little embarrassed, it was recorded that Mary claimed not to know what Jesus was talking about. But I think she just didn't want to draw the attention of the priests and of the church to Jesus at such a young age. And as the story ended, not drawing the attention of the church while Jesus was so young was very probably a wise thing to do.

Thus, from a developmental perspective, this passage of Jesus wandering off to the temple may very well mark the moment in which Jesus's identity became clear to Him. Being fully human, Jesus would not have been able to begin the process of identity development until He developed a ToM, which occurs at about the age of four. It is conceivable that Jesus could have been born with gifted capacity for learning scripture. Nevertheless, being born with a blank slate, as all humans are, Jesus's knowledge of scripture would have to have been learned. I would think that He probably had exceptional learning skills, but He definitely did not have savant-like skills, in which He would have had to have read the scriptures only once to have them committed to memory. Individuals with such skills generally do not have extraordinary social skills, as Jesus must have had to have so many followers and speak so decisively in the face of adversary. He would have had started studying very diligently at a very young age to be able to impress people who have probably studied for decades.

It is also safe to assume that Jesus was not only a bookworm. We know His father (legal guardian) was a carpenter; we know after the incident at the festival, He was obedient to His parents; and we know He had a physically strong stature. Thus, Jesus, as the oldest son, was probably not a stranger to hard and long workdays. However, there are only twenty-four hours in a day. If the young Jesus was working hard as a carpenter by day and then also diligently studying scripture, when did He have time for friends? I doubt He had much of a social life. Growing up knowing that He was destined to die a horrible death and not being able to talk to anyone about that makes me wonder whether John the Baptist may have played a role in supporting Jesus in some way during His child development.

The *Home Alone*–like scenario of Jesus's family riding back from the festival that I wrote is of course totally speculative, but the Bible scholars amongst you will recognise some truths to the story. One of those is that Elizabeth (Aunt Lizzy), the mother of John the Baptist, and Mary, the mother of Jesus, were related and apparently good friends. After Mary is told by an angel that she will give birth to a child as a virgin, the angel tells her that Elizabeth is also going to have a child. So Mary goes to visit Elizabeth, who is already pregnant. When the two greet each other, Elizabeth's baby leaps for joy in her womb (Luke 1:35–45).

John the Baptist is one of my favourite characters in the Bible. Like Jesus, his coming was foretold in the Old Testament (Isaiah 40:3; Malachi 3:1). He was described as a burly man of the wilderness, a misfit of sorts, which is why I like him so much. He was given the job to prepare a way for the coming Messiah, and he did a good job in doing so. By the time Jesus started His ministry, John had already begun to preach the coming of the Messiah. He had quite a large following, so when Jesus finally let it be known that He was the Messiah, John's disciples were set and ready to go.

But I wonder—and this is pure speculation—whether John's role as a 'preparer of the way' also included supporting Jesus in some way as a teen. We know Jesus was the oldest of four brothers and an unknown number of sisters. Of course, the circumstances of His birth would have made Him very special to His mother. But still, ten to fifteen years later, there were up to six other kids in the family who had wants and needs. Jesus was the oldest, and I doubt very much that He was treated, in His teenage years, like the king as He was treated at the time of His birth. On top of all the typical family stress, learning stress, and work stress, Jesus grew up knowing that He was going to suffer a horrible death. It is not clear at which point He came to know this, but we do know that His coming death was no surprise to Him. He spoke of it many times before it happened. And He will have learned of His fate from the reading of Isiah 53 and other prophecies. If He knew the scriptures so well at the age of twelve, it is very likely that He will have come to know His fate as the Messiah during the course of His identity development. In any case, from a developmental standpoint, having one good friend like John preparing the way would have been helpful, if not necessary, to ensure healthy development into adulthood.

This is also totally speculative, and there is no evidence that Jesus and John hung out as kids, but the Bible does say Jesus's mother and John's mother had close contact, and both knew of the circumstances of each other's children's births. John was commissioned by God to 'prepare a way for Jesus'. Perhaps that meant being a good friend to Him in His teenage years, which may have been quite lonely under the known circumstances.

Nevertheless, the Bible mentions only three incidents in which Jesus and John had contact. The first was when John jumped in his mother's womb, which I already discussed. The second was at Jesus's baptism. Two things about this event are of particular importance. First, John knew that Jesus was the Lamb of God who takes away the sin of the world (John 1:29). This statement makes their third encounter particularly interesting. In their third contact, John is in jail waiting to be beheaded; he sent his disciples to ask Jesus if He was the one to come, or whether someone else be expected (Matthew 11:2–3). This question actually has deeper theological implications than I wish to get sidetracked with at this point. But Jesus answers, 'Go back and report to John what you hear and see: The blind receive sight, the lame walk, those who have leprosy are cleansed, the deaf hear, the dead raised, and the good news is proclaimed to the poor' (Matthew 11:4–6).

What I've been taught about this passage coincides with my notion that John and Jesus may have been childhood friends. If we assume for a moment that John's calling to 'prepare a way for Jesus' included being a childhood friend, then they would have talked about all the things they were going to do when they grow up, as kids do. And what they were planning to do when they grew up is give the blind sight, make the lame walk, cleanse leprosy, make the deaf hear, raise the dead, and proclaim the good news to the poor. Jesus knew this would come to pass because it was embedded into His very identity; it was who He was. John also knew this was who Jesus was. But just like knowing that the sun will rise in the east tomorrow and experiencing a sunrise are not the same thing, John's knowing that Jesus was the Messiah was not the same as the certainty of the experience. Since their (proposed childhood) plans of serving God, a lot has happened. And at the time, John was in jail, knowing that the king wanted him dead. I think John simply wanted to know if his job was done. And this is how Jesus told him, 'Well done, good and faithful servant.'

The second significant thing about Jesus's baptism concerning His childhood development is the dove that descends upon Jesus immediately after his baptism. 'At that moment heaven was opened, and he saw the Spirit of God descending like a dove and alighting on him' (Matthew 3:16). But John 1:32 reports that the Spirit came down on Him as a dove. The point is not the dove. Whether like a dove or as a dove, it doesn't matter. The problem is some people think that this is the moment in which Jesus became empowered by the Holy Spirit. I strongly disagree.

This was a significant moment. It was the moment in which Jesus began His ministry. For Jesus, John, the Holy Spirit, God the Father, and all the angels, even the fallen ones, this was the kick-off and the sounding trumpet to the battle, which ended with Jesus having a bruised heel and the devil getting his head crushed (Genesis 3:15). However, this was not the moment in which Jesus was first empowered by the Holy Spirit. Jesus was empowered by the Holy Spirit at the moment of His conception (Matthew 1:18), as was John the Baptist (Luke 1:15).

Those who have accepted Jesus into their lives know that the Spirit grows in us. However, our fleshly desires and our animalistic nature oppose this growth. Paul explains this in Romans 5–8, detailing how the flesh and spirit struggle against each other in the strongest of believers. But in Jesus's case, the Spirit grew in him even before His flesh began to grow. So He experienced the same struggle between His flesh and the Spirit. But in His case, the Spirit had a decisive advantage, having been able to take root from the moment of conception. By the time His fleshly, animalistic desires arose in Him, the Spirit of God was much stronger, giving Him an enormous capacity to override any sinful urges.

Thus, as interesting as the idea may be that Jesus may have had a childhood friend in little bug-eating Johnny B, having been born with the Spirit of God growing in Him from birth would have been all the help He needed to get through what must have been a very difficult human development.

Becoming Like-Minded with God

As previously stated, the Bible encourages us to become like-minded with God. But how do we do that? We can ask ourselves, 'What would Jesus do?' in the midst of various situations. But even if we knew the definitive answer to that question in all situations, that does not make it any easier to do what Jesus would do. Very often, if not most of the time, we do not want to do what Jesus would do. Very often we would rather continue to hate instead of forgive and love. We want to hurt others who have hurt us. We want to do unto others before they do unto us. We want for ourselves what others have. We take what we can but give only what we don't need or want. That is simply human nature, and it is sinful in God's sight. Believers and non-believers know and understand that behaving in such a way is not right, but such behaviour is quickly rationalised and justified through thoughts and ideas of self-preservation.

So how can we change our human nature, and should we? After all, if we are human and this is our human nature, are we really doing anything wrong if we behave as humans do? Why isn't it enough to simply follow our human morals? If we do not murder, rape, steal, deceive, or otherwise cause malicious harm, shouldn't that be enough for God? And if He wants more than that, then He should have made us differently. If He is God, all-powerful and all-loving, why is this life so damn hard? It's God who needs to change, not us!

The previous statements are both the standpoint of humanity and the very nature of sin. God gives a direct answer to the above arguments that are frankly not very reassuring to believers and not reassuring to non-believers:

> It is not as though God's word had failed. For not all who are descended from Israel are Israel. Nor because they are his descendants are they all Abraham's children. On the contrary, 'It is through Isaac that your offspring will be reckoned.' In other words, it is not the children by physical descent who are God's children, but it is the children of the promise who are regarded as Abraham's offspring. For this was how the promise was stated: 'At the appointed time, I will return, and Sarah will have a son.' Not only that, but Rebekah's children were conceived at the same time by our father Isaac. Yet, before the twins were born or had done anything good or bad—in order that God's purpose in election might stand: not by works but by him who calls—she was told, 'The older will serve the younger.' Just as it is written: 'Jacob I loved, but Esau I hated.' What then shall we say? Is God unjust? Not at all! For he says to Moses, 'I will have mercy on whom I have mercy, and I will have compassion on whom I have compassion.' It does not, therefore, depend on human desire or effort, but on God's mercy. For Scripture says to Pharaoh: 'I raised you up for this very purpose, that I might display my power in you and that my name might be proclaimed in all the earth.' Therefore God has mercy on whom he wants to have mercy, and he hardens whom he wants to harden. One of you will say to me: 'Then why does God still blame us? For who is able to resist his will?'

> But who are you, a human being, to talk back to God? 'Shall what is formed say to the one who formed it, 'Why did you make me like this?' Does not the potter have the right to make out of the same lump of clay some pottery for special purposes and some for common use? (Romans 9:6–21)

Wow, right? I'll let that sink in for a moment before pointing out that this follows directly after the part I mentioned earlier, in which Paul writes about the struggle between his sinful nature and his desire to submit to God's command: 'Be holy, because I am holy' (1 Peter 1:16; Leviticus 11:44–45; Leviticus 19:2; Leviticus 20:7).

The simple fact of the matter is this: God has allowed us to be in this impossible situation and then tells us, more or less, 'I'm God, and I can do what I want, so deal with it.' At first—and even second or third—glance, that seems so incredibly harsh that one could begin to question whether God is at all-loving. In response to this, Richard Dawkins wrote, 'The God of the Old Testament is arguably the most unpleasant character in all fiction: jealous and proud of it; a petty, unjust, unforgiving control-freak; a vindictive, bloodthirsty ethnic cleanser; a misogynistic, homophobic, racist, infanticidal, genocidal, filicidal, pestilential, megalomaniacal, sadomasochistic, capriciously malevolent bully' (Dawkins, 2006b, p. 51).

From this perspective, this world likens a backyard football game in which a child says, 'It's my ball and my backyard, so I get to make the rules.' What is one to do? One can simply say, 'F you,' stop playing, get a ball of your own, find another yard to play in, and find some other kids to play with. Or one can submit to the desires of the owner of the ball and yard continue to play according to his rules. But why on heaven or earth would one choose to submit to such a person? So what if he has the best ball and yard? That is the struggle against our sinful nature: our opposition against God. How could anyone get past that and choose not only to believe in such a God but also submit to Him?

From a child's perspective, just as I've illustrated, the notion that one could come to love and follow such a God is hard to imagine. But now let's take a father's perspective. What do we say, and how do we react to our children, when they persistently and penetratingly ask, 'Why do I have to go to bed? Why do I have to eat that? Why can't I eat that? Why do I have to do this? Why can't I do that? Why, why, why?' I know this too is a highly debated issue, but parents who find it necessary and correct to answer all these why questions will find themselves being raised by their children rather than them raising their children.

The simple fact of the matter is that God, like a good parent, is less concerned with the happiness of His children and more concerned with the growth and development of His children. If all I cared about was the immediate happiness of my children, that would be easy to facilitate. All I would have to do is let them do whatever they wanted all of the time. Then they would grow up happy—but very incapable of a self-sustaining life.

Thus, the first step to becoming like-minded with God is to assume the perspective of a good parent and understand that we, as God's children, do not know all that God knows, just like our children do not know all that we as adults know. We may not like God's rules. We may think He is unfair, just like our children think of us more often than we know. But in the end, it comes down to a choice. We can choose to believe in God, choose to believe that He loves us, and choose to believe that in the midst of all of our trials and tribulations, all of this has meaning and purpose, and that purpose is growth. Or we can bitch and whine about how tough everything is.

I recognise that the world is indeed hard and unfair, but I also recognise God's Word and value it more.

> In your struggle against sin, you have not yet resisted to the point of shedding your blood. And have you completely forgotten this word of encouragement that addresses you as a father addresses his son? It says, 'My son, do not make light of the Lord's discipline, and do not lose heart when he rebukes you, because the Lord disciplines the one He loves, and He chastens everyone he accepts as His son.' Endure hardship as discipline; God is treating you as his children. For what children are not disciplined by their father? If you are not disciplined—and everyone undergoes discipline—then you are not legitimate, not

> true sons and daughters at all. Moreover, we have all had human fathers who disciplined us and we respected them for it. How much more should we submit to the Father of spirits and live! They disciplined us for a little while as they thought best, but God disciplines us for our good in order that we may share in his holiness. No discipline seems pleasant at the time but painful. Later on, however, it produces a harvest of righteousness and peace for those who have been trained by it. Therefore, strengthen your feeble arms and weak knees. 'Make level paths for your feet,' so that the lame may not be disabled, but rather healed.' (Hebrews 12:4–13)

The Heart and Mind

The key to having a strong mind is having a strong heart. Later, when I write the third book in this series on the heart, I will write that the key to having a strong heart is having a strong mind. The heart, which represents our emotional self, and our mind, which represents our mental self, are the one-two punch against life stress and turmoil. In no other way are the Holy Scriptures and scientific psychology more similar than in how they describe the interactions of the heart and mind.

First of all, both scientific psychology and Christian theology have difficulty defining the lucid border between the heart and mind. This is especially true when one includes the body and soul into the equation. The heart, body, mind, and soul are the four components of the human being. These four components are so interactively entangled that it is very difficult to address any one of the four individually and exclusively without compounding the focus with any of the other three components.

To make matters more complicated, some may be wondering, 'What about the spirit?' Others may equate the spirit with the soul. Let me briefly address the matter of the spirit. Humans are born with a heart, body, mind, and soul. These four components are present at birth and develop over time. The spirit, be it the Spirit of God, school spirit, a spirit of darkness, or any kind of spirit that one can imagine, is not born into a person. Instead, a person adopts, chooses, or takes on a spirit of … whatever.

Furthermore, the little preposition *of* is significant in the matter. Each of us is born with our own body, heart, mind, and soul, but a spirit is always a spirit of something else. It is something that we adopt later on in our lives. This is true for the Holy Spirit, as well as spirits of esoteric or common nature. When we accept Jesus as our Lord and Saviour, we invite His Holy Spirit into our lives to help guide and counsel us. In much the same way, we can adopt the Pittsburgh Steelers spirit, a school spirit, a spirit of darkness, a spirit of nature, a party spirit, the spirit of the wolf, a hippy spirit, or a spirit of any kind. Clearly one can adopt more than one kind of spirit, and one can allow this spirit to guide one's behaviour and essentially one's heart, body, mind, and soul to a varying degree. All of this is true for the Spirit of God as well as the spirit of anything else. The point is that with the exception of John the Baptist (Luke 1:15) and Jesus (Matthew 1:20), no one is born with a spirit of any kind. We are born only with a heart, body, mind, and soul.

The heart represents our emotional self, which is of course not literally located in our heart organ. Nevertheless, the term heart has been used to represent our emotional self since written language was invented. We are now discussing how to strengthen and protect one's mind, so it is necessary to bring the heart into the discussion because, as I said, the heart is the key to a strong mind.

Throughout the Bible, there are very many references to the heart—far too many to list here. What I find particularly interesting is that only about half of these references pertain to emotions in general, and fewer than that pertain to a specific emotion. The majority of the references to the heart in the Bible pertain to an element of cognition or behaviour. One of my favourite verses and a prime example of this is Proverbs 4:23, 'Above all else, guard your heart, for everything you do flows from it.' Earlier, I proved with the experiment of turning the page that the mind controls our behaviour. Now, this verse is saying it is the heart that controls our behaviour. It is in matters like these that the non-believers dance and sing, 'Contradiction!' Not only is this not a contradiction, but it illustrates that scientific psychology is, just in the last one hundred years, catching up to the wisdom of the Bible.

The context of Proverbs 4:23 is about how to deal with problems and stress rather than everyday routine behaviours, like turning the page of a book. Generally, our central nervous system is in charge of our behaviours, but at a moment's notice, at the speed of a reflex, our emotional processing system can take control of our behaviours. This is why when we become emotional, we can do and say things that we do not cognitively mean and later regret. Thus, to guard one's heart and remain cognitively aware of one's emotional state is extremely important. That is, we guard our hearts through our minds. But at the same time, we guard our minds through our hearts.

Just as the term *heart* in the Bible often has cognitive connotations, the term *mind* in the Bible often has emotional connotations. In fact, the words *heart* and *mind* are often used interchangeably from translation to translation. In my Hebrew Bible, I came across thirteen different words used to refer to *mind*, many of which had emotional connotations. Again, these are not contradictions but merely illustrations of how closely interactive our hearts and minds are. Nevertheless, the heart, which is our emotional self, and our mind, which is our mental self, are not the same things. Amazingly, the Bible picks up not only on the interwoven similarities of the heart and mind but also on the distinct differences.

Colossians 3:1–2 and Luke 10:27 are prime examples of the exclusiveness of the heart and mind. Jesus said the most important commandment is to 'Love the Lord your God with all your heart and with all your soul and with all your strength and with all your mind,' naming each of the four components separately and distinctly. Similarly, Paul advises, 'Set your hearts on things above, where Christ is, seated at the right hand of God. Set your minds on things above, not on earthly things.' In these verses, we are told to do the same thing with both our hearts and our minds. The Bible is not being redundant here; it's being effective, a wonderful counsellor.

We need to set both our hearts and our minds on God, not just one or a partial combination of both, but rather very distantly AND. It wasn't until I got my master's degree in psychological counselling that I came to realise how important this 'AND' is. Psychological counsellors are taught that when someone comes with a mood disorder, like depression or anxiety, this disorder can be alleviated with a rational cognitive approach. There are many such therapeutic methods. I use rational emotional behavioural therapy (REBT), but there are others with the same underlining principle. When someone is suffering from anxiety or depression, they generally know in their mind that they should not be feeling this way. They understand in their mind that there is no reason for them to feel afraid or sad. Still, they feel afraid and sad. That is what is so frustrating about mood disorders. Mood disorders do not make any sense. A person with depression can have everything going for them, be totally on top of the world, and have nothing at all to be sad about, and they know it. Likewise, a person with anxiety can be secured in every way possible and know it. Still, fear haunts them continually. In such cases, the therapeutic method is to tap into the mind, the understanding that everything is actually OK, and allow this cognitive understanding to combat the irrational feelings. Thus, in such cases it is the mind that protects the heart.

However, if one is plagued with negative thoughts, then it is the heart that can be used to protect the mind. Negative thoughts can be like someone continually whispering, or in severe cases screaming, into your ear: 'You can't do that. You're nobody, you're nothing. You're ugly, fat, stupid, and a horrible person. Nobody likes you.' Man, it breaks my heart just writing that. But those are the kind of thoughts some people have continually pounding into their minds. In such cases, rational arguments and therapies are often ineffective. If a person is totally convinced in their mind that they are unlovable, telling them, 'Yes, you are loved,' will only prompt the response, 'No, I'm not.' And a continuation of this will only lead to an argument.

In many cases, psychopharmaceuticals are needed to dim the onslaught of negative thoughts that plague the individual so a psychotherapeutic discussion can take place. However, if such an individual is able to combat the negative thoughts with positive emotions, healing can take place. That is, if someone who thinks they are unlovable is generally loved by someone and is able to feel loved, then this love is able to combat the negative thoughts. I know only of one such love. Sure, a love for baking, music, art, pets, and other things have been found to have a positive effect on combating negative thoughts. But these are only Band-Aids on a deep, open wound compared to the healing power of the love of God.

While I was a student, and early in my career as a psychological counsellor, I thought I was so smart and skilled at helping people figure out solutions to their problems. And I was, and I still am. But what I didn't realise then, but do now, is the relentlessness of problems. I would talk to a client about a problem. We would come up with a good plan, and the client would leave feeling better, empowered, and ready to tackle their problems. But the next time we met, we would have to start over from the beginning, again and again. They would come in feeling terrible and leave feeling better. But during the time between sessions, their relentless negative thoughts would pound them so persistently that they were not able to use the techniques we had devised to counteract the perpetual negative thoughts.

As a professional scientific psychologist, I did not evangelise during counselling sessions. That would be very unprofessional, and after all, the client was seeking professional psychological help and not spiritual guidance. Even as a Christian, I saw no problem with this. If I went to my dentist with a toothache, and he asked me if I had prayed about it, I would probably find a new dentist. I would rather have the best surgeon in the world operating on me, regardless of his religion, than the best Christian in the world, regardless of his occupation. Thus at the time, I thought the same would apply to the field of psychology. But when one reads the Beatitudes from a psychological perspective, one may to realise that Jesus was talking about psychological disturbances that occur in people's lives every day. People who are poor in spirit, mourning, anxious, and left wanting for something in their lives do not need Dr Freud, Erikson, Kohlberg, or least of all Dr Kolb. They need Jesus in their lives.

After reflecting upon this, I came to realise that the clients whom I was able to help knew Jesus, and the ones whom I was not able to help did not. I am not saying that Christian psychological counselling is the only thing that can help. The heart of the counsellor is irrelevant. The heart of the client is all that matters. If a client has Jesus in their heart, there is not much that any counsellor needs to do to help this client. But if the client does not have Jesus in their heart, there is not much that any counsellor can do to help this client.

Scientific psychology has devised many various effective techniques that one can use to identify, cast out, and keep negative thoughts out of the mind. I use and teach biofeedback. You can look it up if you are interested. But biofeedback, aromatherapy, art therapy, baking, ice cream, and anything else one may try will never be able to permanently stop the unrelenting onslaught of negative thoughts once they have gained a stronghold in one's mind, because all of these techniques take time and effort, and a considerable amount of it, on the part of the client. Sooner or later, the negative thoughts will begin their attack, and if one does not have the time or energy to go jogging, bake a cake, paint a picture, or dance the name of their spiritual animal, then one will be left unguarded and succumb once again to the negative thoughts.

But if one has hidden the Word of God in their heart, then when the negative thoughts begin to pound, the Word of God will pop up in their mind from out of their heart. When they hear, 'No, one loves you,' Jesus will respond, 'I died for you.' When they hear, 'You are fat and ugly,' Jesus will respond, 'I created you.' When they hear, 'You can't do it,' Jesus will respond, 'I can.' No matter the negative thought, the Word of God has a positive response to it. I have yet to come across a problem common to humans that is not specifically addressed in the Word of God. Thus if you have the Word of God hidden in your heart, you are armed and ready for battle.

> Finally, be strong in the Lord and in his mighty power. Put on the full armor of God, so that you can take your stand against the devil's schemes. For our struggle is not against flesh and blood, but against the rulers, against the authorities, against the powers of this dark world, and against the spiritual forces of evil in the heavenly realms. Therefore, put on the full armor of God so that when the day of evil comes, you may be able to stand your ground, and after you have done everything, to stand. Stand firm then, with the belt of truth buckled around your waist, with the breastplate of righteousness in place, and with your feet fitted with the readiness that comes from the gospel of peace. In addition to all this, take up the shield of faith, with which you can extinguish all the flaming arrows of the evil one. Take the helmet of salvation and the sword of the Spirit, which is the Word of God. And pray in the Spirit on all occasions with all kinds of prayers and requests. With this in mind, be alert and always keep on praying for all the Lord's people. (Ephesians 6:10–18)

If you are plagued with negative thoughts and are a believer and follower of Jesus Christ, memorise Ephesians 6:10–18 and believe and know what it says. From top to bottom, it breaks down like this.

1. The helmet of salvation. The helmet protects the head while also allowing the soldier to see. While a direct hit to the head with a helmet on is still painful, it is no longer immediately a kill shot. While many will say that a helmet is a defensive tool, the old-school NFL will strictly disagree. So it is also in the Christian fight against the evils of this world. With a strong helmet of salvation, one can just drop their head and plough through some problems with the attitude, 'Is that all you got?' Because if you are a believer and follower of Jesus, then you know your salvation is secured. Your name is already written in the book of life. Your eternal life has already begun. Know that you are saved, and nothing can take that away from you.
2. The breastplate of righteousness. A good breastplate protects the heart, lungs, and vital organs without hampering mobility. Like the helmet, a direct frontal attack could pierce a breastplate, but it will no longer be an immediate kill shot. That is, if the ones you love tell you they hate you, it will still hurt, and hurt bad. Your heart may bleed, but you will not bleed out. You may lose your breath, but you will not suffocate. If you know that Jesus's death on the cross has covered all of your sins, past, present, and future, your breastplate of righteousness will enable you to get back up every time you get knocked down. No matter how much you've messed up, that sin is paid for. Get up and get back in the fight. And when you mess up again, you will know that also that is paid for in advance. There is nothing you can do to make you unworthy of God's love. Know that, believe that, and get back in the fight.
3. The belt of truth. A belt has the simple function of holding up your pants. One of the worst things that could happen in almost any situation is to have your pants fall down around your ankles. Imagine you are in a fight, whether physically, verbally, or metaphorically. Now imagine that during this confrontation, your pants keep falling down. You are trying to make a convincing

argument, and your pants keep falling down. No matter how good an argument is, it is very certainly much less effective when your pants are down around your ankles. It is embarrassing, you cannot walk properly, and nothing you do is done better with your pants hanging around your ankles, least of all fighting. The belt of truth keeps that from happening. Jesus is the way, the truth, and the life. Know that and believe that, and no matter who has you cornered in whatever situation, you will be able to stand your ground with confidence because the truth is with you.

4. Shoes of readiness of the gospel. Pirelli, a tire company, created an ad that has made me remember this company's name, although I have no interest in cars, tires, and the like. It was a picture of a sprinter in the starting blocks, wearing elegant high-heel shoes. The caption said, 'Power is nothing without control.' You need the right shoes for the right job. And when the job is fighting negative thoughts, then you need to have your feet fitted with the readiness that comes from the gospel of peace. That is, you must know the Word of God. Carrying a Bible around with you in your pocket won't help combat negative thoughts. You need to read it, study it, and know it as if your life depended on it, because frankly it does. What negative thoughts are you dealing with? Know the scriptures that address that issue. Memorise them. That is what it means to hide the Word of God in our hearts (Psalm 119:11; Deuteronomy 6:6; Job 22:22; Jeremiah 20:9). To know something by heart means to have it memorised. Sorry, but this is a must. Do not know it well, do not know it good enough, and do not say, 'Somewhere in the Bible, it says something like …' If you have it hidden in your heart, whenever you need it in your head, it will pop up there quickly and effortlessly. If you have problems with negative thoughts, memorise scripture. If you don't know a scripture that fits your negative thought, simply google it. Search, 'What does the Bible say about [insert negative thought]?' I'm sure a few will pop up. Pick one out and memorise it, and then the next time that negative thought pops into your head, that Bible verse will pop up next to it, acting as a red flag. You will recognise immediately when a negative thought pops up. That is the first

step. After you catch it, kick it out of your mind; when it pops up again, kick it out of your mind again. It takes some practice, but eventually you will gain control of your mind.

5. The shield of faith. While all other elements can and do break down and fail from time to time, the shield of faith does not. The reason for this is simple and covered in chapter 1: We choose to believe what we want to believe. If this choice is God, then nothing, not even a direct hit from the devil himself, can penetrate it if you have chosen to believe in God. Regardless of the amount of time and effort you have invested in making this choice, the choice is yours and yours alone. No one can make you believe anything else. Moreover, no one except God can know what you really believe. Sure, I guess someone could torture you threaten to harm someone you love if you do not do or say something that they command you to say or do. But that does not really have an effect on what you truly believe in your heart. No one, not even the devil or God, can make you believe something you do not want to believe. A person's faith is indestructible to everyone and everything except that person oneself. The question is what do you believe in your heart? And how is that working for you? If it is not working for you so well, then you might want to rethink your choice.
6. The sword of the Spirit. Like the shoes of readiness of the gospel, the sword of the Spirit is also the Word of God. The difference is that the sword of the Spirit is used as a weapon of attack rather than defence. It is not as an attack weapon against people. Quoting scripture like 'Be still and know I am God' to your loud neighbours will not make them quiet, but it will help you concentrate despite their noise. The Bible is not a magic spell book that you can use to control others. But you can use it to control and strengthen yourself. Reading or even quoting 'when I am weak, then I am strong' will not magically cure me or anyone from muscular dystrophy, but when my MD is really bad, so bad that breathing hurts, then I meditate on these words, and a feeling comes over me like I felt when I went out on to the mat in 1984 and won the Junior Olympics in wrestling. Because I have hidden

these words in my heart, I have come to know—not just believe, but know—that my strength is not despite my physical weakness but rather because of it. Sure, I used to run a sub-five mile, and now I can't even walk down the cereal aisle in the supermarket. But through the Word of God, I have become so much stronger than anyone's muscles ever could. If you learn to wield the sword of the Spirit like a gladiator, not only will you be able to stop the negative thoughts from pounding on you, but also you will be able to empower yourself with positive thoughts that will make you unstoppable.

Prayer

Power (2012) reported on a number of scientific studies that have tried to assess the effectiveness of prayer. At least one of these studies did yield empirical evidence towards the power of prayer, but follow-up studies did not. Most researchers attribute the perceived power of prayer to the placebo effect. That is, merely believing that God will respond positively to a prayer about a specific situation helps the individual feel better about that situation.

However, I argue that prayer is one of the most misunderstood practices in science, theology, and philosophy. So many books have been written about prayer. In my next book on the human soul, I will address the issue of prayer in greater detail, what it should be, its purpose, and why God wants us to do it. Prayer is difficult to understand because it seems contradictory to God's nature of being all-loving and all-knowing. If God is all-knowing and all-loving, why does he tell us to pray and ask Him for the things we want and need? Would not an all-knowing God already know what we want and need? And wouldn't an all-loving God give us what we want and need without us having to ask for it?

Therein lies the misunderstanding. Prayer does not serve the purpose of fulfilling human wants and needs. The purpose of prayer is for us to learn the will of God, to want for ourselves and others exactly what God wants for us and others. As such, prayer, conducted in the way it was intended is more like a learning process than wishful thinking powered by the placebo effect.

Newberg and Waldman (2009) outlined the psychological and

neurological benefits of prayer and meditation and pointed out that any activity that integrates breathing, sound, and movement has been found to increase and optimise neuron activity. The authors defined a five-step process of mediation that has been found to yield positive clinical results: desire for improvement, focus, body control, practice, and expectation of improvement. While this is true, to be fair and remain objective, it should be pointed out that the authors, offering supporting evidence of the benefits of meditation and prayer, neglect to affirm that activities such as brain jogging, puzzling, and reading may produce a similar positive effect in terms of neuroplasticity.

The main question that Newberg and Waldman discuss is, What does meditation and prayer do to the brain? In doing so, the authors address the various physiological parts of the brain and how they each correspond with the cognitive concept of God. While this is a very interesting idea, the author's evidence has the tendency to suggest that the neurological computation of the concept of God is somehow a unique process. However, other cognitive activities that require a similar significant amount of concentration, self-reflection, and awareness may foster similar neuroplastic activity as does prayer. Nevertheless, the authors explicitly point out how prayer changes the physical structure of our brains.

Repetitive chants of any kind, meditation of any kind, and stillness of any kind can and do build structures in the brain which can enable an individual to better cope, relax, reenergise, or in some way gain mental healing. Thus, studies that attempt to investigate the power of prayer with the intention to either prove or disprove the existence of God are hopelessly confounded with the very nature of humans to develop means of mental strength. This is often referred to as emotional intelligence.

Prayer is essentially a mental workout for the brain that, at the neurochemical level, is very similar to meditation, yoga, or brain jogging, but I believe it was intended for so much more. Let us take a close look at what Jesus said about prayer. What has become known as the Lord's Prayer, and is often recited repeatedly in prayer all over the world, was not really intended as a specific prayer but rather as an outline of how to pray. Before starting this outline, Jesus said we should not be redundant or prideful in our prayers. And He affirmed that God knows what we want and need before we ask for it. Thus, the purpose of prayer cannot be to inform God of what we need. Jesus does not specifically tell us what the purpose of prayer is; He simply tells us to do it. And when we do it, we should do it like this:

First, we should acknowledge to whom we are praying. Is it God the Father, another god, a crystal, a tree, or a mountain? Even when we say 'bless you' when someone sneezes, or we knock on wood, who is it we are addressing in such actions? Jesus, of course, suggests that we pray to God the Father, but throughout our day, we lift up many prayers in superstition, habit, and tradition about which we are greatly unaware. As was earlier discussed, increasing one's awareness of one's communication can significantly improve the quality and productivity of that communication. This applies to all forms of communication, and prayer is also a form of communication.

After we have become consciously aware of our mental communication, which is essentially what prayer or meditation is, we begin to bring forth our topics of interest. In doing so, we specifically recognise in our mind the issues with which our mind has been preoccupied. These are essentially our worries, for which we need our daily bread. By taking the time to allow these concerns to surface from our subconscious to our conscious awareness, the negative effects that these worries and fear might have on our mental, emotional, and physical health can be and indeed has proven to be effective. Even if this effect is only attributed to the placebo effect, it is nevertheless very effective.

After we have focused on the bad things that are happening to us, the next step in Jesus's prayer outline is to focus on the bad things we are doing to others and ourselves. Guilt is an emotion that has a tendency to nestle into our subconscious like a tumour. It finds its place there and grows, only surfacing through micro-expressions but seldom communicated verbally and openly. A tumour full of guilt in one's subconsciousness is very bad for mental, emotional, and physical health. Reflecting upon it and expressing it through prayer and meditation is an extremely effective means of alleviating guilt's negative effects, thus increasing one's emotional intelligence. Though right is right and wrong is wrong, the line between poles of the spectrum requires a significant amount of self-reflection in order to be drawn and followed behaviourally so that guilt does not build up in one's mind.

Like guilt, anger can build up into tumours of hate in one's subconscious mind. Thus, likewise through prayer and meditation, one takes the time to reflect upon one's anger and hate in conscious self-awareness. Hate is often described as drinking poison oneself and expecting it to kill one's enemies. Like guilt and fear, hate and anger and build up and become very mentally, emotionally, and even physically harmful. The only way to alleviate it is through forgiveness. One of the most difficult things to do in this life is to forgive and forget the harm others have done to us, especially if they've never asked for forgiveness and continue to cause them harm. Nevertheless, forgiveness is absolutely essential to mental, emotional, and physical health. And prayer is an effective means of gaining awareness of, reflecting on, and forgiving others who have harmed us.

The final element of Jesus's five-step prayer outline is that He does not lead us into temptation but delivers us from the evil one. With temptations, I believe He is simply referring to our choices. Our lives, daily as well as long-term, are marked by choice. Sometimes we make good choices; sometimes we make bad choices. Sometimes we know that the choice that we are about to make is a bad one, and we choose to make it anyway. But very often, we don't come to this realisation until long after the choice is made. By asking God not to lead us into temptation, we are asking Him to guide us through His Holy Spirit. And this is where prayer to God the Father differs from all other forms of prayer and meditation. We are essentially asking God to continue to talk to us through His Holy Spirit, even when we are not praying. This is essentially the opposite of saying goodbye at the end of a phone call. A prayer does not end with a goodbye. It ends with an amen, which means 'so be it'. At the end of our prayer, after we formally acknowledge that we are addressing our heavenly Father with our worries, our wrongdoings, and the wrongs that have been done to us, we do not hang up and say, 'OK, that is all for now.' Instead, we set the phone on speaker and keep the line open. That way, we can shout out any time we need to tell Him something. Essentially, the nature of prayer is like we've butt-dialled God, and He is always listening in. When we pick up the phone again, we find that God has been there the whole time.

Why should we ask God to stay on the phone? Because there is very real evil in this world. Anyone who has young children knows the anxiety of not knowing exactly where your children are for any length of time.

Because I am physically disabled, I am unable to accompany my children everywhere they want to go. For example, I might be able to get to a beach and settle down on a blanket with all our stuff. But I haven't been able to walk for any considerable distance on a sandy beach for years. I can only take about ten steps at a time in deep loose sand. Even if I told my young children they could go only as far as I could see them, at that distance, if something bad were to happen, I could not get to them. This fact made it scary for both my kids and me in places like beaches, amusement parks, malls, zoos, and festivals until I came up with this super idea.

Walkie-talkies were the solution to this problem. If we were at a place like that and one of my small children wanted to go off alone on a discovery tour, I gave them a walkie-talkie set on voice activation mode. Then I could sit in my chair doing what I do and hear my child playing up to ten kilometres away. From time to time, they would report in, using walky-talky language, and tell me what they found or saw. But I could also hear people talking to my kids. I never heard anyone come up to my child and say something like, 'Hey, little girl, do you want a piece of candy?' But, I can imagine anyone who would say something like that wouldn't say it to a child with a walkie-talkie visibly hanging around their neck. But very often, I heard adults address my children, asking something like, 'Hey, little girl where's your daddy or mommy?' To which I had fun replying, 'I am right here. Who are you?' After the initial shock, the concerned adult says something like, 'Oh, your daughter was playing with my kids, but now we are leaving, so … bye, nice meeting you.'

The devil is very real. One can't believe in God without also knowing that the devil is real, is evil, and wants nothing us but to cause harm and pain. Having an open and continuous prayer line to God is the first-line defence against the devil. Like any predator, the devil would rather target an easy victim who is cut off from God than one who has a direct and active line to God. That alone will not always deter the evil one from attacking you, but it will surely lessen the frequency of attacks and help response time.

Conclusion

Becoming like-minded with God is not a fast and easy process, but it is obtainable. Reading, and moreover studying scripture, is an important part of it. Many have read or even said the following words, but most do so in a redundant, non-reflective manner.

> This, then, is how you should pray: Our Father in heaven, hallowed be your name, your kingdom come, your will be done, on earth as it is in heaven. Give us today our daily bread. And forgive us our debts, as we also have forgiven our debtors. And lead us not into temptation, but deliver us from the evil one. (Matthew 6:9–13)

Becoming like-minded with God is not something that one achieves but rather something that one strives for. He has created us in His image. Whether you believe that or not is your choice. Whatever your choice may be, I hope that after having read this book, you feel like you have made a more informed choice. I hope you have gained an understanding of the human mind, and more specifically your mind. This book was not written with the direct intent to be a self-help book, but if you have had mental or emotional issues in the past, I hope you have found here some insight that might help you along your way.

We have discussed how the mind is built upon one's beliefs and how it develops from there on various levels and directions. Perhaps the most significant aspect of the mind is our identity. You are who you are in your mind, and this is the identity that you set into reality for all others to see. But each person has a mind of their own, distinctly different from yours, and only you know who you are in your mind. It is through a complex, three-level system of communication that is unique to humans alone that we are able to express others' ideas in our minds and receive ideas from others' minds into our own. So also is prayer nothing more than communication with God, in which we express to Him our ideas, and He expresses to us His ideas. In doing so, humans can become like-minded with God.

REFERENCES

Adolphs, R., Tranel, D., Hamann, S., Young, A., Calder, A., Phelps, E. Anderson, A., Lee, G., & Damasio, A. (1999). Recognition of facial emotion in nine individuals with bilateral amygdala damage. *Neuropsychologia, 37*(10), 1111–1117.

Alexander, R. (1987). *The biology of moral systems*. New York: Aldine de Gruyter.

Alonso, D., & Fernandez-Berrocal, P. (2003). Irrational decisions: Attending to numbers rather than ratios. *Personality and Individual Differences, 33*, 1537–1547.

Andersen, H. (2006). Two causal mistakes in Wegner's illusion of conscious will. *Philosophical Science Archive*, http://philsci-archive.pitt.edu/3008/.

Aquina, T. (1975). *Summa contra gentiles* (Joseph Rickaby and Danial Kolak, Trans.). New York: Random House.

Atamian, H., Creux, N., Brown, E., Garner, A., Blackman, B., & Harmer, S. (2016). Circadian regulation of sunflower heliotropism, floral orientation, and pollinator visits. *Science, 353*(6299), 587–590.

Bader, C. D., Froese, P., Johnson, B., Mencken, F. C., & Stark, R. (2005). Baylor religion survey. Retrieved from http://thearda.com/archive.

Barbour, I. (1990). *The Gifford lectures vol. 1: Religion in the age of science*. San Francisco: Harper Collins.

Baron-Cohen, S. (1987). Autism and symbolic play. *British Journal of Developmental Psychology, 5*, 139–148.

Baron-Cohen, S. (1988). Without a theory of mind one cannot participate in a conversation. *Cognition, 29*, 83–84.

Baron-Cohen, S. (1995). *Mindblindness: An essay on autism and theory of mind*. Cambridge, MA: MIT Press.

Baron-Cohen, S., Leslie, A. M., & Frith, U. (1985). Does the autistic child have a 'theory of mind'? *Cognition, 21*(1), 37–46.

Baron-Cohen, S., Leslie, A. M., & Frith, U. (1986). Mechanical, behavioral and intentional understanding of picture stories in autistic children. *British Journal of Developmental Psychology, 4,* 113–125.

Barrow, J., & Tipler, F. (2009). *The anthropic cosmological principle.* Oxford: Oxford University Press.

Bartsch K, Wellman HM. (1995). *Children talk about the mind.* New York: Oxford University Press.

Bartussek, S. (2000). *Bewusst sein im Körper.* Mainz: Matthias-Grünewald-Verlag.

Baumeister, R. (2008). Free will in scientific psychology. *Perspectives on Psychological Science,* 3(1), 14–19.

Baumeister, R., Masicampo, E. J., & DeWall, C. N. (2009). Prosocial benefits of feeling free: Disbelief in free will increases aggression and reduces helpfulness. *Personality and Social Psychology Bulletin,* 35(2), 260–268.

Behrens, R. (1998). Art, Design and Gestalt Theory. *Leonardo, 31*(4), 299–303.

Berk, L. E. (1994). Vygotsky's theory: The importance of make-believe play. *Young Children, 50,* 30–39.

Berzonsky, M. D., & Adams, G. R. (1999). Reevaluating the identity status paradigm: Still useful after 35 years. *Developmental Review, 19,* 557–590.

Boeree, G. (2008). *Gestalt psychology.* http://webspace.ship.edu/cgboer/gestalt.html.

Bosma, H., & Kunnen, E. (2001). Determinants and mechanisms in Ego identity development: A review and synthesis. *Developmental Review, 21,* 39–66

Bourdieu, P. (1990) *The logic of practice.* Stanford, CA: Stanford University Press.

Bucci, W. (1995). The power of the narrative: A multiple code account. In J. W. Pennebaker (Ed.), *Emotion, disclosure, & health* (pp. 93–122). Washington, DC: American Psychological Association. doi: 10.1037/10182-005.

Bucci, W. (2001). Pathways of emotional communication. *Psychoanalytic Inquiry, 21*(1), 40–70.

Bucci, W. (2002). The referential process, consciousness, and the sense of self. *Psychoanalytic Inquiry, 22*(5), 166-794. doi: 10.1080/07351692209349017.

Bucci, W. (2003). Varieties of dissociative experiences: A multiple code account and a discussion of Bromberg's case of 'William'. *Psychoanalytic Psychology, 20*(3), 542–557. doi: 10.1037/0736-9735.20.3.542.

Buss, D. (1999). *Evolutionary psychology: The new science of the mind.* Needham Heights, MA: Allyn and Bacon.

Cacioppo, J. T., & Petty, R. E. (1982). The need for cognition. *Journal of Personality & Social Psychology, 42,* 116–131.

Caldas-Coulthard, C., & Alves, A. (2008). 'Mongrel selves': Identity change, displacement and multi-positioning. In Identity trouble: Critical Discourse and Contested Identities.

Capps, D. (2004). Decades of life: Relocating Erikson's stages. *Pastoral Psychology, 53*(1), 3–32.

Casby, M. W., & Ruder, K. F. (1983). Symbolic play and early language development in normal and mentally retarded children. *Journal of Speech and Hearing Research, 26,* 404–411.

Cat, J. (2007). Switching gestalts on gestalt psychology: On the relation between science and philosophy. *Perspectives on Science, 15*(2), 131–177.

Chan, A., & Sze S. (2007). Quantitative electroencephalographic profiles for children with autistic spectrum disorder. *Neuropsychology, 21*(1), 74–81.

Cheung, C. (2010). *Environmental and cognitive factors influencing children's theory of mind development.* Dissertation, University of Toronto.

Cialdini, R. (2007). *Influence: The psychology of persuasion.* New York: Harper Collins.

Courchesne, E. (2004). Brain development in Autism: Early overgrowth followed by premature arrest of growth. *Mental Retardation and Developmental Disabilities Research Reviews, 10,* 106–111.

Courchesne, E., Townsend, J., Akshoomoff, N. A., Saitoh, O., Yeung-Courchesne, R., Lincoln, A. J., ... & Lau, L. (1994). Impairment in shifting attention in autistic and cerebellar patients. *Behavioral Neuroscience, 108*(5), 848.

Courchesne, E., Karns, C. M., Davis, H. R., Ziccardi, R., Carper, R. A., Tigue, Z. D., ... & Courchesne, R. Y. (2001). Unusual brain growth patterns in early life in patients with autistic disorder: An MRI study. *Neurology, 57*(2), 245-254.

Crespo-Picazo, J. L., Rubio-Guerri, C., Jiménez, M. A., et al. (2021). Bottlenose dolphins (Tursiops truncatus) aggressive behavior towards other cetacean species in the western Mediterranean. *Scientific Reports,* 11, 21582. https://doi.org/10.1038/s41598-021-00867-6.

Dacey, A. (2003). Human nature is ___ (fill in the blank). *The Skeptical Inquirer, 27*(3), 49–51.

Dael, N., Mortillaro, M., & Scherer, K. R. (2012). Emotion expression in body action and posture. *Emotion, 12*(5), 1085–1101. doi: 10.1037/a0025737.

Damasio, A. (2000). *The feeling of what happens.* London: Heinemann.

Damasio, A. (2006). *Descartes' error: Emotion, reasoning, and the human brain.* London: Vintage.

Darwin, C. (1994). *The origin of species: by means of natural selection.* London: Studio Editions. Original work published in 1872.

Dauphin, B. (2003). *The blank slate: The modern denial of human nature: A review by Barry Dauphin, Ph.D.* Originally published in *MSPP News,* October 2003.

Dawkins, R. (2006a/1986). *The blind watchmaker.* London: Penguin.

Dawkins, R. (2006b). *The God delusion.* London: Bantam.

De Gelder, B. (2006). Towards the neurobiology of emotional body language. *Nature Reviews Neuroscience, 7*(3), 242–249. Retrieved September 20, 2009 from Academic Search Premier.

Dennet, D. (1978). Beliefs about beliefs. *Behavioral & Brain Sciences, 1,* 568–570.

Dennett, D. (1988). Quining qualia. In *Consciousness in modern science.* Oxford University Press.

Dennett, D. (2020). Daniel C.—What Is Consciousness? Youtube. https://www.youtube.com/watch?v=K26fo6QRc_k.

De Waal, F. (2005). A century of getting to know the chimpanzee. *Nature*, 437, 56–59. https://doi.org/10.1038/nature03999.

Dilley, F. (2004). Taking consciousness seriously: A defence of Cartesian dualism. *International Journal for Philosophy of Religions*, 55(3), 135–153.

Dovidio, J. F., Hewstone, M., Glick, P., & Esses, V. M. (2010). Prejudice, stereotyping and discrimination: Theoretical and empirical overview. In J. F. Dovidio, M. Hewstone, P. Glick, & V. M. Esses (Eds.), *The SAGE handbook of prejudice, stereotyping and discrimination* (pp. 3–29). London: Sage. doi:10.4135/9781446200919.n1.

Dumsday, T. (2019). Breathing new life into the world soul? Revisiting and old doctrine through the lens of current debates on special divine action. *Modern Theology, 35*(2), 301–322. doi: 10.1111/moth.12448

Duval, S., & Wicklund, R. (1972). *A theory of objective self-awareness*. New York: Academic.

Edgar, I. I. (1935). Shakespeare's psychopathological knowledge: A study in criticism and interpretation. *Journal of Abnormal and Social Psychology, 30*(1), 70–83. doi: 10.1037/h0059943.

Ekman, P. (1992). Are there basic emotions. *Psychological Review, 99*(3), 350–553. http://dx.doi.org/10.1037/0033-295X.99.3.550.

Ekman, P. (2003). *Emotions revealed: Recognizing faces and feelings to improve communication and emotional life*. New York: Henry Holt.

Ekman, P., Friesen, W., & Hager, J. (2002). *Facial action coding system*. [CD ROM]. Salt Lake City: Research Nexus Division of Network Information Research Corporation.

Endres, L. (2003). *Role of theory of mind in the social competence of preschoolers*. Dissertation, Miami University of Ohio.

Epley, N., Converse, B. A., Delbosc, A., Monteleone, G. A., & Cacioppo, J. T. (2009). Believers' estimates of God's beliefs are more egocentric than estimates of other people's beliefs. Proceedings of the National Academy of Sciences, 106(51), 21533–21538.

Epstein, S. (1990). Cognitive-experiential self-theory. In L. Pervin (Ed.), *Handbook of personality theory and research* (pp. 165–192). New York: Guilford.

Epstein, S. (1993). Implications of cognitive experiential self-theory for personality and developmental psychology. In D. Funder, R. Parke, C. Tomlinson-Keasey, & K. Widaman (Eds.), *Studying lives through time: Personality and development* (pp. 399–438). Washington, DC: American Psychological Association.

Epstein, S. (1994). Integrating the cognitive and psychodynamic unconscious. *American Psychologist, 49*, 704–724.

Epstein, S. (1998). Personal control from the perspective of cognitive experiential self-theory. In M. Kofta, G. Weary, & G. Sedek (Eds.), *Personal control in action: Cognitive and motivational mechanisms* (pp. 5–26). New York: Plenum.

Epstein, W., & Hatfield, G. (1994). Gestalt psychology and the philosophy of mind. *Philosophical Psychology, 7*(2), 163–181.

Epstein, S., Pacini, R., Denes-Raj, V., & Heier, H. (1996). Individuals, ghosts, UFOs, and magic: Differences in intuitive-experiential and analytical-rational thinking styles. *Journal of Personality and Social Psychology, 71*, 390–405.

Erikson, E. (1950). *Childhood and society*. New York: Norton.

Erikson, E. H. (1968). *Identity: Youth and crisis*. New York: Norton.

Farris, J. (2015). Considering souls of the past for today: Soul origins, anthropology, and contemporary theology. *Neue Zeitschrift für Systematische Theologie und Religionsphilosophie*, 57(3), 368–397. DOI 10.1515/nzsth-2015-0018.

Fivush, R., Haden, C. A., & Reese, E. (2006). Elaborating on elaborations: Role of maternal reminiscing style in cognitive and socioemotional development. *Child Development, 77*, 1568–1588. doi:10.1111/j.1467-8624.2006.00960.x.

Flavell, J. (1999). Cognitive development: Children's knowledge about the mind. *Annual Review of Psychology*, 50(1), 21–45.

Flavell, J. (2004). Theory-of-mind development: Retrospect and prospect. *Merrill-Palmer Quarterly, 50*(3), 274.

Forguson, L., & Gopnik, A. (1988). The ontogeny of common sense. In J. W. Astington, P. L. Harris, & D. R. Olson (Eds.), *Developing theories of mind* (pp. 226–243). New York: Cambridge University Press.

Fowler, J. (1981). *Stages of belief.* San Francisco: Harper and Row.

Frankl, V. (1959). *Man's search for meaning: An introduction to logotherapy.* Boston: Beacon.

Frederick, S. (2005). Cognitive reflection and decision making. *Journal of Economic Perspectives, 19*(4), 25–42.

Fromkin, H. L. (1976). The search for uniqueness and valuation of scarcity: Neglected dimensions of value in exchange theory. Institute for Research in the Behavioral, Economic, and Management Sciences, Krannert Graduate School of Management, Purdue University.

Gauvain, M. (1998). Culture, development, and theory of mind: Comment on Lillard (1998). *Psychological Bulletin, 123*, 37–42.

Gaylin, W. (1990). Adam and Eve and Pinocchio: On being and becoming human. New York: Viking Press.

Gazzaniga, M. (1998). *The mind's past.* Berkeley: University of California Press.

Geddes, L. (2015). The baby experiment. *Nature, 527*(7576), 22.

Gervais, W. (2012). Analytic thinking promotes religious disbelief. *Science, 336*(6080), 493–496. doi: 10.1126/science.1215647.

Gould, S., & Eldredge, N. (1977). Punctuated equilibria: The tempo and mode of evolution reconsidered. *Paleobiology, 3*(2), 115–151.

Gopnik, A., & Meltzoff, A. N. (1997). *Words, thoughts, and theories.* Cambridge, MA: MIT Press.

Gopnik, A., & Wellman, H. M. (1992). Why the child's theory of mind really is a theory. *Mind and Language, 7*, 145–171.

Gopnik, A., & Wellman, H. M. (1994). The theory theory. In L. A. Hirschfeld & S. A. Gelman (Eds.), *Mapping the mind: Domain specificity in cognition and culture* (pp. 257–293). New York: Cambridge University Press.

Green, C. (1997). Introduction to Koffka, K. *Perception: An introduction to the gestalt-theorie.* Classics in the history of psychology.

Gumperz, J. (1982). *Discourse strategies.* Cambridge: Cambridge University Press.

Habermas, T., & Reese, E. (2015). Getting a life takes time: The development of the life story in adolescence, its precursors and consequences. *Human Development, 58*, 172–201. doi:10.1159/000437245.

Hallahan, B., Daly, E. M., McAlonan, G., Loth, E., Toal, F., O'brien, F., & Murphy, D. G. M. (2009). Brain morphometry volume in autistic spectrum disorder: A magnetic resonance imaging study of adults. *Psychological Medicine, 39*(2), 337–346.

Hammack, P. L. (2011). *Narrative and the politics of identity: The cultural psychology of Israeli and Palestinian youth.* New York: Oxford University Press.

Happe, F. (1995). The role of age and verbal ability in the theory of mind task performance of subjects with autism. *Child Development, 66*(3), 843–855.

Harris, P. L. (1992). From simulation to folk psychology: The case for development. *Mind & Language, 7*(1), 120–144.

Heiphetz, L., Lane, J., Waytz, A., & Young, L. (2018). My mind, your mind, and God's mind: How children and adults conceive of different agents' moral beliefs. *British Journal of Developmental Psychology, 36*, 467–481. doi:10.1111/bjdp.12231.

Henle, M. (1978). Gestalt psychology and gestalt therapy. *Journal of the History of the Behavioral Sciences, 14*, 23–32.

Hoare, C. H. (2002). *Erikson on development in adulthood: New insights from the unpublished papers.* New York: Oxford University Press.

Hughes, C., Jaffee, S. R., Happe, F., Taylor, A., Caspi, A., & Moffitt, T. E. (2005). Origins of individual differences in theory of mind: From nature to nurture? *Child Development, 76*, 356–370.

Hutson, M. (2013). What kind of thinker believes in God? Cognitive style helps determine religious faith. *Psychology Today*, Feb. 25, 2013.

Huyck, M. H. (1990). Gender differences in aging. In J. E. Birren & K. W. Schaie (Eds.), *Handbook of the psychology of aging* (3rd ed., pp. 124–134). New York: Academic.

Isay, G. (2009). A humanist synthesis of memory, language, and emotions: Qian Mu's interpretation of Confucian philosophy. *Dao, 8*, 425–437. doi: 10.1007/s11712-009-9137-6.

James, W. (1890). *The principles of psychology, vol. 1–2.* New York: Dover.

James, J. B., Lewkowicz, C., Libhaber, J., & Lachman, M. (1995). Rethinking the gender identity crossover hypothesis: A test of a new model. *Sex Roles, 32*, 185–207.

Johnstone, K. (1981). Status. In *Impro: Improvisation and the theatre.* New York: Routledge.

Karadig, E., Caliskan, N., & Yasil, R. (2008). Developing the evaluation scale to determine the impact of body language in an argument: Reliability and validity analysis. *Journal of Instructional Psychology, 35*(4), 396–404.

Kazdin, A. E. (2000). Gestalt psychology. *Encyclopedia of Psychology, Vol. 3*, 486–489.

Kerpelman, J., Pittman, J., & Lamke, L. (1997). Toward a microprocess perspective on adolescent identity development: An identity control theory approach. *Journal of Adolescent Research, 12*(3), 325–346

Keskin, B. (2005). *The relationship between theory of mind, symbolic transformations in pretend play, and children's social competence.* Dissertation, Florida State University, College of Education.

King, L. A., Burton, C. M., Hicks, J. A., & Drigotas, S. M. (2007). Ghosts, UFOs, and magic: Positive affect and the experiential system. *Journal of Personality and Social Psychology, 92*(5), 905–919.

Klapp, S., & Jagacinski, R. (2011). Gestalt principles in the control of motor action. *Psychological bulletin, 137*(3), 443. doi: 10.1037/a0022361.

Koffka, K. (1922). Perception: An introduction to the gestalt-theory. *Psychological Bulletin, 19*, 531–585. http://psychclassics.yorku.ca/Koffka/Perception/intro.htm.

Koffka, K. (1935). *The principles of gestalt psychology.* London: Routledge & Kegan Paul.

Kolb, E. (2009). *Physiological and behavioral aspects of ASD: How can they be reached?* https://www.researchgate.net/publication.

Kolb, E. (2010). Status: The basic grammar of non-verbal communication. *Researchgate.net.* http://www.researchgate.net/publication.

Kolb, E. (2021). *The psychology of God: A psychological view of theological concepts.* Maitland, FL: Xulon.

Köhler, W. (1940). *Dynamics in psychology.* New York: Grove.

Köhler, W. (1969). *The task of gestalt psychology.* Princeton, NJ: Princeton University Press.

Kostrubiec, V., Zanone, P., Fuchs, A., & Kelso, S. (2012). Beyond the blank slate: Routes to learning new coordination patterns depend on the intrinsic dynamics of the learner – experimental evidence and theoretical model. *Frontiers in Human Neuroscience*, 6(222).

Kroger, J. (2006). Identity development during adolescence. In Gerald R. Adams & Michael D. Berzonsky (Eds.), *Blackwell handbook of adolescence*. Malden, MA: Blackwell.

Lane, J. D., Wellman, H. M., & Evans, E. M. (2010). Children's understanding of ordinary and extraordinary minds. *Child Development, 81*, 1475–1489. https://doi.org/10.1111/j.1467-8624.2010.01486.x.

Landro, B. (2019). Body—spirit—soul: Philosophical discussion. *Journal for Spiritual and Consciousness Studies*, 42(1), 4–16.

Lannegrand-Willems, L. & Bosma, H. (2006). Identity development in context: The school as an important context for identity development. *Identity: An International Journal of Theory and Research*, *6*(1), 85–113

Lazarus, R. (1982). Thoughts on the relations between emotion and cognition. *American Psychologist*, *37*(9), 1019–1024. doi: 10.1037/0003-066X.37.9.1019.

Lazarus, R. (1991). Cognition and motivation in emotion. *American Psychologist*, *46*(4), 352–367. doi: 10.1037/0003-066X.46.4.352.

Lemke, J. L. (2008). Identity, development and desire: Critical questions. In *Identity trouble* (pp. 17–42). Palgrave Macmillan, London.

Leslie, A. M. (1987). Pretense and representation: The origins of 'theory of mind'. *Psychological Rev*iew, *94*, 412–426.

Leslie, A. M. (1994). Pretending and believing: Issues in the theory of mind. *Cognition*, *50*(1), 211–238.

Leslie A, & Roth D. (1993). What autism teaches us about metarepresentation. In S. Baron-Cohen, H. Tager Flusberg, & D. J. Cohen, *Understanding other minds: Perspectives from autism* (pp. 83–111). Oxford: Oxford University Press.

Lillard, A. S. (1993). Young children's conceptualization of pretense: Action or mental representational state? *Child Development*, *64*, 372–386.

Lillard, A. S. (1998). Ethnopsychologies: Reply to Gauvain and Wellman. *Psychological Bulletin*, *123*, 43–46.

Liu, D. (2005). *Neural correlates of children's theory of mind development.* Dissertation, University of Michigan.

Lloyd, G. (1996). *Spinoza and the ethics.* London: Routledge Philosophy Guidebook.
Lovejoy, O. (1981). The origin of man. *Science, 211*(4480), 341–351.
Luhrmann, T. M. (2012). When God talks back: Understanding the American evangelical relationship with God. New York: Alfred A. Knopf.
Mach, E. (1890). The analysis of the sensations. *The Monist, 1*(1), 48.
Marcia, J. E. (1966). Development and validation of ego-identity status. *Journal of Personality and Social Psychology, 3,* 551–558.
Marcia, J. E. (1976). Identity six years after: A follow-up study. *Journal of Youth and Adolescence, 5,* 145–160.
Marcia, J. E. (1980). Identity in adolescence. In J. Adelson (Ed.), *Handbook of adolescent psychology.* New York: Wiley.
Marcia, J. E. (1993). The status of the statuses: Research review. In J. E. Marcia, A. S. Waterman, D. R. Matteson, S. L. Archer, & J. L. Orlofsky (Eds.), *Ego identity: A handbook for psychosocial research* (pp. 22–41). New York: Springer-Verlag.
Matsuzawa, T. (2009). The chimpanzee mind: In search of the evolutionary roots of the human mind. *Animal Cognition, 12*(1), 1–9. doi: 10.1007/s10071-009-0277-1.
Maslow, A. (1973). Dominance, feeling, behavior, and status. In Lowry, R. (Ed.), *Dominance, self-esteem, self-actualization: Germinal papers of A. H. Maslow.* Monterey, CA: Brooks/Cole.
May, R. (1967). *Psychology and the human dilemma.* Princeton, NJ: D. Van Nostrand.
McCredie, Scott. (2007). *Balance: In search of the lost sense.* New York: Little, Brown.
McLean, K. & Pasupathi, M. (2012). Process of identity development: Where I am and how I got there. Identity. *International Journal of Theory and Research, 12,* 8–28.
McLean, K., & Syed, M. (2015). Personal, master, and alternative narratives: An integrative framework for understanding identity development in context. *Human Development, 58,* 318–349.
Meadors, J., & Murry, C. (2014). Measuring nonverbal bias through body language responses to stereotypes. *Journal of Nonverbal Behavior, 38,* 209–229. doi: 10.1007/s10919-013-0172-y.

Mehrabian, A. (1968). Relationship of attitude to seated posture, orientation, and distance. *Journal of Personality & Social Psychology, 10*(1), 26–30. doi: http://dx.doi.org/10.1037/h0026384.

Mehrabian, A. (1969). Significance of posture and position in the communication of attitude and status relationships. *Psychological Bulletin, 71*(5), 359–372. doi: 10.1037/h0027349.

Meinong, Alexius (1899). Über gegenstände höherer ordnung und deren verhältnisse zur inneren wahrnehmung. *Zeitschrift für Psychologie Und Physiologie Der Sinnesorgane, 21*, 182–272.

Meyer, J. (1995). *Battlefield of the mind: Winning the battle of your mind.* London: Hodder & Stoughton.

Miele, F. (2004). The revival of human nature ≠ The denial of human nature. *Skeptic, 11*(2), 44-54.

Mooney, C. G. (2000). *Theories of childhood: An introduction to Dewey, Montessori, Erikson, Piaget, and Vygotsky.* Minnesota: Redleaf.

Muuss, R. E. (1996). Erik Erikson's theory of identity development. In *Theories of adolescence* (pp. 42–75). New York, NY: McGraw-Hill.

Naude, F. (2015). Foundation-phase children's causal reasoning in astronomy, biology, chemistry, and physics. *South African Journal of Childhood Education, 5*(3), 1–9.

Navarro, J., & Karlins, M. (2008). *What everybody is saying.* New York: Harper Collins.

Newberg, A., & Waldman, M. (2009). *How God changes your brain.* New York: Ballantine.

Nyhof, M., & Johnson, C. (2017). Is God just a big person? Children's conceptions of God across cultures and religious traditions. *British Journal of Developmental Psychology, 35*, 60–75. doi: 10.1111/bjdp.12173.

Oderberg, D. (2008). Concepts, dualism, and the human intellect. In Antonietti, A., Corradini, A., & Lowe, J. E. (Eds.). (2008). *Psycho-physical dualism today: An interdisciplinary approach* (pp. 211–33). Lexington Books.

Panagariya, A. (2018). The human brain, human mind and consciousness connectome: An unresolved enigma. *Neurology India, Neurological Society of India, 66*(4), 904. doi: 10.4103/0028-3886.236985.

Patten, K. (2011). The somatic appraisal model of affect: Paradigm for educational neuroscience and neuropedagogy. *Educational Philosophy and Theory, 43*(1), 87–97. doi: 10.1111/j.1469-5812.2010.00712.x.

Peacocke, A. (1993). Theology for a scientific age: Being and becoming—natural, divine, and human. In *Theology and the Sciences*. Minneapolis: Fortress.

Pearson, D. (2013). *Effect of language background on metalinguistic awareness and theory of mind*. Dissertation, University of Stirling.

Penn, D., Holyoak, K., & Povinelli D. (2008). Darwin's mistake: Explaining the discontinuity between human and nonhuman minds. *Behavioral and Brain Sciences, 31*, 109–178. doi: 10.1017/S0140525X08003543.

Pennycook, G., Cheyne, J., Seli, P., Koehler, D., & Fugelsang, J. (2012). Analytic cognitive style predicts religious and paranormal belief. *Cognition, 123*, 335–346.

Penuel, W., & Wertsch, J. (1995). Vygotsky and identity formation: A sociocultural approach. *Educational Psychologist, 30*, 83–92.

Petru, S. (2012). Man, animal or both? Problems in the interpretation of early symbolic behaviour. *Documenta Praehistorica, 39*, 269–276. doi: 10.4312\dp.39.19.

Perner J. 1991. *Understanding the Representational Mind*. Cambridge, MA: MIT Press.

Pinker, S. (1997). *How the mind works*. New York: W.W. Norton.

Pinker, S. (2003). *The blank slate: The modern denial of human nature*. New York: Viking.

Pinker, S. (2006). The blank slate. *General Psychologist, 41*(1), 1–8.

Plonka, L. (2007). *Walking your talk: Changing your life through the magic of body language*. New York: Penguin.

Power, M. (2012). Adieu to God: Why psychology leads to atheism. West Sussex: Wiley-Blackwell.

Polkinghorne, J. (1994). *The faith of a physicist: Reflections of a bottom-up thinker*. Minneapolis: Fortress.

Rana F., & Ross, H. (2015). *Who was Adam?*. Covina, CA: RTB Press.

Richert, R., Saide, A., Lesage, K., & Shaman, N. (2017). The role of religious context in children's differentiation between God's mind and human minds. *British Journal of Developmental Psychology, 35*, 37–59. doi: 10.1111/bjdp.12160.

Read, S., Vanman, E., & Miller, L. (1997). Connectionism, parallel constraint satisfaction processes, and gestalt principles: (Re) introducing cognitive dynamics to social psychology. *Personality and Social Psychology Review, 1*(1), 26–53.

Reiss, S. (2000). *Who am I? The 16 basic desires that motivate our action and define our personalities.* New York: Berkley

Rhyne, J. (2001). The gestalt approach: To experience, art, and art therapy. *American Journal of Art Therapy, 40*(1), 109.

Rich, Y., & Schachter, E. (2012). High school identity climate and student identity development. *Contemporary Educational Psychology*, 37, 218–228.

Richer, R., Saide, A., Lesage, K., & Shaman, N. (2017). The role of religious context in children's differentiation between God's mind and human minds. *British Journal of Development, 35*, 37–59.

Rock, I., & Palmer, S. (1990). The legacy of gestalt psychology. *Scientific American, 263*(6), 84–91

Rose, R. (1995). Genes and human behavior. *Annual Review of Psychology, 46*, 625–654.

Ross, L. D., Lelkes, Y., & Russell, A. G. (2012). How Christians reconcile their personal political views and the teachings of their faith: Projection as a means of dissonance reduction. *Proceedings of the National Academy of Sciences of the United States of America, 109*, 3616–3622.

Ruse, M. (1986). *Taking Darwin seriously: A naturalistic approach to philosophy.* New York: Basil Blackwell.

Russell, B. (2008). *The analysis of mind.* Stilwell, KS: Digireads.

Russell, E. (1916). *Form and function: A contribution to the history of animal morphology.* London: ProQuest.

Ryle, G. (1949). Th*e concept of mind.* London: Hutchinson's University Library.

Sadock, B., & Sadock, V. (2007). *Synopsis of Psychiatry tenth Edition.* Philadelphia PA, USA: Lippincott Williams & Wilkins

Sarbin, T. R. (1986). The narrative as a root metaphor for psychology. In T. R. Sarbin (Ed.), *Narrative psychology: The storied nature of human conduct* (pp. 3–21). Westport, CT: Praeger.

Sayette, M., Cohn, J., Wertz, J., Perrott, M., & Parrott, D. (2001). A psychometric evaluation of the facial action coding system for assessing spontaneous expression. *Journal of Nonverbal Behavior, 25*(3), 167–185. http://www.ri.cmu.edu/publication_view.html?pub_id=4008.

Schachter, E. P., & Rich, Y. (2011). Identity education: A conceptual framework for educational researchers and practitioners. *Educational Psychologist, 46*(4), 222–238.

Scherer, K. R., & Ceschi, G. (1997). Lost luggage: A field study of emotion—Antecedent appraisal. *Motivation and emotion, 21*(3), 211–235. doi: 10.1023/A:1024498629430.

Schlinger, H. (2004). The almost blank slate: Making a case for human nurture. *Skeptic, 11*(2), 34–44.

Schneider, S. (2007). Daniel Dennett on the nature of consciousness. In Schneider, S., & Velmans, M. (Eds.). (2017). *The Blackwell companion to consciousness* (pp. 313–324). John Wiley & Sons.

Sfard, A., & Prusak, A. (2005). Telling identities: In search of an analytic tool for investigating learning as a culturally shaped activity. *Educational Researcher*, 34(4), 14–22.

Shani, L. (2010). Mind stuffed with red herrings: Why William James' critique of the mind stuff theory does not substantiate a combination problem for panpsychism. *Acta Anal, 25*, 413–434

Shenhav, A., Rand, D., & Greene, J. (2012). Divine intuition: Cognitive style influences belief in God. *Journal of Experimental Psychology: General, 141*(3), 423–428.

Sieratzki, J., & Woll, B. (1996). Why do mothers cradle babies on their left? *Lancet, 3347*, 1746–1748.

Sokol, J. (2009). Identity development throughout the lifetime: An examination of Erikson Theory. *Graduate Journal of Counseling Psychology, 1*(2), 14.

Spolin, V. (2002). *Improvisations Techniken für Pädagogik, Therapien & Theater [Improvisation techniques for education, therapy, & theater].* Paderborn: Junfermann Verlag.

Sproul, R. C., & Mathison, K. (1994). *Not a chance: God, science, and the revolt against reason.* Grand Rapids, MI: Baker.

Stapp, H. P. (2004). A quantum theory of the mind-brain interface. In *Mind, Matter and Quantum Mechanics* (pp. 147–174). Springer, Berlin, Heidelberg.

Stein, L., & Belluzzi, D. (1988). Operant conditioning of individual neurons. In M. Commons, M., Church, r., Stellar, J. & Wagner, A. (Eds), *Quantitative analysis of behavior: Biological determinants of reinforcement* (pp. 249–264). Hillsdale, NJ: Erbaum.

Thomson, J. (2009). Who are we? Where did we come from? How religious identity divides and damns us all. *The American Journal of Psychoanalysis, 2009, 69, (22–42). DOI:10.1057/ajp.2008.46*

Tegmark, M. (2015). Consciousness as a state of matter. *Chaos, Solitons & Fractals, 76*, 238–270.

Tononi, G. (2008). Consciousness as integrated information: a provisional manifesto. *Biological Bulletin, 215*(3), 216–242.

Van Inwagen, P. (1997). Materialism and the psychological-continuity account of personal identity. *Philosophical Perspectives, 11*, 305–319.

Velmans, M. (2007). The co-evolution of matter and consciousness. *Synthesis philosophica, 22*(44), 273–282.

Volker, M., & Lopata, C. (2008). Autism: a review of biological bases, assessment, and intervention. *School psychology quarterly*, 23(2), 258-270

Vygotsky, L. S. (1978). *Mind in society.* Cambridge, MA: Harvard University Press.

Wagemans, J., Feldman, J., Gepshtein, S., Kimchi, R., Pomerantz, J. R., Van der Helm, P. A., & Van Leeuwen, C. (2013). A century of gestalt psychology in visual perception II: Conceptual and theoretical foundations. *Psychological Bulletin, 138*(6), 1218–1252. doi: 10.1037/a0029334.

Walton, M. D. (1985). Negotiation of responsibility: Judgments of blameworthiness in a natural setting. *Developmental Psychology, 21*, 725–736.

Washburn, S., & Moore, R. (1974). *Ape into man: A study of human evolution.* Boston: Little, Brown.

Waterman, A. (1982). Identity development from adolescence to adulthood: An extension of theory and a review of research. *Developmental Psychology, 18*(3), 341–358.

Waterman, A. S. (1993). Developmental perspectives on identity formation: From adolescence to adulthood. In J. E. Marcia, A. S. Waterman, D. R. Matteson, S. L. Archer, & J. L. Orlofsky (Eds.), *Ego identity: A handbook for psychosocial research* (pp. 42–68). New York: Springer-Verlag.

Waterman, A. S. (1999). Identity, the identity statuses, and identity status development: A contemporary statement. *Developmental Review, 19*, 591–621.

Waytz, A., Morewedge, C., Epley, N., Monteleone, G., Gao, J., & Cacioppo, J. T. (2010). Making sense by making sentient: Reflectance motivation increases anthropomorphism. *Journal of Personality and Social Psychology, 99*, 410–435. https://doi.org/10.1037/a0020240.

Wegner, D. (2017). *The illusion of conscious will.* London: MIT Press.

Wellman, H. M. (1988). First steps in the child's theorizing about the mind. In J. W. Astington, P. L. Harris, & D. R. Olson (Eds.), *Developing theories of mind* (pp. 64–92). New York: Cambridge University Press.

Wellman, H. M. (1990). *The child's theory of mind.* Cambridge, MA: MIT Press.

Wellman, H. M. (1992). *The child's theory of mind.* Cambridge, MA: MIT Press.

Wellman, H. M., Cross, D., & Watson, J. (2001). Meta-analysis of theory-of-mind development: The truth about false belief. *Child Development, 72*, 655–684.

Wellman, H. M., & Gelman, S. A. (1998). Know ledge acquisitions in foundational domains. In W. Damon, D. Kuhn, & R. Siegler (Eds.), *Handbook of Child Psychology, Vol 2: Cognition, perception, and language* (5th ed., pp. 523–574). New York: Wiley.

Wellman, H. M., & Liu, D. (2004). Scaling of theory-of-mind tasks. *Child Development, 75*(2), 523–541.

Wellman, H., M., Fang, F., Liu, D., Zhu, L., & Liu, G. (2006). Scaling of theory-of-mind understanding in Chinese children. *Psychological Science, 17,* 1075-1081.

Williams, D., Botting, N., & Boucher, J. (2008). Language in autism and specific language impairment: Where are the links. *Psychological Bulletin, 134*(6), 944–963.

Printed in the United States
by Baker & Taylor Publisher Services

Printed in the United States
by Baker & Taylor Publisher Services